Employment Law for HR and Business Students

Kathy Daniels teaches at Aston Business School and is a tutor for ICS Ltd in employment law and related topics. She is also a tutor on the Advanced Certificate in Employment Law for the Chartered Institute of Personnel and Development. She is a lay member of the Employment Tribunals, sitting in Birmingham. Prior to these appointments she was a senior personnel manager in the manufacturing sector.

The CIPD would like to thank the following members of the CIPD Publishing Editorial Board for their help and advice:

- Pauline Dibben, Middlesex University Business School
- Edwina Hollings, Staffordshire University Business School
- Caroline Hook, Huddersfield University Business School
- John Sinclair, Napier University Business School

The Chartered Institute of Personnel and Development is the leading publisher of books and reports for personnel and training professionals, students, and all those concerned with the effective management and development of people at work. For details of all our titles, please contact the Publishing Department:
Tel: 020–8263 3387
Fax: 020–8263 3850
E-mail: publish@cipd.co.uk
The catalogue of all CIPD titles can be viewed on the CIPD website:
www.cipd.co.uk/bookstore

Employment Law for HR and Business Students

Kathy Daniels

Chartered Institute of Personnel and Development

Published by the Chartered Institute of Personnel and Development, CIPD House, Camp Road, London, SW19 4UX

First published 2004

Designed and typeset by Fakenham Photosetting, Fakenham, Norfolk
Printed in Great Britain by The Cromwell Press, Trowbridge, Wiltshire

British Library Cataloguing in Publication Data
A catalogue record for this book is available from the British Library

ISBN 184398 028 2

The views expressed in this book are the author's own and may not necessarily reflect those of the CIPD.

The CIPD has made every effort to trace and acknowledge copyright holders. If any source has been overlooked, CIPD Enterprises would be pleased to redress this for future editions

Chartered Institute of Personnel and Development, CIPD House,
Camp Road, London, SW19 4UX
Tel: 020-8971 9000   Fax: 020-8263 3333
E-mail: cipd@cipd.co.uk   Website: www.cipd.co.uk
Incorporated by Royal Charter.   Registered Charity No. 1079797

Contents

Cases Referred to in This Book

Legislation Referred to in This Book

Access to Medical Records Act 1998
Asylum and Immigration Act 1996
Conduct of Employment Agencies and Employment Businesses Regulations 2003
Control of Substances Hazardous to Health Regulations (Amendment) 2002
Copyright Designs and Patents Act 1988
Data Protection Act 1984
Data Protection Act 1998
Disability Discrimination Act 1995
Disability Discrimination Act 1995 (Amendment) Regulations 2003
Disabled Persons (Employment) Act 1944
Employment Act 2002
Employment Equality (Religion and Belief) Regulations 2003
Employment Equality (Sexual Orientation) Regulations 2003
Employment Protection Act 1975
Employment Protection (Part-time Employees) Regulations 1995
Employment Relations Act 1999
Employment Rights Act 1996
Employment Rights (Dispute Resolution) Act 1998
Employment Tribunals (Constitution and Rules of Procedure) Regulations 2001
Equal Pay Act 1970
Equal Pay (Amendment) Regulations 1983
Flexible Working (Eligibility, Complaints and Remedies) Regulations 2001
Flexible Working (Procedural Requirements) Regulations 2002
Health and Safety at Work Act 1974
Health and Safety (Display Screen Equipment) Regulations 1992
Health and Safety Information for Employees (Modifications and Repeals) Regulations 1995
Human Rights Act 1998
Immigration and Asylum Act 1999
Industrial Training Act 1964
Law Reform (Contributory Negligence) Act 1945
Management of Health and Safety at Work Regulations 1999
Manual Handling Operations Regulations 1998
Maternity and Parental Leave Regulations 1999
National Minimum Wage Act 1998
Part-time Workers (Prevention of Less Favourable Treatment) Regulations 2000
Patents Act 1977
Personal Protective Equipment at Work Regulations 1992
Protection from Harassment Act 1997
Provision and Use of Work Equipment Regulations 1998
Public Disclosure Act 1998
Race Relations Act 1976
Race Relations Act 1976 (Amendment) Regulations 2003
Rehabilitation of Offenders Act 1974
Regulation of Investigatory Powers Act 2000
Reporting of Injuries, Diseases and Dangerous Occurrences Regulations 1995
Right to Time Off for Study or Training Regulations 2001
Sex Discrimination Act 1975
Sex Discrimination (Gender Reassignment) Regulations 1999

Preface

This book has been written specifically for non-lawyers. It is particularly suitable, therefore, for those studying employment law as part of a non-law degree such as Human Resource Management or Business Studies. It covers the entire standards set by the Chartered Institute of Personnel and Development for their employment law elective, and hence is also suitable for students studying towards CIPD membership.

To make the subject of employment law more accessible for such students, legal cases referenced in the book are explained in some detail, bringing the subject to life and giving a clear illustration of the legal point in question.

In addition to understanding the facts of employment law it is also important that students take time to evaluate the impact of employment law. To stimulate such evaluation the book has four particular features:

- *Task.* These are activities that the student can carry out to understand more of how employment law impacts on an organisation. Many of the tasks are specifically focused on an organisation within which the student works, or an organisation with which the student is familiar.

- *Relationship Balance.* Employment law primarily provides legislation that determines the way in which the employee/employer relationship is conducted. These sections require the student to give more consideration to impacts on this important relationship.

- *Further Exploration.* These sections give suggestions for further study and stimulate further thought for students who wish to examine a particular issue in more detail. The sections are supported by ideas of further cases to read, which are given at the end of each chapter.

- *Examples to Work Through.* At the end of each chapter are organisational scenarios, giving the students the opportunity to apply the legislation they have learned.

It should be noted that, when referring to an individual, 'he and his' have been used. This is not meant to refer specifically to one gender, but is intended to be gender neutral.

Acknowledgements

I should like to thank Acas and the Employment Tribunals Service for permission to quote from their annual reports. I should also like to thank:

- My husband and parents for reading the draft copy so carefully and making helpful comments.

- Ruth Lake at the CIPD for all her helpful advice.

Kathy Daniels, February 2004

The Formation of Employment Law

CHAPTER 1

The objectives of this chapter are to:

- **Introduce the workings of employment law;**

- **Understand the difference between criminal and civil law;**

- **Examine the sources of employment law;**

- **Understand common terms used in employment law;**

- **Examine the impact of European institutions on UK employment law;**

- **Determine the role of key institutions.**

AN INTRODUCTION TO EMPLOYMENT LAW

Employment law is one of the fastest changing areas of the law in the UK. In the past two decades there has been a steady increase in the introduction of legislation.

In 1979 the Conservative Government came into power with a reforming agenda. Under Margaret Thatcher's leadership it took the view that the balance of power in the employment relationship had swung too far in favour of the employee. The miners' strike in 1984 was a key example of this struggle of power. As a result of this concern over the balance of power a raft of new employment legislation was introduced in the 1980s and 1990s.

In 1997 the Labour Government returned to power. First, it opted into the Social Charter. The Social Charter is a declaration of member states of the European union that they will bring in a level of basic rights as laid out in the 1957 Social Chapter (which is in the original Treaty of Rome). The basic rights include such things as a basic wage, the rights to be consulted by employers and the rights to join or not join a trade union. The signing of the Charter has led to the introduction of a series of changes in employment law.

It was also widely expected that the Labour government would reverse much of the legislation introduced by the Conservative Government. In fact, it has done very little reversal, but it has continued with the ongoing introduction of new legislation. There have been specific themes to some of these introductions. For example, the concern over the increasing difficulty for employees in balancing home and work life led to the introduction of a number of pieces of legislation known as 'family-friendly' policies.

Further legislation is planned for introduction over the coming years, and it is expected that this pace of change will continue. Some of the coming legislation involves relatively minor amendments to existing legislation. For example, in August 2004 there were amendments to the Working Time Regulations 1998, that relate only to junior doctors. However, there will also be more major changes such as the introduction of legislation relating to discrimination on the grounds of age, due in 2006.

This relentless change has serious implications for those involved with employment law. Employers complain that there is a never-ending amount of bureaucracy to face, and HR practitioners struggle to keep updated with the changes. In this book we shall examine current legislation, anticipate some of the planned changes – and try to understand the impact of the major pieces of legislation on organisations.

TASK Find out how your organisation, or an organisation with which you are familiar, ensures that it keeps up to date with changes in employment law. Find out how the organisation made the changes required by one recent change in legislation.

RELATIONSHIP BALANCE

In looking at the political influence on employment law it is important to consider the stance taken on employment issues by the main political parties. The stereotypical view is that the Conservatives are the party of the 'employer' and Labour is the party of the 'employee'.

Consider whether you think this stereotypical view is supported by the actions and manifestos of both parties. Also, as you work through this book and consider the various areas affected by employment legislation, consider how the introduction of each piece of legislation impacted on the balance of the relationship between the employer and the employee.

Further Exploration

All the major political parties have their own websites. Browse through the sites of the main parties, paying particular attention to their policies and manifestos. What would be the likely impact on employment law if one of the opposition parties came into power?

CRIMINAL AND CIVIL LAW

Employment law is primarily governed by civil law. However, there is some criminal law that relates to employment matters, and hence the issue of criminal law cannot be ignored.

Criminal law

Criminal law focuses on the punishment of crimes, usually through proceedings brought by the Crown Prosecution Service. There is also the possibility of proceedings being brought by other bodies, such as the Health and Safety Executive. The punishment brought by criminal proceedings can be imprisonment or fines. In employment law the main cases of criminal law are brought through the:

- Trade Union and Labour Relations (Consolidation) Act 1992 – some aspects relating to illegal activity during industrial action (we shall examine this in Chapter 10);
- Data Protection Act 1998 – for improper use of confidential and personal data (we shall examine this in Chapter 11);

- Health and Safety at Work Act 1974 – for criminal breaches of health and safety legislation (we shall examine these in Chapter 12).

Criminal proceedings are usually first brought in the Magistrates Court. Serious offences can be referred direct to the Crown Court. Appeals on issues of fact go to the Crown Court, whereas appeals on issues of law go to the Divisional Court. From here any further appeals go to the Court of Appeal and then on to the House of Lords.

Examples of criminal cases relating to employment law are given next.

HSE v *Zeneca Ltd* [1999]

A breach of the Health and Safety at Work Act (1974) led to the Health and Safety Executive bringing a case against Zeneca Ltd. While preparing to decant a highly flammable liquid an employee suffered facial burns after electrostatic ignition of the liquid. A lack of training in electrostatic awareness was identified. Zeneca was fined a total of £5000.

R v *The Mansfield Justices ex parte Sharkey & others* [1984] IRLR 496

Nine striking miners, who were members of the Yorkshire National Union of Miners, were arrested under the Public Order Act 1936. They were remanded on bail, with the condition that they did not visit any place for the purposes of picketing in relation to the existing employment dispute. They were allowed, however, to picket peacefully at their usual place of work.

TASK During your studies take note of any employment cases you read of which relate to criminal law. It is unlikely that you will find a great number of such cases, because most employment cases will relate to civil law.

Civil Law

Most employment law will fall under the remit of civil law. Civil law is concerned with resolving a dispute between two parties. Most employment disputes will be resolved in the employment tribunal – which deals only with civil cases. In resolving the dispute a monetary award can be given to the wronged party (referred to as compensation or damages), and in some cases an injunction can be made. Civil law is based on the law of:

- *Contract*: In employment law a contract is made between the employer and the employees, consisting of a number of obligations on both sides of the agreement. If one of those obligations is breached in some way there can be a dispute under the law of contract. For example:

Wiluszynski v *London Borough of Tower Hamlets* [1989] IRLR 279

Following a dispute between the employer and the recognised trade union, Wiluszynski refused to carry out all his duties as agreed under his contract of employment. Although he carried on performing other duties the employer decided to withhold all his wages. The Court of Appeal ruled that the employer was allowed to take this action because Wiluszynski was not acting in accordance with his contract of employment.

- *Tort*: A tort is a wrong, such as the wrong of negligence. If an employee is injured at work through the negligence of the employer (the employer has provided inadequate equipment, for example) a claim would be made based on the law of tort. For example:

Walker v *Northumberland County Council* [1995] IRLR 35

In this case Walker was employed as a social worker by Northumberland County Council. Due to the stressful nature of his work, and the lack of support he received, he suffered a nervous breakdown. While he was absent from work due to this breakdown he agreed with his employers a series of measures to help him in his work. He returned to work, but the agreed support was withdrawn. Walker suffered a further breakdown. It was found that his employers had been negligent in not giving him the support that he needed to carry out his duties. (We shall examine this case in more detail in Chapter 12.)

- *Property*: If an employee uses inventions designed at work, under the employer's copyright, for personal gain there can be a claim under the law of property. For example:

Reiss Engineering v *Harris* [1985] IRLR 23

Harris was a sales manager working for a company that sold valves. Reiss Engineering did not have a research and design department, and had never designed a valve or improvements or modifications to a valve. Harris invented a new type of valve. Reiss Engineering claimed that the patent for the new valve should belong to them, because they claimed Harris had invented it during the course of his normal duties. The court held that it had not been part of Harris's normal duties to invent anything, and hence the patent belonged to Harris. (We shall examine this case in more detail in Chapter 11.)

In employment law most cases are first heard in the Employment Tribunal. If there is an appeal, which must be based on a point of law, it is referred to the Employment Appeals Tribunal. Any further appeal is directed to the Court of Appeal and then to the House of Lords.

The present Labour Government is currently consulting about the creation of a Supreme Court, which, if created, would be the ultimate court of appeal.

A civil law claim that is not related to employment is first brought in the County Court. Any appeal is then directed to the Court of Appeal and finally the House of Lords.

Not all employment related issues must start in the Employment Tribunal. For example, certain cases of wrongful dismissal (see Chapter 9) can be brought in the County Court or the High Court, as well as in the Employment Tribunal.

SOURCES OF LAW

Legislation is created in a number of different ways, as follows.

Statute

Statutes are Acts of Parliament, and they are the main source of legislation. Recent examples of statutes are the Employment Act 2002 and the Employment Relations Act 1999.

An Act of Parliament has to go through a lengthy process before it is finally accepted as statute. Typically it starts as a Green Paper, which is a consultation document. This Green Paper will pass through a number of parliamentary committees, depending on the range of its content. When all comments have been received and considered it is issued as a White Paper – which is a statement of the government's policy. This White Paper (known as a bill) is then discussed and reviewed by the House of Commons, and then the House of Lords before being finalised. It becomes a statute when it receives royal assent.

Some statutes are implemented immediately. However, it is more common for there to be a time lag between the royal assent and the enforcement of the content. This is usually for the practical reason that employers need time to implement the requirements.

For example, The Employment Act came into existence in October 2002. Within the act there were new provisions relating to maternity leave, that were only enforced for women whose babies were due after 6 April 2003, and new dismissal, disciplinary and grievance rules that did not come into force until October 2004.

Statute is created for a variety of reasons. Some will be directly related to the political policies of the party in government, eg the National Minimum Wage Act 1998 was a result of a manifesto promise of the Labour government to bring a minimum basic wage.

Some statute results from British membership of the European Union, as we shall discuss later in this chapter.

Some statute results from concern regarding specific aspects of working life in the UK. For example, a significant part of the Employment Act 2002 relates to family-friendly policies (which the Labour Government highlights as a major concern). Prior to introducing this legislation, the government undertook a survey of working life. It identified concerns about the quality of family life, and concerns about the amount of time parents were spending with their children. The content relating to maternity leave, paternity leave, adoption leave and flexible working were all intended to address this issue of the balance between working and family life.

Codes of Practice

Codes of practice are not law, but if they are broken the court would expect to see a good reason for such a breach. They are, therefore, important and should be breached only if there is good reason for doing so. The most commonly quoted example of a code of practice, although not relevant to employment law, is the Highway Code.

Employment codes are issued by a number of bodies such as:

Acas – Advisory, Conciliation and Arbitration Service

CRE – Commission for Racial Equality

EOC – Equal Opportunities Commission

HSE – Health and Safety Executive.

 TASK Look at the Acas website (www.acas.org.uk) and read one of the codes of practice that are there. Become familiar with the style and content of codes of practice.

Common law

This is also known as case law. Case law is law based on judgments made by judges or employment tribunal chairmen on cases brought before them in the court or the employment tribunal. Most cases give judgments specific to the person before them. For example, I could take a case to the Employment Tribunal saying that my contract of employment expressly stated that I should be paid my full holiday entitlement on leaving the company. The company did not pay that holiday pay. There is no dispute over the calculation of the holiday pay, the only issue is whether the money should have been paid. The Tribunal read the contract, agree that the money is owed and order that it should be paid. That judgment affects me alone.

However, a case could be brought to the Tribunal where there is a disagreement over the legal definition of holiday pay (as defined in the Working Time Regulations 1998). In determining what the correct definition of holiday pay is the tribunal is determining how the law should be interpreted – and is setting a precedent that is then referred to by any subsequent cases relating to the definition of holiday pay. This is case law.

Case law is interpreted by the most senior court in the relevant legal system, so if a decision is overturned by an appeal court that decision forms case law and not the decisions of previous courts. So, if the employer thinks that the decision over the definition of holiday pay is wrong, he can appeal to the Employment Appeals Tribunal (EAT). The EAT reviews the decision made by the Employment Tribunal (ET), and either supports it or changes it. If the EAT changes it, the EAT's interpretation takes precedent over the ET, and the case law is based on the EAT's decision.

If the employee is unhappy with the reversal of the decision made by the EAT he can appeal to the Court of Appeal. Any decision made by the Court of Appeal overrules the EAT. Ultimately, the decision of the House of Lords overrules all previous decisions.

THE ROLE OF EUROPE

The UK has been a member of the European Community since 1973. As already noted, the Labour Government signed the Social Charter on coming into power in 1997. The Social Charter is a declaration that the member state will adhere to a basic level of rights as spelled out in the 1957 Social Chapter. These basic rights include a right to a basic wage; the rights to join or not join a trade union; the right to strike and the right to be consulted by employers. The Social Chapter is important, because it is the basis for many of the directives that have been introduced by the EC.

European Law is given precedence over UK national law. Therefore, if there is any dispute between UK national law and European law the European law will be enforced. There are four main sources of European law:

1   Treaties are the primary source of all European law. A treaty is a framework within which a member state can implement legislation. The first treaty was the Treaty of Rome (1957) that created the European Economic Community (as it was then named). Subsequent treaties include the Maastricht Treaty (1992) and the Treaty of Amsterdam (1997).

2   Regulations automatically become part of the national laws of the member state, by virtue of treaties previously entered into. There might be the requirement for the Member State to pass legislation to incorporate them. Examples of regulations are the Working Time Regulations 1998 and the Part-time Workers (Prevention of Less Favourable Treatment) Regulations 2000.

3   Directives lay down objectives that the Member State is 'directed' to implement, by making them part of national law. The Member State decides exactly how they will achieve this. There is usually a time period given in which to carry out this implementation, and there have been occasions where an extension to this time period has been negotiated. If the Member State does not implement the directive in the given time period it can be forced to pay damages to any individual who has suffered loss as a result of the non-implementation. Examples of Directives are the Working Time Directive 1993 and the Information and Consultation Directive 2002.

4   Decisions relate to specific Member States, individuals, or organisations. They are binding.

> **TASK** Find further examples of treaties, regulations, directives and decisions. Consider the impact that each of your examples had on UK legislation.

Within the European Community the European Commission introduces new legislation. The European Parliament has the right to be consulted over any proposals but, unlike the UK parliament, cannot introduce any proposals.

The European Court of Justice (ECJ) has an important role in defining and interpreting EC law. The final court of appeal in a member state can refer a case to the ECJ for an interpretation of a specific aspect of European Law. The ECJ makes the ruling and then returns it to the courts in the Member State for that ruling to be acted upon.

A good example of this is the following case.

R v Secretary of State ex parte Equal Opportunities Commission [1995] 1 AC 1

The Equal Opportunities Commission (EOC) claimed that the differing qualifying periods to bring a claim of unfair dismissal for full-time and part-time employees was discriminatory. At the time, full-time workers had to have two years' continuous service to bring a claim for unfair dismissal, whereas part-time workers had to have five years' continuous service.

The EOC showed that significantly more women than men have part-time jobs, and hence the law discriminated against female employees. The case was referred to the ECJ which judged that the different qualifying periods were discriminatory against women, and hence had to be changed. The ruling was referred back to the UK, which subsequently introduced new legislation eliminating the difference in qualifying period for full- and part-time workers. (Note: The current qualifying period is one year for both full- and part-time workers.)

Further Exploration

What do you think the impact would have been on UK law if the ECJ had not been there to rule in the case of R v *Secretary of State ex parte Equal Opportunities Commission* [1995] 1 AC 1? What ongoing repercussions might this have had?

The ECJ carries out a number of additional functions, including:

- hearing challenges that the Member State has failed to fulfil some aspect of a treaty. An individual or a group of individuals can bring these challenges
- hearing complaints regarding the way in which European law has been interpreted and applied.

The European Court of Human Rights (ECHR) is the court that hears any claims that an individual, or groups of individuals has suffered a violation of the European Convention on Human Rights 1950. Much of this convention has been incorporated into the Human Rights Act 1998. In the same way as with the ECJ, any legislation of a Member State that is found to be incompatible with European Law is referred back to the government of the Member State for amendments to be made to national legislation.

The Human Rights Act 1998 contains a number of articles, which will be explored in detail in Chapter 11.

RELATIONSHIP BALANCE

The ECJ allows a further stage of appeal in employment disputes. Both the employer and the employee can seek redress to the ECJ. On this basis, does the role of the ECJ maintain the relationship balance, or does it alter it in some way?

Further Exploration

Look at recent changes in employment legislation in the UK. Identify which are the result of European directives and which are not. Are there underlying differences relating to the two sources of legislation? Identify any other Member State of the European Union. Contrast and compare key areas of legislation of this Member State and the UK. Are there any areas of commonality appearing? If there are not, how can this be explained?

KEY INSTITUTIONS

There are a number of institutions within the UK that have a direct impact on the creation and workings of employment law. These include the following.

Acas (Advisory, Conciliation and Arbitration Service)

Acas (www.acas.org.uk) is a service funded by the government, but independent of any government control. Acas is run by a council of 12 members from business, unions and the independent sector. It has about 800 employees working from 11 regional offices and a head office in London. It has been in existence since 1974.

Acas is a service for both the employer and the employee. Its duty is to remain impartial, and to try to help both sides find solutions to their difficulties. Specifically, the functions include:

- *Advice*: Any person can phone Acas for advice about an employment-related matter. For example, an employer might phone to ask for information about recent developments in employment law, or an employee might phone asking for advice in taking a claim to the Employment Tribunal. In 2002–03 Acas dealt with 760,000 telephone enquiries. According to the Acas annual report, the top three topics that people rang the helpline about were: wages/holiday entitlement (29%), notice period pay (27%) and sick pay/absence (27%). Acas can also be asked to carry out employment-related surveys or more lengthy projects.

- *Conciliation*: Conciliation is the process of bringing both sides of a dispute together, and helping them to find a solution to their difficulties. Acas might perform this role before any conflict has actually occurred, or when it has already commenced. In addition, Acas tries to help both parties in an employment tribunal to resolve the dispute before the case reaches the tribunal. All cases lodged with the employment tribunal are copied to Acas and they will contact both parties and try to help them to reach an agreement. In 2002 Acas helped to resolve 71 per cent of cases before they reached a tribunal hearing.

- *Arbitration*: Arbitration is the process of bringing in an independent body (eg Acas) and letting them evaluate the situation and determine a solution. Although there is not always a legal requirement to implement the recommended solution, there is a moral obligation. This process can work only if both sides agree to be bound by the process of arbitration.

In addition, Acas publishes codes of practice, runs training sessions and is involved in consultation with the government about new initiatives relating to employment.

Look through the Acas website (www.acas.org.uk) and make sure you are familiar with the range of services that it provides. You might find it particularly interesting to read its annual report.

CAC (Central Arbitration Committee)

The CAC (www.cac.gov.uk) is an independent body with statutory powers, whose specific role is to determine the outcome of applications relating to the statutory recognition or derecognition of trade unions for collective bargaining purposes (see Chapter 10). The CAC is also responsible for determining the outcome of disputes between employers and employees over the disclosure of information for collective bargaining purposes, and in dealing with complaints relating to the establishment of Works Councils in the UK. All these issues will be looked at in more detail in Chapter 10.

The Committee consists of a chairman, 10 deputy chairmen, 16 members representing workers and 16 members representing employers. The Secretary of State for Trade and Industry appoints the Committee after consulting with Acas.

EOC (Equal Opportunities Commission)

The EOC (www.eoc.org.uk) is an independent statutory body, funded by grant-in-aid. It is independent from the government, although it is responsible to the Equality Minister. It was set up as a result of the Sex Discrimination Act (1975) to work towards the elimination of discrimination on the grounds of sex or marriage and:

- to promote equality of opportunity for women and men
- to keep under review the Sex Discrimination Act (1975) and the Equal Pay Act (1970)
- to provide legal advice and assistance to individuals who have been discriminated against.

To achieve its aims the EOC:

- provides up-to-date advice on rights relating to equality to both employers and employees
- runs high profile campaigns and lobbies decision makers at every level
- carries out relevant research and publishes the results
- represents employees at landmark legal cases under the Sex Discrimination Act (1975) and the Equal Pay Act (1970).

CRE (Commission for Racial Equality)

The Commission for Racial Equality (www.cre.gov.uk) is a publicly funded, non-governmental body set up under the Race Relations Act (1976) to tackle racial discrimination and promote racial equality. The CRE:

- works in both the public and private sectors to encourage fair treatment and to promote equal opportunities for everyone, regardless of their race, colour, nationality, or national or ethnic origin
- provides information and advice to people who think they have suffered racial discrimination or harassment

- works with public bodies, businesses and organisations from all sectors to promote policies and practices that will help to ensure equal treatment for all

- runs campaigns to raise awareness of race issues, and to encourage organisations and individuals to play their part in creating a just society

- makes sure that all new laws take full account of the Race Relations Act and the protection it gives against discrimination.

DRC (Disability Rights Commission)

The Disability Rights Commission (www.drc-gb.org) is an independent body, established by Act of Parliament to eliminate discrimination against disabled people and promote equality of opportunity. The DRC:

- provides an advice and information service for disabled people, employers and service providers

- supports disabled people in securing their rights under the Disability Discrimination Act (DDA)

- supports legal cases to set new precedents and test the limits of the law through representing and/or advising applicants

- campaigns to strengthen the law so that it works better and protects more disabled people

- organises campaigns – such as the Educating for Equality campaign – to change policy, practice and awareness so that disabled people get a fairer deal

- puts on events and conferences to raise public awareness of disability issues

- produces publications about rights for disabled people and good practice for employers and service providers

- publishes policy statements and research on issues that affect disabled people.

The role of the key institutions relating to health and safety (the Health and Safety Executive and the Health and Safety Commission) will be discussed in Chapter 12.

TASK It is important that, throughout your studies, you keep abreast of the changes and developments in employment law. This can be achieved by reading such publications as the CIPD magazine *People Management*, reading quality newspapers and browsing websites such as www.dti.gov.uk and the websites already given for specific employment institutions. Decide now what will be your main sources of reference and be sure to make regular referrals to them.

RELATIONSHIP BALANCE

Both the employer and the employee can seek advice and support from all the bodies outlined above. Are you aware of any evidence, therefore, of any of these bodies affecting the balance of the relationship?

EXPLANATION OF COMMON TERMS

There are some standard terms that are used in employment law, which it is important to understand:

- An *Act* is always cited in a standard way – that is the name of the Act followed by the date the Act was passed. For example, Employment Act 2002.
- The person who brings a case to a tribunal is called an *Applicant*.
- The employer who defends a case in the tribunal is called the *Respondent*.
- The person who brings a case to the appeal court is called an *Appellant*.
- The person who brings a case in the civil court is called a *Claimant*. (Until 2000 the person was known as a *Plaintiff*.)
- A *case* is always described as the two parties 'versus' each other, with the date it was heard in the court following in brackets. For example, *Delaney* v *Staples* [1992] IRLR 191.
- If a case is brought by the *State* it is listed as *R* v *A N Other* [2003], where R stands for Regina (the Queen – as Head of State).
- *Ex parte* literally means 'from a party' – meaning that only one party is making the initial application. So, in the case *R* v *Secretary of State ex parte Equal Opportunities Commission* [1995] 1 AC 1 the challenge was coming from a party called the Equal Opportunities Commission.
- When cases are cited in literature only a brief description of the facts is usually given. To read the full report you need to refer to the given *source*. For example, *Delaney* v *Staples* [1992] IRLR 191 means that the full script can be found in the Industrial Relations Law Reports (www.irsonline.co.uk). A case followed by ICR is reported in the Industrial Case Reports (www.lawreports.co.uk). (The hard copies of these reports can be found in many university libraries.)

CHAPTER REVIEW

1. Employment law is a rapidly changing area of law.
2. Employment law is primarily governed by civil law, although there are situations in which criminal law might be applied. Civil law is based on the law of contract, tort and property.
3. Legislation is created by statute, common (case) law and the influence of codes of practice.
4. European law has precedence over UK law.

WEBSITES REFERENCED IN THIS CHAPTER

www.acas.org.uk	Advisory, Conciliation and Arbitration Service
www.cac.gov.uk	Central Arbitration Committee
www.cre.gov.uk	Commission for Racial Equality
www.drc-gb.org	Disability Rights Commission
www.dti.gov.uk	Department of Trade and Industry
www.eoc.org.uk	Equal Opportunities Commission

OTHER USEFUL WEBSITES

www.cbi.co.uk	Confederation of British Industry
www.cipd.co.uk	Chartered Institute of Personnel and Development
www.curia.eu.int	European Court of Justice
www.dfes.gov.uk	Department for Education and Skills
www.dwp.gov.uk	Department for Work and Pensions
www.echr.coe.int	European Court of Human Rights
www.tuc.org.uk	Trades Union Congress

It is important to note that some legislation and legal terms are different in Scotland to that in England and Wales. A number of the websites will direct Scottish students to particularly relevant information. In addition, it might be helpful to access the following specific websites:

www.scottishlaw.org.uk
www.scottish.parliament.uk

EXAMPLES TO WORK THROUGH

1 Your managing director asks you to give a brief presentation about the impact of Europe on UK employment legislation. Map out the main areas you would cover in this presentation.
2 A longstanding employee has been involved in a car accident, and is returning to work with a significant loss of mobility. What organisation might be able to advise you in the best way to assist this employee, and what type of questions do you need to ask this organisation?
3 Your managing director is concerned that employees have the right to bring criminal proceedings against the company. Explain to him the most likely situations in which this could occur.

The Employment Tribunals and Employment Appeal Tribunal

The objectives of this chapter are to:

■ **Analyse the history of the Employment Tribunals;**

■ **Understand the operation of the Employment Tribunals;**

■ **Outline the impact of the Employment Appeal Tribunal;**

■ **Analyse the Acas Arbitration Scheme;**

■ **Consider the future of the Employment Tribunals.**

THE HISTORY OF THE EMPLOYMENT TRIBUNALS

The Employment Tribunals were created by the Industrial Training Act 1964 (and at this stage were named Industrial Tribunals). They were initially created to hear appeals relating to the assessment of training levies under this 1964 Act. Over the next three years their brief was extended to include such things as the determination of the right to a redundancy payment and issues surrounding the lack of, or inaccuracy of, a written statement of terms and conditions of employment.

In the mid-1960s the Government became concerned about the number of unofficial strikes, wage inflation and the general existence of restrictive practices in industry. It commissioned Lord Donovan to lead an investigation into these issues. As a result of the investigation the Donovan Report was published in 1968 and gave a comprehensive overview of industrial relations at the time. In particular the report observed two systems of industrial relations that had developed. There was the formal system of negotiation at industry level, and the informal level happening more locally within the organisation. Donovan suggested that many of the problems identified by the Government were due to the conflict between these two systems. His main recommendation was the formalisation of industrial relations systems at organisational and industry level.

As part of those recommendations Donovan saw the need for an industrial tribunal system to which employees could bring their grievances. He described this system as needing to be easily accessible, informal, speedy and inexpensive. At first the industrial tribunal system was just this. However, over the years the workload of the tribunals has increased significantly, and many believe the system has moved far from the ideal that Donovan initially described.

It is easy to see some of the key reasons that the workload increased so dramatically. When the Donovan report was published there was no legislation relating to unfair dismissal (introduced in 1971), sex discrimination (1975) and race discrimination (1976). Today more than half of the claims to the Employment Tribunals relate to these areas of legislation.

Despite this increasing workload it was still hoped that the employment tribunals system could meet Donovan's ideal. The idea was that an employee who felt he had been badly treated by an employer should have the means to get an independent judgment on the issue, quickly and without cost. How are those criteria met today?

Accessibility

The Donovan report suggested that there should be Employment Tribunals operating in all major industrial centres, making them easily accessible. In 1971 Employment Tribunals were heard in 84 locations. Today there are 31 permanent centres at which Employment Tribunals are heard. In addition to this there are a number of hearings that take place at non-permanent centres. There is also the ability to hear cases almost anywhere if people have particular needs (eg disability) that make it difficult to attend a permanent centre. It is difficult, therefore, to give a specific number of centres, but the system is certainly still very accessible to those who want to use it.

Accessibility can also refer to the ease of registering a claim with the Employment Tribunal. The system is open to everyone, and the actual process of registering a claim is relatively straightforward (as we shall see later in this chapter). Forms to apply to the Employment Tribunals (IT1) are readily available at places such as the Citizens' Advice Bureau. It is also possible to complete the IT1 on line through the Employment Tribunals' website (www.ets.gov.uk).

Informality

This is perhaps now the area which least meets the original Donovan ideal. There are definitely ways in which the employment tribunals system is much less formal than other court systems. There are no wigs and gowns, and the hearing rooms are less imposing than many courtrooms. In higher courts the parties are expected to present their case, and challenge the case of the opposite side. An unrepresented applicant who is struggling to explain their case in the employment tribunal will usually be given some assistance by the chairperson to make sure all facts are communicated.

However, it is widely accepted that the employment tribunals have moved away from the picture of the potentially wronged employee presenting his grievance in a simple manner, with the employer responding to the accusations. It is now very common for one or both parties to be represented by solicitors or barristers, and the simple arguments are often weighed down by substantial legal arguments. This has impacted on the aspect of informality – but is probably inevitable given the growing amount of legislation relating to employment issues.

Speed

The original Donovan ideal was of a very quick resolution to the grievance. This allowed the employee and employer to put the issue behind them and continue with a good working relationship or, if the employee had left the employer, allowed the employee to leave the issue and move on to find new employment.

All the employment tribunals have targets to hear claims speedily. However, typically many months elapse between the application to the employment tribunals and the hearing. The actual time lapse will depend on the area of the country where the application is lodged and the expected length of the hearing. There are simply too many applications for the process to work any quicker. In the late 1960s there were around 9500 applications registered at the Employment Tribunals each year. In the year 2002–2003, 91,793 applications were received.

Inexpensive

There is currently no charge for bringing an application to the employment tribunals – although we shall see when we review the future of the employment tribunals that this might change in the future.

If an employee chooses to represent himself, and many do, there are obviously no legal costs. If the employee chooses to seek legal representation then legal aid is not available, and hence the employee must meet those costs. If the employee is a member of a trade union then that union will typically represent the employee, presuming that they do not feel the case is totally unfounded. In some cases the employee might get representation or support from one of the bodies we looked at in the last section – such as the Equal Opportunities Commission or the Disability Rights Commission.

In many courts the unsuccessful party has to meet all or part of the costs of the opposing side. In the Employment Tribunals this is unusual, although the practice is increasing. In 2002–2003 costs were awarded in just 998 cases (307 times to applicants and 691 times to respondents). The average amount of costs awarded was £1524.

We can see, therefore, that there are ways in which the 'Donovan ideal' is far away from the reality of today. However, the employment tribunals are still a court at the lowest rung of the court hierarchy and there is still a desire to ensure that the employee is able to bring his case and present it in a simple format.

Further Exploration

How relevant do you think the 'Donovan ideal' is for today's world of employment? Are the issues of accessibility, informality, speed and expense of primary importance? Any students particularly interested in this should read the original Donovan report. Compare and contrast that report with the report of the Employment Tribunal System Taskforce (www.dti.gov.uk/er/individual/taskforce.htm).

RELATIONSHIP BALANCE

An application to the Employment Tribunals is usually brought by an individual (although there are cases when a group of employees with the same grievance bring a joint claim). This focus on the individual reflects the increasingly individualised nature of employment rights. As we work through the various areas of employment law in this book you will notice that most of the legislation gives right to the individual, rather than rights to a group of individuals (eg a trade union). Note which legislation is focusing on the group, and which is focusing on the individual.

THE PROCESS OF THE EMPLOYMENT TRIBUNALS

The Employment Tribunal consists of a chairperson and two lay members. The chairperson is a fully qualified lawyer, who either works full time as a chairperson, or who practises law part time. The lay members are appointed by the Secretary of State for Trade and Industry. They have extensive experience and knowledge of employment issues. In each employment tribunal one lay member will come from an 'employee' background (eg a trade union official) and one from an 'employer' background (eg a personnel manager). The three members of the Employment Tribunal have an equal vote in deciding the outcome of each case.

In certain cases the Chairman can sit alone to hear a case. These are specific claims under legislation such as the Pension Schemes Act 1993 and the National Minimum Wage Act 1998.

The employment tribunals have jurisdiction to hear cases relating to over 80 different pieces of legislation. In the 2002–2003 Employment Tribunals Service's Annual Report the most common types of claims were reported as:

Table 2.1

	Number of claims (total 91,793)
Unfair dismissal	38,612
Wages Act	20,987
Breach of contract	9,417
Sex discrimination	8,128
Redundancy pay	4,414
Equal pay	3,077
Race discrimination	3,039
Disability discrimination	2,716
Working Time Directive	1,403

Bringing a claim to the Employment Tribunals

An employee makes an application to the employment tribunals by completing the form known as an IT1. This form must be lodged at the Employment Tribunals within three months of the alleged incident occurring.

For example, if the employee has been dismissed the application must reach the employment tribunals within three months of the date of dismissal. If the employee is alleging that an act of sex discrimination has occurred the application must reach the employment tribunals within three months of the last date of the alleged act of discrimination occurring.

If the application is presented after this date, and the applicant can show a justifiable reason for the delay, the application can be referred to a preliminary hearing of the Employment Tribunals to consider whether the reason is indeed justifiable and whether the case should go forward to a full hearing.

The possible reasons for a late application include (although these will not necessarily be accepted as justifiable reasons – it will depend on the details of each case):

- ignorance of rights
- ignorance of the time limit
- advisers not being aware of the time limit, or not giving clear advice regarding it
- the applicant being ill or too distressed to make a claim
- the applicant being disabled and needing to seek help, which took time to arrange
- waiting for internal procedures within the organisation to be completed
- applications being lost or delayed in the post
- waiting for the outcome of other legal proceedings.

It is not possible to have clear rules on when an application presented out of time could still be accepted because the details of each application will vary. The following cases illustrate this issue.

Avon County Council v *Haywood-Hicks* [1978] ICR 646

In this case the applicant was a polytechnic manager. He had been dismissed, and he claimed it had been an unfair dismissal. His application was received by the employment tribunal six weeks after the three-month period had elapsed. He claimed that he was not aware of the existence of Employment Tribunals, and the possibility of bringing a claim, until he read an article in a newspaper. The Employment Tribunal ruled that he ought to have investigated his rights and ought to have claimed in time. They ruled that the idea that a well-educated and intelligent man had no idea of his rights 'offended their notion of common sense'. Hence, the time limit was not extended in this case.

House of Clydesdale v *Foy* [1976] IRLR 391, EAT

In this case Foy had become aware of his right to claim unfair dismissal when he saw Department of Employment literature at the local employment exchange. However, he did not realise there was a time limit. The Employment Appeal Tribunal found that, if he had read the literature carefully, he would have been aware of the time limit and hence ignorance was no defence. Again, the application to extend the time limit was rejected.

Shultz v *Esso Petroleum Ltd* [1999] IRLR 488

The applicant became depressed during the last six weeks of the three-month period for application, and claimed he was too depressed to instruct solicitors. The employment tribunal and the employment appeal tribunal both found in favour of the respondent. However, the Court of Appeal held that it had not been practicable for the applicant to lodge a claim. The Court of Appeal stressed that the issue of practicability was paramount.

Responding to a claim in the Employment Tribunal

The relevant Regional Office of the Employment Tribunal receives the application to the tribunal and a copy is sent to the respondent. The respondent is also sent a form known as an IT3 to complete and return to the employment tribunal within 21 days. As well as confirming details of the applicant and the respondent, the IT3 requires the respondent to outline their defence of the claim.

When the 21-day period has elapsed the case will be listed for a hearing in the employment tribunal. If the respondent does not respond within the 21-day period the case will still be listed, although the respondent can apply for a time extension if there are grounds for this request. A copy of the completed IT3 is sent to the applicant by the employment tribunal.

It should be noted that the Government is consulting about proposed changes to the application and response forms. It is expected that the use of the new forms will be mandatory from 6 April 2005. Progress with the consultation, and draft forms, can be found on the DTI website (www.dti.gov.uk).

 TASK Find out what preparations each party needs to make before a hearing. Looking at the Employment Tribunals Service website (www.ets.gov.uk) will help in doing this.

Hearings prior to a full hearing

There are circumstances in which an application can be listed for some form of review prior to a full hearing. These are:

Pre-hearing review

The purpose of the pre-hearing review is to act as a deterrent to a party to pursue a claim that has little or no chance of success by ordering payment of a deposit. It is unusual for a party that has been ordered to pay a deposit to go on and win their case.

The review considers whether the application or the response has any likelihood of being successful. A chairperson may instruct that a pre-hearing is needed, or it might be requested by either party (usually the respondent). At this hearing the contents of the IT1 and the IT3 are reviewed and both sides are able to make representations. No witnesses are called. The Employment Tribunal (or the Chairperson sitting alone) has to decide whether to order one party to pay a deposit before proceeding. If that party goes on to lose the case and is ordered to pay costs the money will be deducted from the deposit. The maximum deposit that can be ordered is £500.

Preliminary hearing

The purpose of a preliminary hearing is to consider an issue that might affect the right of an individual to bring a claim to the Employment Tribunal. We have already considered the role of the preliminary hearing in determining whether a claim can be considered when it is presented outside of the three-month qualifying period. A preliminary hearing might also be requested when a claim for disability discrimination has been brought and there is dispute over whether the applicant is disabled as defined by the Disability Discrimination Act 1995 (see Chapter 6).

Settlement prior to the hearing

In most employment law cases Acas has a statutory duty to contact both parties and try to reach a conciliated settlement. According to the Acas Annual Report 2002–03, settlements of claims through Acas in that year were:

Table 2.2

Unfair dismissal	46%
Disability discrimination	45%
Breach of contract	38%
Race discrimination	38%
Wages Act	35%
Working time	35%
National minimum wage	28%
Sex discrimination	27%
Redundancy pay	17%
Equal pay	15%
Others	25%

It is usual for the conciliation to involve a payment of some financial sum, although reinstatement or re-engagement can occur in some cases. When both sides have agreed a settlement it is confirmed on a form COT3 and the case is then withdrawn from the Employment Tribunal. The signing of the COT3 prohibits either side from pursuing any issue relating to the case.

Outside of the Acas process a compromise agreement can be reached. These agreements have the same status as a COT3 (ie the parties cannot take the claim any further) but are not negotiated through Acas. A compromise must be in writing and can be reached only when the employee has received advice from a relevant, independent adviser. An independent adviser is a qualified lawyer, a certified adviser from an independent trade union, or a worker at an advice centre who has been certified as an adviser for this purpose.

In addition, the applicant can withdraw their application at any stage.

In 2002–03 70 per cent of cases lodged with the employment tribunals were withdrawn or settled before the full hearing.

RELATIONSHIP BALANCE

The number of cases withdrawn before a full hearing is very significant. For what reasons do you think applicants might withdraw their claims? Is the high level of withdrawal a concern? How are employees protected in situations where they have no legal representation, but the respondent is represented by highly qualified lawyers?

THE OPERATION OF THE EMPLOYMENT TRIBUNALS

Before the case is listed, a chairman will have reviewed the file and estimated how long the case will take to hear. The majority of cases are listed for one day (or part day), but it is quite possible for a hearing to go beyond this time, especially if a group of applicants is bringing a case against a respondent. Unless there are good reasons, all hearings are open to the public. Exceptions to this include situations where national security might be at risk, or where a juvenile is involved in some way.

After all the evidence has been presented, and all witnesses have been heard, the Employment Tribunal retires to reach a verdict. The verdict has to be a majority view, not necessarily a unanimous view. The Employment Tribunal can give its judgment in summary form (ie identifying just the key facts and concluding with the judgment) or give extended reasons. Extended reasons give a thorough summary of the facts of the case, an explanation of the reasons behind the decision of the Employment Tribunal and a summary of the merits of the case. A party requiring extended reasons must request them within 21 days of the summary reasons being given. It is not unusual for summary reasons to be given before the parties leave the tribunal building. This will depend on the time available and the complexity of the case.

TASK Find out more about the procedure that is followed during an Employment Tribunal hearing. You will find useful Information on the Employment Tribunals Service website (www.ets.gov.uk).

The decision of the Employment Tribunal is not only who has 'won' the case, but also what remedies are to be made. The remedies will vary according to the type of claim brought. For example, if the claim brought is for an unlawful deduction of wages, and the Employment Tribunal finds that there has been an unlawful deduction, the remedy will be to pay the money that has been unlawfully deducted.

In cases such as unfair dismissal and discrimination (when employment has ended) there are three options available to the Employment Tribunal: reinstatement, re-engagement and compensation.

Reinstatement

The employee returns to the job he had – this was awarded in 0.2 per cent of unfair dismissal claims in 2002–03. (This is a rare remedy because the relationship between the employee and the previous management is usually too badly damaged for a working relationship to be resumed. In addition, it is quite possible that the employee has gone on to find new employment whilst waiting for the hearing.)

Re-engagement

The employee returns to the company, but in a different role – this was awarded in 14.7 per cent of unfair dismissal cases in 2001–02.

Compensation

The company is ordered to pay an amount of money to the employee – this was awarded in 28.2 per cent of unfair dismissal cases in 2002–03. (The remaining cases were settled before coming to the Employment Tribunal.)

Compensation awards for unfair dismissal are currently capped at £55,000 – this figure is reviewed annually. There is no maximum compensation for a successful discrimination claim. However, large awards are still relatively rare. In 2002–03 average awards of compensation are given in Table 2.3.

Table 2.3

	£
Unfair dismissal	£6,776
Sex discrimination	£8,787
Race discrimination	£27,041
Disability discrimination	£10,157

TASK Attend the local Employment Tribunal. Hearings typically start at 10am, so arrive at least 15 minutes before. Explain to the clerk the purpose of your visit, and ask advice for a suitable hearing to watch. Try to attend the full hearing, and (if the decision is given that day) stay to hear the decision.

THE ROLE OF THE EMPLOYMENT APPEAL TRIBUNAL

Both the applicant and the respondent have the right to appeal against the decision of the Employment Tribunal. An appeal is referred to the Employment Appeal Tribunal (EAT). It is usual for the composition of the EAT to be one legally qualified chairman and two lay members. In this case, however, the chairman is a judge from the High Court or the Court of Appeal nominated by the Lord Chancellor. As with the Employment Tribunal, one lay member comes from an 'employer' background and one from an 'employee' background. On rare occasions (usually when a matter of great importance is being heard) a Chairman might sit with four lay members, two from each side.

An appeal can be made only on a point of law, or on a claim that the finding of the Employment Tribunals is 'perverse'. In addition, there can be an appeal if the decision has been subject to some fundamental flaw, such as one member of the Employment Tribunal has been found to be known to one of the parties; or a member of the Employment Tribunal behaved in a way that clearly demonstrated bias; or if the Employment Tribunal refused to hear a witness, allow cross-examination, or to take note of a piece of relevant evidence. An appeal is also allowed if a member of the Employment Tribunal falls asleep during the hearing!

An appeal must be lodged within 42 days of the date that the extended reasons were sent to the appellant. The appeal is lodged by serving a notice of appeal along with a copy of the Tribunal's decision and a copy of the extended reasons.

All appeals are listed for a preliminary hearing/directions (PHD). The main purpose of the PHD is to determine whether there are adequate grounds for appeal and, if there are, to give directions to both parties on preparation for the full appeal hearing.

In claiming that a finding was perverse the appellant must show that the conclusion reached by the Employment Tribunal was one that no reasonable tribunal could have reached. This is very difficult to present successfully. For example:

Williams & ors v *Whitbread Beer Co* [1996] CA

Williams was attending a works-related course and after a course session went to the hotel bar. He had a number of drinks and became loud and abusive to a fellow employee. When his manager told him to 'tone it down' he became loud and abusive towards his manager. Whitbread held a disciplinary hearing and Williams was summarily dismissed for gross misconduct.

The Employment Tribunal found that the dismissal was not within the band of reasonable responses of a reasonable company, and hence concluded that the dismissal was unfair.

Whitbread appealed and the appeal was upheld because the EAT concluded that a reasonable employment tribunal could have concluded that dismissal was a fair response.

The Court of Appeal overturned the EAT's decision, stating that the role of the EAT was to determine whether the tribunal had reached a conclusion that no reasonable tribunal could have reached. They ruled that the Tribunal's conclusion was reasonable, and even if it was not the conclusion the EAT would have reached there was no evidence of 'perversity' and hence the decision of the Employment Tribunal had to stand.

TASK Read the Annual Report of the Employment Tribunals Service (www.ets.gov.uk/annualreport). The statistics quoted in this chapter largely come from this report – by reading the report you will learn a lot of supporting information.

Further Exploration

Many of the cases we shall study in this book have been referred to appeal – some to a higher level of appeal than the Employment Appeal Tribunal. Look at a number of these cases and identify the reasons that the appeal was made. What are the most common reasons that you identify? Do you think there is any way that the procedure of the Employment Tribunals needs to be changed to reduce the number of cases that go to appeal?

EMPLOYMENT RIGHTS (DISPUTE RESOLUTION) ACT 1998

As we noted earlier in the chapter, claims to the Employment Tribunals have grown sharply over the years. However, the level of growth seemed to reach a peak in 2000–01, with the number of applications falling in 2001–02 and then falling further in 2002–03. Although no precise reason for the drop is known it could well be linked to a number of initiatives to address the overloaded Employment Tribunals Service.

Although there has been a slight drop in applications, the current Employment Tribunals system is one that was originally designed to cope with a very limited range of legislation, and a few thousand claims each year, which is now coping with an increasingly wide range of legislation and over one hundred thousand claims each year.

Why have the claims increased?

1 *Every time new legislation is introduced there are new claims that can be brought to the Employment Tribunal.* An interesting example of this is the introduction of the Employment Act 2002 (which we shall examine in more detail at various times throughout this book). In this Act the ability for an employee to request flexible working hours if they have a child aged 6 years or less is introduced. Any complaints about the way this request is handled by the organisation are referred to the Employment Tribunals – new legislation for the Employment Tribunal to address. In addition, the Act introduces new rules for the handling of disciplinary and grievance procedures. This is partly to reduce the number of claims to the Employment Tribunals, because it introduces the requirement to have internal procedures that must be exhausted before a claim can be brought to the Employment Tribunals. However, it also brings in a change to the way an important principle of unfair dismissal is dealt with (known as the 'Polkey rule' – we shall examine this in Chapter 8) and that is likely to increase the number of claims to the Employment Tribunals whilst this area is being clarified by case law.

2 *More people can bring claims to the Employment Tribunals.* Until February 1995, part-time employees had to have five years' continuous service before they could bring a claim for unfair dismissal to the Employment Tribunals. As we shall see in Chapter 6, this was challenged as being discriminatory against women – because significantly more women than men work part time. Hence, under the Employment Protection (Part-time Employees) Regulations 1995 the qualifying period for part-time employees was brought into line with full-time employees. Up until 1999, full-time employees were required to have two years' continuous service before they brought a claim to the Employment Tribunals. In a similar way to the part-time case explained above, the two-year rule was challenged on the grounds of indirect discrimination. In *R* v *Secretary of State for Employment ex parte Seymour Smith* [1997] 1 WLR 473 it was shown that, on average, women have significantly shorter periods of continuous service than men, and hence the two-year rule discriminated against women. On this basis the qualifying period was reduced to one year in 1999 in the Unfair Dismissal and Statement of Reasons for Dismissal (Variation of Qualifying Period) Regulations 1999. Again, we shall look at this case in more detail in Chapter 6.

3 *Employees are more aware of their rights.* It is certainly true that employees are more aware of their rights. They might not be certain exactly what those rights are, but they know enough to be prompted to go and find out more. It is more likely, therefore, that employees will think about the possibility of bringing a claim.

Further Exploration

Can you think of any other reasons that the claims to the Employment Tribunals might have fallen? Would you predict that the number of claims will fall further, or do you think that there will be an increase? What are the reasons for your predictions? Make sure you read the next annual report of the Employment Tribunals Service, and see if you are right.

RELATIONSHIP BALANCE

It is hard to determine what a really hopeless case is until all the facts have been heard. However, there will always be employers who defend cases that are indefensible and employees who bring cases that are truly hopeless. The measures we have looked at try to deter this occurring. However, do you think that the employers and employees who bring/defend such claims really believe that they do have grounds for their actions? If so, should they be deterred from bringing a claim?

ACAS ARBITRATION SCHEME

The Employment Rights (Dispute Resolution) Act 1998 introduced a new scheme to try to reduce the pressure on the employment tribunals system. It is known as the Acas Arbitration Scheme. The scheme was launched in May 2001 and it was hoped that this would take the strain off the Employment Tribunals system. In reality it has had little impact, indeed it handled only 13 cases in 2001–02 and 23 cases in 2002–03. However, it is an important step and needs examination.

The Acas Arbitration Scheme addresses only unfair dismissal cases. Although that limits its jurisdiction, we must remember that nearly half of all claims to the Employment Tribunals do relate to unfair dismissal.

The main advantage of the scheme is that it will hear claims quickly, it will be informal and it will be speedy – remember the Donovan ideal we examined at the start of this chapter.

The initial lodging of the claim is still to the Employment Tribunals, through submitting an IT1. If both parties agree, the claim may then be taken out of the employment tribunals process and directed to the Acas Arbitration process. At the stage an Acas Arbitrator (not an Acas member of staff, but an independent person appointed by Acas who is deemed to have specialist relevant knowledge) is appointed to the case. The Acas Arbitrator then arranges a time for the hearing as quickly as possible, with a target of being heard within a period of two months.

The hearings are conducted informally, and as locally as possible to the parties. There is no cross-examination of witnesses (witness statements may be presented, but the witnesses are not questioned), no formal pleadings and the proceedings are confidential. The two parties simply explain their side of the case to the Acas Arbitrator, bringing to his attention any relevant documents. Each party is also allowed the opportunity to comment on the other party's written submission. The Acas Arbitrator then questions both parties and also seeks views on any remedy that might be awarded. Both parties are then invited to make closing statements. The Acas Arbitrator determines whether the dismissal was fair or unfair and, if the dismissal is deemed to be unfair, determines remedies. The decision is not given at the hearing, but is communicated to both parties in writing after the hearing.

The decision of the Arbitrator is final – there is no route of appeal unless there is a challenge on the grounds of substantive jurisdiction, or on grounds of serious irregularity.

Why has the system been so little used?

1   The limited focus of jurisdiction can be a problem. It is not unusual for a claim to relate to more than one area of legislation. For example, there could be a claim for unfair dismissal and unlawful deduction of wages. If such a claim went through the Acas Arbitration route, only the part relating to unfair dismissal could be heard. The matter relating to unlawful deduction of wages would have to be referred to the Employment Tribunal, meaning that the parties would need to attend two hearings. This is unlikely to be popular with applicants or respondents.

2   In addition, if there are any disputes relating to the claim (eg was the applicant actually dismissed, was the application to the Employment Tribunal made in time, etc) the Acas Arbitrator cannot hear the claim. Again, it is not unusual for these types of issues to accompany a claim for unfair dismissal.

3   There is no right of appeal. Although this means the claim is finalised more quickly, people might be apprehensive about committing themselves to a scheme where there is no appeal – especially as there is an alternative (ie the Employment Tribunal) where there is the right of appeal.

4   The hearings are in private and hence representatives are not able to assess how effective the process is and decide if they want to use this route. In reality this is a small issue, as there have been so few hearings. However, a representative has a responsibility to give the best advice possible to his client. Hence, he might find it difficult to recommend a process he has never seen in operation and knows relatively little about.

5   The Acas Arbitrator is not required to be legally qualified. Although the Acas Arbitrator will be thoroughly trained, and will have been selected for his depth of knowledge and experience, some applicants or respondents might feel uncomfortable that no formal legal qualification is required.

Acas, in their 2001–02 annual report, commented that the reason the scheme has been so little used is that people do not understand the benefits of the scheme, or have not appreciated that the outcome is likely to be the same as going through the Employment Tribunal scheme.

Whatever the reasons for the poor uptake, the scheme is currently under review. There could be alterations made to it, or it could simply be relaunched with more publicity and more explanation.

TASK   Relate the Acas Arbitration Scheme back to the Donovan 'ideal'. On the basis of that analysis do think the scheme is well designed? What would you alter to make the scheme more attractive?

EMPLOYMENT TRIBUNALS (CONSTITUTION AND RULES OF PROCEDURE) REGULATIONS 2001

The Acas Arbitration Scheme addresses only unfair dismissal claims. In addition, it only provides an alternative route to the Employment Tribunals. It does not help to resolve some of the difficulties with the tribunal system itself. The Employment Tribunals (Constitution and Rules of Procedure) Regulations 2001 were brought into effect to try to address specific problems within the employment tribunals system.

In the explanation of the regulations it is explained that their purpose is to deal with cases fairly, cost effectively, expeditiously and justly. The main changes that were introduced were: costs, deposit and strike out.

Costs

As we have already noted, in 2002–03 costs were awarded in just 998 of cases, with an average award of £1524. These regulations tried to address the issue of costs in relation to unmeritorious claims. Prior to the regulations there was the possibility for the Employment Tribunals to award costs if they considered that the applicant bringing the case or either party's conduct during the case had been 'frivolous'. The maximum possible costs award prior to the regulations was £500.

The regulations broadened the range of situations in which costs can be awarded. There is now the opportunity to award costs when the application or the conduct of the proceedings has been 'misconceived'. 'Misconceived' means that the case has no reasonable prospect of success.

Those who bring misconceived cases will mostly be employees who are not represented who have a real (but misplaced) belief that the employer has acted in some illegal manner. The potential for costs to be awarded should encourage employees to seek more advice before pursuing a claim. However, this does presume that employees realise they might have a weak case, and that they need that advice. It could be argued that if they realised they had such a weak case they might never have considered a claim in the first place!

The awarding of costs against the unrepresented employee does require a change of attitude of the Employment Tribunals. Although the 'Donovan ideal' might be very distant from today's reality, there is still the underlying idea that Tribunals are there for the employee to bring a case against the employer in a simple way, looking for an independent judgment on the issue. Awarding costs might deter the employee who has genuinely been treated badly, going against the whole philosophy of the Employment Tribunals.

As well as widening the grounds for costs to be awarded, the maximum was also increased from £500 to £10,000. This is very likely to see more applications for costs being made – many employers (or employees) will not have seen it worthwhile to pursue a possible £500, but £10,000 is much more attractive. It is also likely to deter employees with weak cases from applying to the Employment Tribunals. There is also the possibility that employers with weak defences to a claim will be more likely to settle out of court, reducing the numbers of claims coming to the Employment Tribunals.

The impact of the changes in costs will depend on how widely costs are awarded. In 2002–03 the number of occasions when costs are awarded would have resulted in no significant impact on the number of cases coming to the Employment Tribunals. It will be interesting to track the numbers and amounts of costs awarded and to determine if there is a significant increase.

Deposit

As we have already noted, the Employment Tribunals can require an applicant to pay a deposit, following a review of the case at a pre-hearing review. The regulations increased this deposit from £150 to £500 – again trying to reduce the number of weak claims to the employment tribunals. However, deposits are rarely awarded and this increase will be of no relevance unless deposits become more widely used.

Strike Out

Prior to the regulations an Employment Tribunal could 'strike out' a claim on the basis that it was 'scandalous, frivolous, or vexatious'. As with the definitions relating to costs, the term 'frivolous' was replaced with the term 'misconceived' in these regulations. As before, this covers cases that the Employment Tribunal judges to have no reasonable chance of success. This aspect of the regulations does give more powers to the Employment Tribunal but is largely thought to be unlikely to have much effect. Not only are Employment Tribunals reluctant to judge a case before all the facts have been presented, but the strike out could be challenged under the Human Right Acts 1998, specifically the right to a fair trial.

THE FUTURE FOR THE EMPLOYMENT TRIBUNALS

Despite all the changes outlined above, the Government remained concerned about the effective working of the Employment Tribunals. In July 2001, therefore, it published a consultation document entitled 'Routes to Resolution: Improving Dispute Resolution in Britain'. The focus of the consultation document is on reforming the current employment tribunal process and on encouraging more resolution of disputes back in the workplace. If more disputes are resolved at the place of work there will be fewer cases for the Employment Tribunals to handle.

The consultation document had a number of recommendations under three main headings: resolving disputes at work, promoting conciliation, and modernising Employment Tribunals.

Resolving disputes at work

This section focused on the suggestion that applications can be made to the employment tribunal only once disciplinary or grievance procedures have been completed in the workplace. In addition it looked at the possibility of allowing Employment Tribunals to ignore minor procedural mistakes in the way in which an issue has been handled in the workplace. Most of the issues under this heading went on to be addressed in the Employment Act 2002, and we shall examine them in more detail in Chapter 7.

The reasons behind this section are primarily to reduce the number of cases coming to the Employment Tribunals, and to resolve conflict more speedily and at the source of the conflict.

Promoting conciliation

This set of proposals moved on from the workplace resolution, to disputes that it has not been possible to settle in this way. The main issues were to remove Acas's duty to conciliate in all cases, not requiring them to get involved in cases where the facts are not in dispute but the concern is a technical point on how the law should be applied. This section also looked at having a fixed period for conciliation to try to achieve more timely settlements and broadening the scope of compromise agreements and the number of bodies that can carry out conciliation.

The purpose of this section is to handle the conciliation of cases more speedily, and to try to settle more cases before they come to the Employment Tribunals.

Modernising Employment Tribunals

The proposals then went on to look at ways of improving the process for claims that cannot be resolved outside of the Employment Tribunals. The proposals covered the possibility of charging for an application to the Employment Tribunals. No figure was suggested in the report. This suggestion caused a lot of concern amongst both employer and employee bodies consulted as a result of the report. At present it has not been taken any further, but it is always a possibility for the future.

In addition there were suggestions giving a clearer focus on costs. There was the suggestion that costs are presumed to be awarded to the winning party when faced with a weak application or response – therefore taking away the requirement for the Employment Tribunal to justify the awarding of costs. The proposals to allow costs to be awarded directly against representatives who have conducted a case unreasonably and to award costs compensating for time spent in preparation, were included in the Employment Act 2002.

As a result of the consultation document, an Employment Tribunal System Taskforce was set up in October 2001. Its purpose was to consider all the proposals put forward by the Government and to publish a report making clear recommendations on the way forward for the Employment Tribunals. This report was published in July 2002.

In the report's introduction, it gives a vision of the Employment Tribunals Service as being appropriate to the needs of the 21st century, and being able to deal with cases in a just and fair manner. In considering how this vision will be achieved it emphasises the importance of such issues as accessibility, being easily understandable, speed, consistency and the need to be properly resourced.

It is interesting to note that the vision is not dissimilar to the original vision of Donovan back in 1968.

TASK Read the full report of the Employment Tribunal System Taskforce (www.dti.gov.uk/er/individual/taskforce.htm). Track the progress of any changes to the Employment Tribunal Service during your studies.

Following the publication of the Employment Tribunal System Taskforce Report, and as a result of issues within the Employment Act 2002, revised regulations relating to the employment tribunals system are expected to come into force on 1 October 2004. The key reforms proposed (and not confirmed at the time of writing) are:

- The IT1 and IT3 will disappear and be replaced by 'Claim' and 'Response' forms. The forms will contain certain specified information, and if this is not included they will be rejected.

- There will be new procedures to sift out claims and responses that should not proceed.

- Acas's duty to conciliate will be limited to a fixed period (either a seven-week short period or a standard thirteen-week period), depending on the nature of the case. This will discourage the practice of settling just before the Tribunal hearing takes place. Conciliation periods in discrimination cases (which are usually more complicated) will remain unlimited.

- There will be a new provision for costs award in respect of preparation time in some circumstances and it will be possible for representatives (except not-for-profit representatives) to incur a costs award on account of their own conduct.

- The rules will apply to the whole of Great Britain, replacing the current separate (but largely similar) rules for England, Wales and Scotland.

Further Exploration

Read the consultation document and the draft regulations (www.dti.gov.uk/er/individual/etregs). (Note: Once these drafts become legislation the DTI will remove the consultation and draft from their website.)

CHAPTER REVIEW

1 The Employment Tribunals system was originally intended to be easily accessible, informal, speedy and inexpensive

2 The Employment Tribunals have jurisdiction to hear cases relating to over 80 pieces of legislation, the most common being unfair dismissal.

3 An applicant lodging an IT1 at the Tribunals within three months of an alleged incident occurring starts the process of a claim to a Tribunal. The respondent must reply to this claim within 21 days using an IT3.

4 The Employment Appeal Tribunal reviews cases when there is dispute over a point of law, or the judgment of the Employment Tribunal is viewed as 'perverse'.

5 There has been a significant increase in the numbers of cases coming to the Employment Tribunals. This is because of increased legislation, more people being eligible to bring claims, and an increased awareness of employee rights.

6 The Acas Arbitration Scheme was introduced to reduce the number of claims being heard by the Employment Tribunals, focusing only on unfair dismissal claims. To date, it has not been widely used.

7 The Employment Tribunals (Constitution and Rules of Procedure) Regulations 2001 were brought into effect to try to address specific problems within the tribunal system.

8 An Employment Tribunal System Taskforce has been set up to make recommendations and oversee ongoing changes to the Employment Tribunal Service.

WEBSITES REFERENCED IN THIS CHAPTER

www.dti.gov.uk	Department of Trade and Industry
www.dti.gov.uk/er/individual/taskforce.htm	Employment Tribunal System Taskforce
www.ets.gov.uk	Employment Tribunals Service

OTHER USEFUL WEBSITE

www.employmentappeals.gov.uk	Employment Appeal Tribunal

EXAMPLES TO WORK THROUGH

1   In your post this morning has arrived an IT1 from a previous employee who was sacked for gross misconduct. He was dismissed on 2 February 2003, and today's date is 23 May 2003. How do you proceed?

2   Peter was an employee of yours for 20 years. He worked as a sales representative, and was a successful employee. Two months ago it was discovered that Peter had been falsifying his expenses. After an investigation it was decided to dismiss him for gross misconduct. You have now received an IT1 from Peter claiming unfair dismissal. He claims that he was never given an adequate opportunity to explain the situation, which you strongly deny. He also claims that he is owed some outstanding commission. You have been informed that Peter would like the unfair dismissal part of the claim to be heard through the Acas Arbitration Scheme. You have been asked whether you agree to this request. Your managing director has asked you to prepare him a short report arguing for and against using the scheme, and recommending a decision. Prepare that report for the managing director.

3   You have been asked to give a presentation to your colleagues on the current issues facing the Employment Tribunals system, and the most effective solutions. Summarise the key points you would make within the presentation.

Contract of Employment

CHAPTER 3

The objectives of this chapter are to:

- **Understand the tests used in law to determine whether a person is an employee;**

- **Examine the component parts of the contract of employment;**

- **Outline the detail to be contained in the statement of initial employment particulars;**

- **Understand the duties of the employee and employer;**

- **Outline the concept of continuity of employment.**

WHO IS AN EMPLOYEE?

This is an important question, because most of the legal protection we shall look at in this book relates only to employees. For example, an employee can make a claim for unfair dismissal but someone else who is working in an organisation and who is not an employee cannot make a claim, even if they are dismissed in exactly the same way. Some legislation extends to both employees and those working within an organisation without employment status – anti-discrimination legislation is an example of such legislation.

There are two alternatives for those that work in an organisation. They can be hired to work under a contract *of* service (an employee) or under a contract *for* services (an independent contractor).

Section 230 (1) of the Employment Rights Act 1996 defines an employee as 'an individual who has entered into or works under a contract of employment'. Section 230 (3) of the same Act states that a worker is 'an individual who either works under a contract of employment or works under any other contract where that individual agrees to personally perform work or services for another party'. Although these definitions are of some use they do not tell us exactly who should be given a contract of employment. This is primarily because situations of employment are very varied and hence there can be no one clear rule.

Where there is any doubt over employee status, it is the responsibility of the courts (usually the Employment Tribunals) to take each individual case and to apply its judgment. They do this through a mix of using case law and applying a number of tests that have been developed over the years. This task is often carried out in a preliminary hearing – to determine, for example, whether a claim for unfair dismissal can be heard because the respondent is claiming that the applicant was never an employee.

Tests used by the courts to determine an employment relationship:

Control test

This test originates from a judgment in 1881 from the case of *Yemens* v *Noakes* QBD 530. The judge stated that 'an employee is subject to the command of his master as to the *manner* in which he shall do his work'.

The idea was that, if a person was being told how to do his work, then he was an employee. This is an outdated test for two main reasons. First, we have a much more skilled workforce than 120 years ago, and many employees are expected to work without specific instructions, using their skill and expertise. Second, an independent contractor could be told specifically what to do if hired for a specific project (eg a company could hire an electrician to help with a rewiring project, and give very specific tasks).

Organisation test

In *Stevenson* v *MacDonald* [1952] 1 TLR 101 the judge, Lord Denning, stated that 'a person is an employee if that person is an integral part of the business'.

This is of more use than the control test, because it overcomes the problem of skilled people having control over their own work. However, it does not help us in the example of the electrician, if the company is carrying out a refurbishment project completing the rewiring is an important part of the overall process. If there is no other electrician the person who has been hired could be seen to be an 'integral part of the business' (under Lord Denning's ruling). This does not necessarily mean that he has become an employee.

Ordinary person test

In *Collins* v *Hertfordshire County Council* [1947] 1 All ER 633 the judge posed the question, 'Was a contract a contract of employment within the meaning which an ordinary person would give to those words?'

This is also known as the 'man in the street' test – in other words what would ordinary common sense conclude? However, such a simple test does not give us any guidelines as to what should be used to determine an employment relationship, and what should not. On that basis, the test is of little help.

Mutual obligations test

This test looks at the nature of the relationship between the employer and the person in question, and considers whether there is sufficient mutuality for an employment relationship to exist. There are two levels of mutuality to consider. First, is there an obligation to provide work (and an obligation to carry out that work)? Second, is there a promise of future work (both a promise to provide it, ie employer, and a promise to carry it out, ie employee)?

This test definitely helps us to understand the definition of an employee more clearly, but there are still some difficulties. If we go back to our electrician example, he could go on to be hired for a series of future refurbishment projects. Although he has no written contract of employment he starts to assume that he is an employee because there is always work for him, and he always carries it out. The employer then runs out of work for him and simply states he is no longer required. The electrician protests that he is an employee, and hence must be made redundant (see Chapter 9). The employer replies that he has always been an independent contractor, and there has never been an obligation on him to provide work for the electrician. It has simply been coincidence that a series of projects followed one after the other, so is the electrician an employee? The following case helps us to examine this further.

Carmichael v National Power [2000] IRLR 43

In this case Mrs Carmichael and her colleague worked at a power station as visitor guides. The work was part time. There was some correspondence between the ladies and National Power that the ladies relied on as a contract of employment. The relationship between the ladies and National Power was described as a 'station guide on a casual as required basis'. National Power argued, therefore, that the work was on a casual basis and that there was no obligation to provide work. On that basis the relationship was not one of employer and employee. It was also noted that on 17 occasions Mrs Carmichael had been unable to work, and her colleague had been unable to work on eight occasions. On none of these occasions had National Power taken any disciplinary action.

The employment tribunal agreed that there was no employment relationship. Eventually the Court of Appeal overturned this decision. National Power appealed against this decision and the House of Lords found in favour of the employer – therefore, the relationship in this case was not one of employer and employee.

The basis for the decision was that the relationship, as described, failed the first stage of the test of mutuality. National Power had no obligation to provide work, and Mrs Carmichael and her colleague had no obligation to work if there was work available.

Multiple test

The experience of using the tests we have examined have shown the courts that it is not possible to focus on one particular aspect of the working relationship and to use that to determine whether or not there is an employment relationship. On that basis, the most commonly used test in the courts today is the multiple test.

In using the multiple test the courts look at every aspect of the relationship as described, and use them to determine the nature of that relationship. This is best illustrated in the following case.

Ready Mixed Concrete v Minister of Pensions [1968] ER 433

Ready Mixed Concrete decided to separate the making of concrete from the delivery of the concrete. It put in place a system of 'owner drivers', in other words the delivery men would own their own vehicles and would be self-employed.

In determining whether or not the drivers were self-employed the courts looked at a number of aspects of their employment. In favour of the drivers being employees was:

- They had to wear company uniforms (suggesting a level of control from the employer).
- Their lorries had to be available for company work at certain hours (an obligation to work).

- They could use the lorries only for company business (again, suggesting a level of control).
- They had to obey the foreman's orders (definitely an issue of control).
- They could sell the lorries back to the company at an agreed valuation (not typical of an independent relationship).

In favour of the drivers being self-employed:

- The drivers were responsible for the maintenance and running costs of the lorries (suggesting that the expenses of employment were their own).
- The drivers could employ a substitute driver (there was no obligation on the driver to be personally available for work).
- The drivers could own more than one lorry (suggesting that they could work for more than one employer).
- The drivers paid their own tax and NI contributions (an employer typically deducts tax and NI from the employee's pay).

Although there were factors suggesting both types of relationship the court decided that there were three crucial conditions to meet for a contract of employment to exist:

1 Did the employee agree to provide his own work and skill?
2 Has the employer got some element of control?
3 There must not be any term inconsistent with a contract of employment.

(Inconsistency with a contract of employment could be such things as the employee being responsible for payment of his own tax and national insurance contributions – typically the employer deducts these from the employee's pay.)

The court found that the first two conditions were met. However, the third condition was not met because there were factors inconsistent with a contract of employment, and on that basis the drivers were to be classed as self-employed. The relevant factors are those listed above as being in favour of the drivers being self-employed.

In determining the nature of a working relationship in the courts today those three crucial conditions are usually addressed, and the decision is made based on the answers to them.

Further Exploration

Do you think that the courts have arrived at a satisfactory solution to the issue of deciding who is an employee? If not, what potential problems do you see with the current situation? What type of test might improve the current situation?

RELATIONSHIP BALANCE

Even if you think that the courts have not arrived at a satisfactory solution to determining who is an employee, do you think that the solution that has been arrived at is fair to both the employer and the employee? If you do not think it is fair, which party do you think it favours?

It is unlikely that there can ever be a clear-cut test that gives an objective formula to determine employment status. This is because all employment relationships differ in some way. This becomes increasingly true as we see a wider use of atypical contracts – which we shall look at in the next chapter. As we have an increasingly flexible workforce, we have increasing variations on employment relationships.

Although, therefore, we might conclude that there never will be a perfect solution to this dilemma, we must not underestimate the importance of the decisions made. An employee has a wide range of rights, which a non-employee simply does not have. It is often advantageous to be classified as an employee. However, we must remember that an employee also has a wide list of duties to the employer, and not everyone might want to be bound by these duties.

THE CONTRACT OF EMPLOYMENT

The contract of employment describes the basis of the employment relationship. It can be in writing, or it can be agreed orally. It is of great importance in the event of any dispute, because the contract of employment explains the way in which the employer and employee have agreed to work together. The contract of employment is a legal document, and hence employers should take great care in determining the content.

The terms of the contract of employment can be classified as:

- express terms
- implied terms.

Express terms are terms that have been discussed and agreed between the employer and employee. They might not be in writing. It must be emphasised that express terms cannot diminish statutory rights. We shall examine statutory rights in more detail later in this chapter, but in essence these are rights expressed in law (in statute). So, for example, the National Minimum Wage (NMW) is determined by statute. Potentially, the employer can offer a wage of a lower level than the NMW and the employee can accept this. However, if the employee then challenges this wage in the court the employer cannot argue that it is fair because it was agreed between the two parties – because it has diminished the employee's statutory rights.

Implied terms are those that have not been specifically agreed between the employer and employee but are derived from the following sources:

- collective agreements
- statute
- custom
- the courts
- work rules.

Written statement of initial employment particulars

Sections 1–7 of the Employment Rights Act 1996 set out the right of all employees to receive a written statement of initial employment particulars not later than two months after the beginning of employment. The statement must include:

- The names of the employer and the employee.
- The date when employment began.
- The date when continuous service with the employer began (ie taking into account any previous service with the employer prior to this appointment).
- The job title, or a brief description of the job duties.
- The rate of remuneration, the way in which it is to be calculated (eg the terms of a bonus scheme) and the periods at which the employee will be paid. This includes all financial benefits as well as basic pay.
- Terms and conditions relating to hours of work (eg this should include basic hours, shift patterns and rules regarding overtime).
- Terms and conditions relating to holiday pay (eg this must specify the numbers of days holiday to which the employee is entitled each year, and the period in which this is to be taken).
- The place of work, or the employer's address if the employee will be moving between a number of places of work.
- Terms and conditions relating to payments given if incapacitated due to sickness or injury.
- Details of pension schemes.
- The length of notice the employee is required to give, and the employer is entitled to receive, to terminate the contract of employment.
- Where the employment is not intended to be permanent the period for which it is expected to continue must be stated, or if it is a fixed-term contract the date it is to end.
- Any collective agreements that will directly affect the employee including, where the employer is not a party, the persons by whom they were made.
- If the employee is required to work outside of the UK for more than one month the period of work outside of the UK must be specified, the currency of the remuneration must be specified and any additional remuneration or benefits applicable to the work must be detailed. In addition, any terms and conditions relating to his return to the UK must be detailed.
- Details of disciplinary rules that apply to the employee.
- Details of grievance procedures, and the name of the person the employee should apply to if they are dissatisfied with any disciplinary decision or with whom to air a grievance.

TASK Look at the statement of initial particulars issued by your organisation, or one with which you are familiar. Does it meet all of the above criteria?

Despite this lengthy list of contents, the statement is not the contract of employment; it is simply a statement of the main terms and conditions of employment. Indeed, it should be noted that the law does not actually require employees to sign the statement, or to give any indication that they have received the statement. The statement is the employer's version of the terms and conditions, and is not an indication of any agreement being reached between the employer and the employee. If the employee accepts the terms and conditions, and works in accordance with them, it could be argued that the employer's version has contractual effect because of the lack of any challenge. In practice, a court will usually accept that the statement is strong evidence of the terms agreed by the employer and employee. However, as the statement is not a contract, either party can challenge the accuracy of the statement, as happened in the following case.

System Floors (UK) Ltd v *Daniel* [1985] IRLR 475

Daniel brought a claim of unfair dismissal against System Floors. System Floors challenged his right to bring the claim, stating that he had insufficient continuity of service. They challenged the date when employment commenced, stating it was actually one week later than stated in the written statement of initial employment particulars. The EAT allowed the employer to show that the actual starting date was different to the one stated, although it did emphasise that it is a 'heavy burden' to show that actual terms differ from the statement.

RELATIONSHIP BALANCE

When an employee seeks employment from an employer it is usually the employer who determines the terms and conditions of employment. Apart from senior employees who typically negotiate the terms of their employment in some detail, employees are usually offered a job on the basis of 'these are the terms, if you don't like them don't take the job'. Given this situation it is not surprising that the initial statement is seen as the employer's interpretation of the terms and conditions of employment.

However, as the statement can be issued at any time during the first two months of employment it is quite possible that the employee has started employment when the statement is received and has possibly left other employment to take the job. 'Don't take the job' might not be a fair solution if the statement is not as the employee expected. Do you think, therefore, that the current legislation relating to the statement protects the rights of the employee? Alternatively, do you think the employer is protected sufficiently if the employee has the right to challenge the statement after the employment has commenced? In what circumstances might each situation be fair?

IMPLIED TERMS

Collective agreements

A collective agreement is an agreement made between the employer and the employee's trade union or association. As the term suggests, the agreement applies 'collectively' to all employees covered by the negotiating group. Typical topics for collective agreements are pay, bonus schemes, shift patterns, redundancy agreements, disciplinary and grievance procedures.

A collective agreement can be incorporated into (become part of) a contract of employment by express incorporation or implied incorporation:

Express incorporation
Here there is a clear statement that the employer and employee agree to be bound by a collective agreement. This is typically a statement within the collective agreement that

expressly incorporates the collective agreement into the contract of employment. An example of express incorporation is found in the following case.

NCB v *Galley* [1958] 1 WLR 16

The pit deputies working for the National Coal Board had contracts of employment that stated that they were regulated by any national agreements. After negotiation with the trade unions a national agreement was revised, and a clause requiring pit deputies to work on such days as reasonably practicable was inserted. This could potentially involve working on Saturdays. Galley refused to work on Saturdays and was held to be in breach of his contract. This was because his contract of employment stated that his employment was governed by national agreements, and hence the revised collective agreement had been expressly incorporated into his contract.

Implied corporation

If there is no express term, an alternative is to claim that the collective agreement has been incorporated into a contract of employment by 'implication'. If the employer and employee have always conducted the employment relationship in accordance with the collective agreement then it can be implied that they agreed to be bound by that agreement. However, this is less certain than a term that has been expressly incorporated, as the intention to be bound by an agreement can always be challenged, as in the following case.

Campbell v *Union Carbide* [2002] EAT 0341/01

Campbell was employed as a chemical plant operator, initially with ICI. ICI entered into a collective agreement with the recognised trade union that included a clause covering redundancy payments, that was stated to be legally binding, and another clause headed 'Discretionary Severance in Non-Redundancy Cases'. The part of ICI in which Campbell worked was transferred to Union Carbide Ltd, along with all terms and conditions of employment. After a period of time Campbell was given notice of termination on the grounds of ill-health. He claimed that he was entitled to payments under the 'discretionary severance in non-redundancy cases' clause because these payments had been made by the organisation in all previous cases when an employee had been terminated following a lengthy period of sickness absence. Union Carbide refused to make the payment stressing that the payments were classed as 'discretionary'.

The EAT ruled that, although the payments had always been made, this did not give rise to incorporation by implication or evidence of a contractual term. The important question was whether there was evidence that both parties intended the payments to form a term of the contract. Because the payments had specifically been called 'discretionary' payments it ruled that the employer had indicated that there was no intention for the payments to be contractual and hence there was no requirement to make the payments.

What collective agreements exist in your organisation (or an organisation with which you are familiar)? Are they expressly incorporated into the contract of employment? If they are not, is there evidence that they have been incorporated by implication?

Statute

As already noted, a contract of employment cannot diminish any rights of the employee determined by statute. Any relevant statute automatically forms a part of the contract of employment. Two examples are:

1 National Minimum Wage Act 1998 (see Chapter 5). The employer must pay at least the minimum wage as determined by the Secretary of State.

2 Working Time Regulations 1998 (see Chapter 5). The employer must allow all employees covered by this legislation the breaks, holidays, rest periods and maximum weekly hours as laid out in the regulations.

Custom and practice

Before written particulars and written contracts of employment were widely used custom and practice was of importance, because looking at the 'way it has always been done' gave a good indication of the terms by which the employer and employee intended to be bound. Since the introduction of written documents, custom and practice has become less important.

However, it can still be argued that if there is a definite practice that is reasonable and is generally applied, it could form part of the contract of employment. In determining whether the practice has become part of the contract a full range of issues must be considered, including how long the custom has been in place, whether the policy regarding the custom has been brought to the attention of employees by management, and whether there is evidence that both parties intended the custom to be part of the contract of employment.

Custom and practice can be useful in helping the courts to interpret a contractual term that is not clear.

If we look back at the case of *Campbell* v *Union Carbide Ltd* (2002) EAT 0341/01 we see the issue of custom and practice highlighted. Although Union Carbide had always paid the ill-health severance payment (evidence of custom and practice), it was judged not to have formed part of the contract because it was clearly highlighted as discretionary.

Sagar v *Ridehalgh* [1931] Ch 310

In this case a weaver working in the mills in Lancashire challenged the company for reducing wages for faulty work. Although this practice had never been brought to the attention of the employee there was a clear custom of trade showing that reductions were always made for faulty work. In this case, custom and practice was judged to form part of the contract of employment.

Although this is an old case, it is a useful illustration of a factor that could be considered to form part of the contract of employment through custom and practice.

TASK Are there any practices that could be incorporated by custom and practice into the contracts of employment in your organisation (or one with which you are familiar)? What are they? Are they important to the organisation? Should they be expressly agreed between the employer and employee?

The courts

The role of the courts in determining implied terms has developed through a series of cases. The initial view was based on the 'officious bystander test' (derived from *Shirlaw* v *Southern Foundries* [1939] ER 113 – see Further Reading). This test questioned whether a term would be implied if an officious bystander asked two parties who had a contract if a term that they had not specifically mentioned was part of the contract. If they replied 'of course' then the term was implied.

This is a very limited way of looking at implied terms, and the courts now take a much wider view. One issue to be considered is 'reasonableness', as illustrated in the following cases.

Courtaulds Northern Spinning Ltd v *Sibson* [1988] ICR 451

Sibson resigned from the trade union and, as the trade union operated a closed shop (all employees had to join the trade union – a practice no longer allowed in law) the trade union insisted he was moved to another site. Sibson was offered employment one mile from his current place of work, but he refused to go and resigned claiming unfair and constructive dismissal (see Chapter 8). The Court of Appeal ruled that the agreement to move sites should be implied if it was satisfied that both parties would have agreed to it if they were being reasonable. It was judged that a move of one mile was reasonable, and hence there was no dismissal.

Johnstone v *Bloomsbury Health Authority* [1991] QB 333

This case is a more recent decision. Johnstone was a senior house officer in a hospital. His contract gave a standard working week of 40 hours, plus he had to be available on call for an average of 48 hours each week. As we shall see when we examine the duties of the employer, there is an implied term that the employer will take reasonable care of the employee's health and safety. In stating an average of 48 hours per week, it was actually possible for Johnstone to work over 100 hours in a week, which breached that implied term. The Court of Appeal ruled that the right for the employer to request overtime work had to be limited by the implied term of care for the employee's health and safety. However, one judge dissented stating that however burdensome the requirements might be, they were express terms of the contract of employment.

In summary, the courts will look at all factors regarding the employment relationship, and determine whether there is an implication that both parties would agree to be bound by the term under question. They will then look wider than this, and consider whether the implied term is reasonable. They will also consider a wider approach, and determine whether the implication of the term is necessary, or of benefit to, the contract of employment.

Work rules

Many organisations have a set of rules governing the way in which they require employees to act. These might cover such things as no smoking, not bringing alcohol or drugs on to site, the correct way to wear uniforms, etc. These rules are clearly devised by management and, unlike collective agreements, do not require any prior negotiation.

If a rule has been expressly incorporated into a contract of employment, then it will be contractual. For example, if the rule of no smoking on company premises is expressly written into a contract of employment, that requirement is contractual. However, if something is simply contained in the set of rules, and is not referred to in any contractual documents it is not part of that contract.

Dryden v Greater Glasgow Health Board [1992] IRLR 469

Greater Glasgow Health Board introduced a smoking ban in the workplace (a new work rule) and Dryden resigned and claimed constructive dismissal. It was held that the introduction by the employer of a smoking ban did not constitute a breach of contract. It was also held that there was no implied right to smoke (despite the employee trying to argue custom and practice). In addition, it was held that the employer did have the right to make rules for the conduct of employees, even changes such as a smoking ban.

RELATIONSHIP BALANCE

As we have seen, there are a number of terms of the contract of employment that can be implied, rather than specifically stated. Do you think that this implication is fair on both the employer and the employee? Is it possible that the two parties have a different understanding of the contract of employment, and discover these conflicting views only when a dispute occurs? How might this be prevented?

IMPLIED TERMS OF LAW

As well as terms that can be implied into the contract of employment, there are also obligations placed on both the employer and the employee by law. These obligations are implied into the contract of employment.

Duties on the employer

To pay wages

There is a duty of the employer to pay the employee during the period of employment.

Devonald v Rosser [1906] KB 728

The employer closed the works (tinplate) through lack of business. Two weeks later the employer gave all employees one month's notice of the termination of this contract. Devonald claimed pay for the two weeks before the notice was given. This was granted because there was an implied duty that the employer would pay the employee.

To provide work

This duty is unclear. It is possible that the failure to provide work might be a breach of contract if:

1 earnings depend on work being provided (eg a sales person remunerated by commission)

2 the employee needs the opportunity to practise skills (eg a trainee).

William Hill Organisation Ltd v Tucker [1998] IRLR 313

Tucker had been involved in developing a new approach to betting. When he gave notice of his intention to resign, William Hill tried to put him on 'garden leave' (stay away from work whilst on full pay) for six months. During that period he would not be allowed to work. Tucker challenged this on the basis that he needed to keep practising his skills, and six months was too long a period to be away from work. He was successful in his claim.

However, providing that the employee is paid, it *can* be concluded that there is no duty to provide work, as in the following case.

Langston v AUEW [1974] ICR 180

When the employee worked on night shifts or worked overtime he was paid his basic wage plus premium payments. His employers suspended him without pay, and hence took away his opportunity to earn the premium payments. It was judged that, although they had no obligation to provide work, they did have an obligation to make the payments.

To provide references

An employer has a duty to take care when writing references and the following case highlights the difficulties that can arise in this area.

Spring v Guardian Assurance plc [1994] IRLR 460

Spring was a sales representative for an insurance company, which was sold to Guardian Assurance. Upon the sale Spring and the new management felt unable to work together and he was subsequently dismissed. At this time Spring decided to set up in business selling insurance for another organisation. Under the rules of the insurance business Guardian Assurance was required to give a reference about Spring to the new organisation. The reference was written on the basis of information from Spring's previous superiors and included references to a serious case of mis-selling, and suggested that Spring was not honest and was a man of little or no integrity. On this basis the new insurance company refused to accept Spring as selling for them, and other insurance companies also rejected him. Spring brought an action in the High Court claiming damages for loss of earnings based on malicious falsehood, breach of an implied term of contract and negligence arising from the preparation of the reference.

The High Court judge described the reference as a 'kiss of death' to Spring's career in insurance because it was so bad. It was found that the allegations of dishonesty were untrue – Spring had acted incompetently but not dishonestly. The judge found that there was no malicious action, because the reference writers genuinely believed Spring was a 'rogue'. However, it was accepted that Guardian Assurance had a duty to take due care over writing the reference, and had been negligent because they had not checked that the allegations of dishonesty were true. Therefore, they had breached the duty of due care. This case worked through appeals at the Court of Appeal and then the House of Lords – which upheld the original verdict.

This case confirms the duty of an employer in giving a reference. The employer must take every care to ensure that every detail written in a reference is correct. This must include checking the details before writing the reference. It is also the responsibility of the employer to ensure that the overall impression given by the reference is fair. It is, therefore, important to consider what is not included as well as what is.

The contractual right to receive a reference was also challenged in Spring v Guardian Assurance. In the House of Lords judgment the judges concluded that there was a duty when the kind of employment is such that a reference is normally required. In this instance, the insurance business requires that organisations seek a reference from previous employers, and hence it would seem that a contractual right for a reference could exist. However, the law on other jobs where the same rigour of reference taking does not exist is still unclear.

Although there is a clear requirement to state the truth in giving references, the truth must be related to matters that have been thoroughly investigated and hence are believed to be true.

TSB Bank plc v Harris [2000] IRLR 157

Harris worked for the TSB and during her employment there had been 17 complaints about her by customers. Surprisingly Harris was unaware of these complaints. Harris applied for a job with the Prudential, and they sought a reference from the TSB. In the reference the TSB stated that there had been 17 complaints against Harris: four had been upheld and eight were still under investigation. The Prudential declined to employ Harris.

On hearing of the reference Harris resigned from the TSB and claimed unfair constructive dismissal (see Chapter 8). The EAT upheld Harris' claim, stating that the TSB had breached the implied term of trust and confidence by not ensuring that the complaints cited in the reference were fair and reasonable.

In this case the TSB had reported the facts relating to Harris as they understood them. However, by not bringing the complaints to her attention they had not investigated them thoroughly, and hence they could not be certain they were true.

Although the obligation to give a reference might not be clear there is a clear requirement to ensure that the content is correct. It is also important to note that, under the Data Protection Act 1998, the employee does have a right to see anything written about him. However, in bringing a claim that a reference has damaged an employee's ability to seek alternative employment the employee must be able to show that it was the reference that harmed his prospects and not any other factors.

Further Exploration

As we have seen in this section, the giving of references is fraught with potential difficulties. Look in the personnel and business press for any recent cases that have occurred relating to the giving of references. Are you able to draw up any guidelines on giving references that might be of use to your employer?

To take reasonable care for the health and safety of employees
We shall study this requirement in Chapter 12.

To indemnify the employee against all liabilities and losses incurred in the course of employment
A good example of this is expenses incurred when travelling on company business. Any legitimate business expense should be reimbursed to the employee.

To take reasonable steps to bring to the attention of employees rights of which they would not ordinarily be aware
There are instances where an employee could not be expected to be aware of a particular right. For example, this could be because it has been negotiated with a representative body, and the employee was unaware of the negotiations.

Scally v Southern Health and Social Services Board [1991] IRLR 522

In this case a group of doctors working for the Health Service in Northern Ireland claimed they had not been advised of the ability to purchase extra years that would enhance their pension contributions. When the doctors did find out about the scheme they applied to join, but their application was rejected as being out of time. The House of Lords went on to rule that an employer has an obligation to make employees aware of their rights.

The employer is required to take reasonable steps. It might be deemed reasonable to put notices on a noticeboard. However, if there are employees who are rarely in the building (eg sales representatives who spend most of their time travelling to see customers) it could be argued that it is not a reasonable way of informing that group of employees. In the same way, it would not be sufficient to e-mail information to all employees if some did not have access to a computer.

To give effective support against bullying at work
This can also be linked to the duty to take reasonable care of the safety (and health) of employees. We shall examine the issues associated with bullying, and the employer's duties, in Chapter 7.

To respect the privacy of the employee
This will be explored in Chapter 11.

To deal effectively with grievances
This will be explored in Chapter 8.

To take care not to damage the relationship of trust and confidence that should exist between an employer and an employee
This requirement is one that falls on both the employer and the employee. The issue of trust and confidence is seen to be right at the heart of the contract of employment. If there is no trust and confidence there can be no successful relationship.

One of the first cases outlining this was the following.

Isle of Wight Tourist Board v Coombes [1976] IRLR 413

Mrs Coombes was the personal secretary to the director of the board. One day they had an argument and, in the presence of another employee, the director stated 'she is an intolerable bitch on a Monday morning'. Mrs Coombes resigned and claimed constructive dismissal (see Chapter 8). She was successful in her claim, because it was judged that the words of the director had shattered any trust and confidence in the relationship.

The breach of trust and confidence can also be between a group of employees and the employer.

Malik & another v Bank of Credit and Commerce International SA [1997] IRLR 462

The BCCI collapsed in 1991 after widespread allegations of fraudulent actions. Malik worked for BCCI and alleged that the employer conducting the business in a corrupt and dishonest manner amounted to a breach of the implied term of trust and confidence. The House of Lords held that Malik could bring a claim for damages relating to the stigma of working for BCCI, relating to any damage to future employment prospects.

However in *Husain and another v Bank of Credit and Commerce International SA* [2002] EWCA Civ 82 another two former employees of BCCI were unsuccessful in their claim for damages related to the stigma. In this situation the Court of Appeal ruled that, although the actions of BCCI might well be a breach of trust and confidence, the inability of the individuals to find alternative work related more to personal factors such as inflating their experience and knowledge on job applications.

Further Exploration

The duty of trust and confidence is at the heart of any contract of employment. As we work through this book we shall see other situations when this duty is breached. Read these cases carefully. Is there ever a case when the employment relationship has survived such a breach?

Duties on the Employee

To obey all instructions of the employer

It should be noted that the instructions should be reasonable and they should be legal.

Ottoman Bank v Chakarian [1930] AC 277

The employer instructed Chakarian to remain in Constantinople, although he had previously been sentenced to death there. He disobeyed, and this was found to be justified as the instruction had been unreasonable.

Morrish v Henley Ltd [1973] ER 137

The employee was instructed to falsify the accounts at the garage where he was employed. He refused and was dismissed. This was an unfair dismissal because the instruction was to carry out an illegal act.

To co-operate with the employer

A clear example of lack of co-operation is the taking of industrial action.

Secretary of State for Employment v ASLEF [1972] QB 443

ASLEF instructed its members to carry out a work to rule. The employees worked strictly according to the company's rules, and caused considerable disruption. The Court of Appeal held that by carrying out the work to rule the employees were in breach of the implied term of co-operating with the employer. Lord Denning commented: 'Now I quite agree that a man is not bound positively to do more for his employer than his contract requires. He can withdraw his goodwill if he pleases. But what he must not do is wilfully to obstruct the employer as he goes about his business.'

As we shall see in Chapter 10, employees do have the right to take industrial action if this action is taken in accordance with relevant legislation.

Fidelity

Employees must not carry out activities that clearly conflict with the duty that they owe to their employer. Therefore, they must not compete with the employer.

Sanders v *Parry* [1967] ER 803

Sanders worked for Parry as an assistant solicitor. He had a major client, and was responsible for all his legal work. Sanders entered into an agreement with the client that he would leave Parry and would set up in practice on his own. The client would then transfer all his business away from Parry, to Sander's new practice. Parry sued Sanders for a breach of the implied term of fidelity. This was successful.

To take reasonable care in carrying out the duties of their contract

If an employee injures another person or property in the course of his duties the employee can be liable to indemnify the employer against any damages. In reality the issue is typically dealt with through the employer's insurance.

Lister v *Romford Ice and Cold Storage Ltd* [1956] AC 555

Lister was a lorry driver who negligently injured a fellow employee (his father) when packing his lorry. The injured employee sought damages from Romford Ice and Cold Storage and was successful (the employer was responsible due to vicarious liability – see Chapter 7). The employer's insurers then brought an action against Lister, in the employer's name, claiming damages for the breach of the implied term that he would exercise reasonable care in carrying out his duties. This claim was allowed.

RELATIONSHIP BALANCE

The main purpose of the relationship between the employer and the employee is to work together for the success of the organisation. Do you think that the guidelines we have covered in this chapter help this to be achieved more efficiently? What would you add to or delete from to the duties to improve the achievement of this overall aim?

CONTINUITY OF EMPLOYMENT

The qualification for certain employment rights are dependent on the employee having a specific period of continuous employment. An example of this is the requirement to have one year's continuous service before being able to make a claim of unfair dismissal (see Chapter 8).

Section 212 of the Employment Rights Act 1996 defines continuous service as including any week during which all or part of the employee's relationship with the employer is governed by a contract of employment. This section also allows for continuity of employment to continue although the contract is not in existence. These exceptional situations are:

1 Any week in which the employee is incapable of work through sickness or injury up to a maximum of 26 weeks.

2 A period of absence due to a temporary cessation of work.

3 Any period during which employment is regarded as continuing due to custom. For example, it could be the custom of the employer to allow compassionate leave that is unpaid in certain situations.

It should be noted that maternity legislation (see Chapter 5) allows for the continuity of employment during the period of maternity leave. It should also be noted that an employee's continuity of employment is preserved when that employment is subject to a transfer of undertaking (see Chapter 9).

In all these cases continuity of employment is preserved, and the weeks during which work does not take place actually count towards the calculation of the period of continuous employment. There are also situations when continuity of employment is preserved, but the weeks when work does not take place do not count towards continuous employment. They are:

1 A period of time when an employee is taking part in a strike
2 A period of time when an employee is locked out by the employer (this is when an employer refuses to provide work to the employees with the aim of forcing them to accept certain terms and conditions of employment).

CHAPTER REVIEW

1 There are a number of tests used by the courts to determine who is an employee. The most commonly used test is the multiple test.

2 The contract of employment consists of express and implied terms.

3 Express terms are those that have been discussed and agreed between the employer and employee.

4 The sources of implied terms are collective agreements, statute, custom, the courts and work rules.

5 A written statement of initial employment particulars must be given to all employees within two months of commencing employment.

6 A collective agreement can be part of a contract of employment through express or implied incorporation.

7 A contract of employment cannot diminish any rights of the employee determined by statute.

8 The courts can determine whether a term is implied within a contract of employment, through looking at a wide range of factors within the way the relationship between employer and employee is conducted.

9 Work rules are incorporated into a contract of employment only if they are specifically mentioned in that contract.

10 There is a series of duties on both the employer and the employee that have been imposed by law.

11 Continuity of employment includes any week when the relationship between the employee and the employer is governed by the contract of employment, although certain exceptions to this do apply.

FURTHER READING

- *Adams* v *British Airways* [1996] IRLR 574 – examining the status of collective agreements in the contract of employment.

- *Gascol* v *Mercer* [1974] IRLR 155 – the written statement is described by the employer as a contract of employment.

- *Harris* v *Richard Lawson Autologistics Ltd* [2002] ICR 765 – are terms within a collective agreement incorporated into a contract of employment?

- *Henry & Others* v *London General Transport Services Ltd* [2002] IRLR 472 – determining whether collectively agreed changes to terms and conditions were incorporated into contracts of employment by implication.

- *Jones* v *Associated Tunnelling Company* [1981] IRLR 477 – examining an implied term that Jones should be employed within travelling distance of his home.

- *Mears* v *Safecar Security Ltd* [1982] IRLR 183 – the courts must look at all facts of the employment relationship in determining whether a term should be implied.

- *Quinn* v *Calder* [1996] IRLR 126 – has a 'custom and practice' term been brought to the attention of employees, and has it been followed for a significant period of time?

- *Robertson* v *British Gas* [1983] IRLR 302 – a statutory statement could not be used to aid the interpretation of the contract of employment.

- *Shirlaw* v *Southern Foundries* [1939] ER 113 – a term is implied into a contract of employment if the parties would tell the officious bystander that 'of course' it is included.

- *United Bank* v *Akhtar* [1989] IRLR 507 – a term of the contract was necessary for business efficiency.

- *Western Excavating (ECC Ltd)* v *Sharp* [1977] QB 761 – showing that a breach in trust and confidence must go to the heart of the contract.

EXAMPLES TO WORK THROUGH

1 Bill is a college lecturer. He lectures on four modules, which have weekly sessions. He is expected to do each lecture himself, and must follow the syllabus issued by the college. He is not required to attend the college at any other time. He is paid a fixed fee for each module he teaches. He sends the college an invoice for the fee at the end of each module, and pays his own tax and National Insurance contributions. He is not entitled to any sick pay, and is not part of the college appraisal scheme. At the end of each academic year the college contact Bill and tell him which modules they would like him to teach in the coming year. The actual modules vary each year. Is Bill an employee? Use the multiple test to reach your answer.

2 You have recently been appointed as the regional manager for a well-known supermarket chain. You have received a request for a reference for one of your current store managers. She has applied for a role as manager with one of your competitors. Although you have met her, you have spent little time with her so far. How should you handle the request?

3 A new production manager in your organisation is horrified to find that the old practice (in his view) of allowing employees five minutes of paid time to wash their hands still exists. He

wants to stop this practice, and tell employees that they must wash their hands in their own time. The trade union representatives have stated that he cannot change this practice, as the time allowed is part of their contract of employment. What evidence do you need to seek, and what law must you apply, in advising the production manager?

Atypical Contracts and the Variation of Contracts

CHAPTER 4

The objectives of this chapter are to:

- **Examine specific legislation relating to agency staff; part-time workers, casual workers, temporary workers and the issuing of fixed-term contracts;**

- **Outline the provisions regarding flexible working;**

- **Overview specific situations such as employing asylum seekers and ex-offenders;**

- **Examine the process of varying a contract of employment.**

SPECIFIC CATEGORIES OF EMPLOYEES

The traditional employment contract of 9–5, Monday–Friday is still common, but it does not have the dominance that it once had. Customers demand certain services 24 hours a day, every day of the week; more mothers are returning to work and wanting hours to fit around child care; and more employees are looking to fit working hours around their other interests to try to achieve some sort of work–life balance. This change in working patterns has also led to an increase in the use of atypical workers. In this chapter we examine some of the issues associated with these contracts.

 TASK Is there a need for a wide variety of types of workers (temporary, part-time, casual, agency, etc in your organisation (or one with which you are familiar)? Find out how the organisation manages this variety.

Further Exploration

In this section we address the legal issues relating to a certain number of atypical contracts. However, there are many more types of contracts being used by organisations (eg annual hours contracts, zero hours contracts). Compile a list of as many of these atypical contracts as you can. Then consider what legislation is relevant to both the employees and employers in specific relation to these contracts. Do you think there is a need for further legislation in some areas? Useful sources of information about changing contracts include the 'Labour Force Survey' and 'Labour Market Trends'.

Agency workers

Workers provided to an organisation by an employment agency can potentially claim an employer–employee relationship with the employment agency or with the employer they actually work for. To determine if such employment relationships exist, the tests we examined in the last chapter are used.

Two cases explained here show the difficulties that exist when determining the employment relationship.

McMeechan v *Secretary of State for Employment* [1997] ICR 549

In this case McMeechan was a catering assistant who undertook a number of assignments from an employment agency. When the agency entered insolvency McMeechan claimed entitlement to unpaid wages and redundancy payments from the National Insurance Fund (state funds for employees made redundant – see Chapter 9 – when the employer cannot meet the statutory payments). In favour of him being an employee was that the agency had control over him, because they could terminate his contract and could discipline him. There were also factors consistent with an employment relationship – for example the agency deducted tax and NI from McMeehcan's pay. However, there was a document stating that McMeechan would work as a 'self-employed worker and not under a contract of service'.

This case finally went to the Court of Appeal which found, on the basis of the evidence outlined above, that there was an employment relationship, because there was evidence of control; there was evidence of mutuality and there was nothing inconsistent with a contract of employment.

Montgomery v *Johnson Underwood Ltd* [2001] IRLR 269

Montgomery was placed in an organisation as a receptionist/telephonist by Johnson Underwood (an employment agency). She worked there for two years and then the organisation asked the agency to terminate the contract. She took a claim for unfair dismissal against both the organisation where she worked and the employment agency. This case went through two stages of appeal and it was eventually concluded by the Court of Appeal that Montgomery was not an employee of either organisation. Crucially, they found that Johnson Underwood exercised 'little or no control, direction or supervision' over Montgomery. On the basis of that conclusion one of the three conditions of an employment relationship was not met, hence Montgomery could not be an employee. Although they did exercise control over her work, there were no mutual obligations between her and the organisation, as the contract was between the agency and the organisation. In addition, there were factors inconsistent with an employment relationship – primarily that Montgomery was paid by Johnson Underwood.

The difficulties highlighted might well have been solved by a recent Court of Appeal judgment in the following case.

Dacas v *Brook Street Bureau (UK) Ltd and anor* [2004] IRLR 190

Dacas was placed by Brook Street Bureau as a cleaner for a local authority hostel. This was the only work she was assigned to by the Bureau. She worked in this role for six years, when she was dismissed following an incident in which she swore at a visitor to the hostel. Dacas claimed unfair dismissal, and took the approach that she had either been an employee of the hostel or of Brook Street Bureau. The employment tribunal had to decide whether she was an employee and, if she was, who was the employer.

The Employment Tribunal first considered whether she was an employee of Wandsworth Council (who ran the hostel). They concluded there was not an employment relationship here because there was no direct contract between Dacas and the Council. They then considered whether she was employed by Brook Street Bureau. They concluded that, although a contract existed between Dacas and the Bureau, they could not be her employers because they had no direct control over her daily work. They concluded, therefore, that she could not bring a claim of unfair dismissal because she had no employer–employee relationship.

The applicant appealed to the Employment Appeals Tribunal (only against the decision that she was not an employee of Brook Street Bureau), which overturned the decision of the employment tribunal. They determined that Brook Street Bureau exercised control over Dacas, because they paid her wages, had the right to exercise disciplinary action and had the right to terminate her contract. They also agreed that mutuality of obligations had been shown. In this case all the other evidence pointed to an employment relationship, and hence that was what existed. Therefore, Dacas was an employee of Brook Street Bureau.

Brook Street Bureau then appealed to the Court of Appeal, which overturned the EAT's finding and ruled that Dacas was not an employee of the Bureau. In making the judgment the Court of Appeal made it clear that the Employment Tribunals should always investigate whether an *implied* contract of employment has arisen between the employee and the *end-user* (in this case, Wandsworth Council). Importantly the Court of Appeal stated that in such agency situations the Employment Tribunals must find that someone is the employer, and it will usually be the end-user. It was also noted that one year's employment (which is sufficient to accrue unfair dismissal rights) was sufficient to mean that an implied contract of employment had arisen.

In this case it was not possible to make a finding that Wandsworth Council was the employer because Dacas had not appealed against the earlier decision regarding this employment relationship.

This ruling is of importance because there is clear guidance to the Employment Tribunal to use in considering who the employer is when the person in question has been supplied by an agency.

The uncertainty regarding the employment status of agency workers has also been addressed by legislation introduced in April 2004 when the Conduct of Employment Agencies and Employment Businesses Regulations 2003 came into force (the Dacas case was heard before this legislation was introduced). These regulations require employment agencies to specify the employment status of any individual who obtains work through the agency (ie state whether they are employed or self-employed). The regulations also require the employment agency to give written notice of the terms and conditions on which the individual is either employed or engaged.

Further Exploration

Clarification of the status of agency workers has partly been driven by European legislation. Find out how other Member States treat agency workers in relation to their agency status. A good starting point will be the websites of the European Commission (www.europa.eu.int/comm) or the European Parliament (www.europarl.org.uk). Apply the ruling in the Dacas case to the two earlier cases. Do you think the outcome of the earlier cases would have been different if the Court of Appeal ruling in Dacas had been made previously?

RELATIONSHIP BALANCE

Do you think that the current legislation gives a fair balance to the rights of the agency worker and the organisation that is using those skills? Potentially the organisation can decide at any time to end the services of the agency worker and ask the agency to supply an alternative worker. Do you think that the proposed legislation will give sufficient protection against this, which in an employee/employer relationship would clearly be wrongful or unfair dismissal (see Chapters 8 and 9).

Part-time workers

In Chapter 1 we referred to the case of *R* v *Secretary of State ex parte Equal Opportunities Commission* [1995] 1 AC 1. In this case the ruling that part-time workers needed five years' continuous service to take a claim of unfair dismissal, compared with two years' service for full-time employees was indirect discrimination against women. This was because significantly more women than men tend to work part-time. On the basis of this challenge, the qualification period for part-time workers was brought into line with full-time workers.

In 1997 the European Union put in place a directive dealing with the issue of all employment rights for part-time employees. This directive covered a wide range of contractual issues. Most of the directive was brought into place as UK law in the Part-time Workers (Prevention of Less Favourable Treatment) Regulations 2000 (amended in 2002) – which we shall refer to as PTW regulations.

The first stage in considering part-time workers is to determine who they are. First we have the definition of 'worker' which is the same as that already quoted from Section 230(3) of the Employment Rights Act 1996, namely that 'a worker is an individual who either works under a contract of employment or works under any other contract where that individual agrees to personally perform work or services for another party'.

Having determined that the definition of a worker is the same, whether they may be part-time or full time, the next step is to determine what 'part-time' means. The legislation simply states that a part-time worker is one whose normal hours of work, averaged over a period of up to a year, are less than the normal hours of comparable full-time workers.

The comparator is key to these regulations because they give the right to make a claim of less favourable treatment on the grounds of working part-time. To show that a part-time worker has been treated less favourably he must be able to point to a full-time worker and show that his treatment has been different, and that it has been less preferable. For example, he might state that he does not think the rules regarding access to a pension scheme are fair. If the rules are also applied to full-time workers then the issue is not the part-time employment. However, if the full-time workers had different pension rules that were seen as preferential, and he was able to identify a comparator who was full time, then he could take a claim of less favourable treatment under the PTW regulations.

The comparator should be someone who is employed at the same time, by the same employer, at the same establishment (or if there are no comparators at that establishment at another establishment of the employer), under the same type of contract and doing the same or broadly similar work (given reference to levels of qualification, skill and experience).

There are straightforward examples: In a call centre there might be a core of staff answering calls who all work a basic week of 35 hours. In addition, there are staff that take the same calls at the same call centre who work for only 15 hours each week – they are clearly classified as part time.

The more difficult examples are when there is not a clear comparator. For example, the person claiming to be part-time is a cleaner working in a factory where there are no other cleaners, and no other people doing similar work. In this situation the strict definitions do not allow the cleaner to take any claim under the PTW regulations. This might seem unfair, but the regulations are focused on different treatment for full-time and part-time working, and any difference that is identified must be clearly attributable to the part-time status. If that clear distinction cannot be shown then there can be no claim.

There are exceptions to the rules on comparators:

■ If a full-time worker reduces his hours and becomes part-time he can use his previous terms and conditions of employment as a full-time worker as the comparator.

■ In the same way, a worker returning to work after an absence of less than 12 months, who returns to reduced hours, can use his previous full-time employment as the comparator.

The regulations give the part-time worker the right not to be treated by the employer less favourably because of his part-time status. This covers contractual issues (eg rate of pay, overtime payments, sickness and maternity pay arrangements, and any other benefits). It also gives the right for the part-time worker not to be subjected to any detriment because of the part-time status. This covers issues such as the possibility of promotion and the access to training. In addition, there must be equal rights to have access to schemes such as pensions and share options and access to statutory leave rights (eg maternity, paternity and parental leave). A worker cannot be selected for redundancy only because of his part-time status.

If a worker considers that he is being treated less favourably because of his part-time status he may ask his employer for a written statement explaining the reasons for the treatment. This written statement can be produced as evidence at any subsequent employment tribunal hearing. If the worker is not satisfied with the response from the employer he can take a claim to the Employment Tribunal on the grounds of less favourable treatment or of victimisation. If the worker does take such a claim, the employer has to identify the ground for the less favourable treatment or detriment. The employer is 'vicariously liable' for the actions of its managers, supervisors and other employees. In other words, the employer is responsible for any actions that have been taken by its employees, even if those actions contravene company policy unless the employer can clearly show that he has taken steps to stop such a situation occurring. (We shall examine vicarious liability in more detail in Chapter 7.)

If the worker wins the case at the Employment Tribunal the possible remedies are that the Employment Tribunal can order any or all of the following:

- A declaration of the rights of the worker in respect of the complaint.
- The employer to pay compensation to the applicant.
- Recommend action to be taken by the employer to deal with the issue that has been brought to the tribunal. The employer's failure to comply can result in increased compensation being ordered.

TASK Does your organisation (or one with which you are familiar) employ part-time staff? If so, find out if changes were made to their terms and conditions when the part-time worker regulations were introduced. Do you think any changes have been positive for both the employer and the employee?

Casual Workers

We have already examined the status of casual workers in looking at the case of *Carmichael v National Power* [2000] IRLR 43 (see previous chapter).

If a worker is 'casual' in the sense that there is no obligation on the employer to provide work, and no obligation on the employee to carry out any work, it is unlikely that an employer–employee relationship exists. In this situation the casual worker is not entitled to the same benefits as an employee.

Temporary workers

A temporary worker has exactly the same rights as other workers, presuming that he has acquired the relevant statutory period of employment (eg one year's service to take a claim of unfair dismissal). The exceptions are specific temporary contracts to cover maternity leave or to cover an employee suspended on medical grounds.

A temporary worker will usually be on a fixed-term contract (see next section), or will be an agency worker (as we have already examined) or will be a casual worker (which we have also examined).

Fixed-term contracts

There are situations when an employer wants to employ someone, but for a fixed period of time only. For example, there might be a special project to complete, but once that project is completed it is expected that there will be no further work for the employees involved. In this situation an employer can issue a fixed-term contract – which clearly states when the employment will end. The following case shows how this can also be abused.

Booth v *United States of America* [1999] IRLR 16

This case centred on three employees who worked at a USAF airbase. They were employed on a series of fixed-term contracts. At the end of each contract there was a short break in service after which a new contract of employment was issued. Upon the issuing of each contract they returned to the same job with the same tools and equipment; however the breaks in employment meant they never amassed sufficient continuity of service to claim statutory rights (such as the right to take a claim of unfair dismissal). The EAT ruled that they had been unable to show evidence of continuity of service. The employer's actions were lawful, if undesirable, and if this loophole was to be addressed it needed to be done through legislation.

The Employment Act 2002 introduced new legislation relating to fixed-term contracts. The employee on a fixed-term contract should not receive less favourable treatment when compared to a permanent employee who is employed by the same employer, is engaged in the same or broadly similar work and is based at the same establishment. Less favourable treatment includes contractual terms (including pay and benefits), opportunities to receive training and secure permanent employment, and qualifying periods for benefits.

In addition, the legislation has limited the issuing of fixed-term contracts to a maximum of four years. If fixed-term contracts are issued beyond that period of time the contract will automatically become permanent. Only contracts issued from, or running from, 10 July 2002 are covered by the legislation.

RELATIONSHIP BALANCE

Do you think that the revised legislation with regard to fixed-term contracts gives adequate protection to the employer and the employee? Does it restrict the ability of the employer to address the resourcing issues relating to specific projects? Do you think the legislation should be refined in any way?

Flexible working

The demographics of the workplace have changed greatly over recent years. In particular, there are more women working, and more mothers returning to work after childbirth. In addition, there are more parents raising children alone, and needing to work as they are the only source of income in the family.

It is these changing demographics of the workplace that have prompted the Government to consider a number of aspects of legislation to address the needs of family life. As well as the changing statistics there is also the issue of work–life balance and the amount of time that families have to spend together. The Government wants to encourage people to work – and wants to encourage women to return to the workplace to use their skills. However, family life is important, and an appropriate balance must be struck between work and outside commitments.

In response to these needs the government has introduced legislation giving a statutory right to request flexible working. The statutory rights are set out in Section 47 of the Employment Act 2002, and the main substance of the rights are found in the Flexible Working (Eligibility, Complaints and Remedies) Regulations 2001 and the Flexible Working (Procedural Requirements) Regulations 2002. The rights came into force on 6 April 2003.

It is important to note that the legislation gives a statutory right to *request* flexible working. It does not give a right to be *granted* flexible working hours.

It is also important to note that the rights are available only to those who have a child aged under 6 years, or a disabled child aged under 18 years. This aspect of the regulations has given employers some concern. Is it fair to expect those with no children, or older children, to work 'non-flexible' hours, whilst colleagues with younger children are treated differently? In looking at the detail of the legislation we shall attempt to address this concern.

To qualify for the right to make a request for flexible working the employee must have had at least 26 weeks' continuous service on the date of making the request, must be the mother, father, adopter, guardian or foster parent of the child or be married to the child's mother, father, adopted, guardian or foster parent, and must expect to have responsibility for the child's upbringing.

In considering these qualification criteria it is important to note that:

- the legislation is not restricted to women
- the request does not have to be made at the end of maternity leave; it can be made any time that the child is aged under 6 years (18 for a disabled child)
- the purpose of the request must be to care for the child – it cannot just be because the parent would like to work different hours for their own benefit.

In requesting flexible working, employees can request changes to:

- the hours they work
- the times they work
- the place they are required to work.

An employee must write to his employer requesting a change to flexible working. There is no prescribed format for this, although the DTI has published some standard forms on its website (www.dti.gov.uk) to suggest the type of information that should be included in the request. The application must be made at least 14 days before the child's sixth birthday.

Once the employer has received the request it must arrange a meeting with the employee within 28 days to discuss the request. The employee has the right to be accompanied to this meeting by a fellow worker or a trade union representative. Within 14 days of the meeting the employer must give a written response to the request.

If the request is granted the changes that have been agreed must be specified in writing, and a date for the start of the changes must be confirmed. This will be a change of contract (see later in this chapter) and will be considered a permanent change. In other words, the employee has no right to expect a change back to the current terms and conditions of employment at some future date. Therefore, it should also be noted that the new working patterns will continue after the child reaches his sixth birthday.

The legislation sets out a number of grounds on which the employer can turn down the request. They are:

- burden of additional costs
- detrimental effect on the ability to meet customer demand
- inability to reorganise work among existing staff
- inability to recruit additional staff
- detrimental impact on quality
- detrimental impact on performance
- insufficiency of work during the periods the employee proposes to work
- planned structural changes
- any other ground the Secretary of State may specify by regulations.

If the employee is refused his request he may appeal against the decision. This must be done in writing within 14 days of the decision being received. The legislation suggests that the appeal should be on the grounds that the procedure was not followed correctly, that the business reasons are incorrect or that they have not been explained sufficiently. Within 14 days of the request for an appeal there must be a meeting convened, preferably with a more senior manager. Again, the employee has the right to be accompanied. The decision of the appeal should be communicated in writing within 14 days of the appeal meeting.

If the employee's request is still turned down they can refer the issue to an Employment Tribunal. The Employment Tribunal has a limited role to play. It cannot challenge the validity of the employer's decision, and it cannot make its own judgment on whether the request should have been granted. Its role is simply to consider whether the employer has given the request serious consideration, whether the reason for refusal was one permitted by the legislation, whether the facts used to assess the request were correct and whether the employer has acted in accordance with the statutory procedure.

If the Employment Tribunal finds that the employer has erred in the way it has handled the request it can either award compensation to the employee (at a maximum of eight weeks' pay the statutory definition of a maximum week's pay applies, which is £270 at the time of writing – February 2004) or it can make an order that the request is reconsidered.

It is possible for an employee to bring other claims associated with the way they consider the application has been handled. These might include sex discrimination; race discrimination and disability discrimination (we shall look at all these claims later). It is important, therefore, that the employer is careful to ensure a consistent approach to all requests.

TASK How has your organisation, or an organisation with which you are familiar, dealt with requests for the legislation relating to flexible working? Do you think the organisation has followed a correct procedure?

As the legislation is so recent there are currently no cases that have been brought to the Employment Tribunal for us to consider. However, it is worth noting the following issues that might cause employers difficulties.

- *Setting precedents*. An employer might receive a request from an employee for flexible working, and decide to grant the request. If another employee in the same department then makes the same request can the employer refuse that employee? Each request is handled separately, so it might be possible to refuse a further request because, for example, the employer was able to reorganise work amongst existing staff when only one employee was working different hours – but cannot achieve this when two employees are working in this way.

- *Interpretation of the business grounds*. How much inconvenience is the employer expected to accept? It might be possible, for example, to still meet customer demands – although the flexible working of a member of staff makes this more difficult. To what extent must the employer accept a certain level of difficulty before it becomes classed as a 'detrimental effect'?

- *Expectations of employees*. It is true that the legislation was heralded in the popular press as the opportunity for all parents of young children to work the hours they requested. Although the legislation does not state that, there is definitely an increased expectation of some level of flexibility. How does the employer address this and maintain good employee relations?

Many employers have addressed these types of issues by formulating a clear policy on dealing with employee requests. Obviously, the policies must incorporate the statutory procedure but writing a company policy gives time for employer and employees to consider the issues before any conflict occurs.

Concern has been expressed about the strength of the legislation. At the CIPD's annual employment law conference (2003) there was debate over the likelihood of the legislation being flouted. The concern is that employers have only to give a 'business reason' for refusing the request, and that employment tribunals cannot investigate those reasons, they can only instruct firms to 'go back and think again'. It was confirmed by the head of the DTI's employment relations directorate that the Government was committed to reviewing the new rights in April 2005, and would consider bringing in some test of objective justification, or possibly a right to flexible working, if there was widespread evidence that the rules were being ignored.

Further Exploration

At the time of writing (early 2004) the early indications are that there has not been a great flood of applications from employees under the flexible working regulations. Keep abreast of any developments in this area, noting any reports in the personnel press on numbers using this legislation (www.dti.gov.uk will also be a useful source of information). Try to understand the reasons behind the level of usage that is reported.

VARYING A CONTRACT OF EMPLOYMENT

A contract of employment is an agreement between two parties, and hence an employer cannot unilaterally vary that contract. If the employer, unilaterally, does make a change to the contract the employee has two options:

- to resign and seek damages for wrongful dismissal (see Chapter 9)
- to continue working, but try to seek damages for any loss that has been suffered.

If the employee does continue working, without making protest, and continues to work in accordance with the new terms for a significant period of time, it can be interpreted that the employee has accepted the changes to the contract by his actions.

If the employee does not agree to the proposed changes it can be very difficult for the employer to proceed. The options open to the employer are:

- to terminate the contract of employment, and offer new contracts under the new terms. This option runs a strong risk of claims for unfair dismissal from the employee (see Chapter 8)
- to negotiate the proposed new terms with the employee representative body, and to try to seek agreement. If there is a reasonable period ('reasonable' will be the time required for all the issues raised by the employee representatives to be seriously considered and addressed) of negotiation and no agreement can be reached the employer can give notice that the variation will go ahead, if it can be justified for business reasons. This option will be particularly strong if the majority of employees affected have already agreed to the change.

Hepworth Heating Ltd v Akers & others [2003] EAT 846/02

Two hundred and eighty of the employees at Hepworth Heating were entitled to be paid in cash. Hepworth Heating proposed moving all the employees to pay by direct transfer to a bank account. This had security and cost benefits for the employer. Some of the employees objected on the grounds of inconvenience and security issues surrounding the use of cashpoint machines. Negotiation took place and was unsuccessful. The employer then wrote to the employees telling them that the change would go ahead, and giving notice of dismissal if the employees refused to accept the change. A number of employees returned the required forms but wrote 'under duress' against their signatures. They carried on working after the cashless pay was introduced. The EAT ruled that there had been no 'duress' and hence by continuing to work the employees had agreed to the variation in the terms and conditions of their employment.

International Packaging Corporation (UK) Ltd v Balfour & others [2003] IRLR 11

IPC was experiencing problems with falling orders and reduced its employees' working hours (and hence their wages) without their consent. A number of employees brought claims that this was an unfair variation of contract, leading to an unlawful deduction of wages (see Chapter 5). The EAT ruled that no implied term existed that allowed the company to unilaterally reduce employees' hours of work (although short-time working had been introduced on two previous occasions with no objections). On that basis, the employees' claim was upheld.

RELATIONSHIP BALANCE

Organisations change in order to survive, and hence it is inevitable that there will be occasions when terms and conditions of employment need to change. How can it be ensured that the process for varying a contract of employment is used when necessary for organisational reasons, rather than being used to the detriment of the employees? Do you think employees have sufficient protection in the process of variation that is described above?

A change should always be preceded by a period of negotiation, when it is hoped that the employer and employee will be able to explore the issues regarding the change. However, the employer does have the right to impose the change. If the employee wants the right to impose his opposition, the most effective way is to actually leave employment and claim constructive dismissal. Even if that claim is successful, the employee no longer has a job.

EMPLOYING ASYLUM SEEKERS, EX-OFFENDERS AND THOSE REQUIRING WORK PERMITS

Asylum Seekers

Under the Asylum and Immigration Act 1996 it is an offence for an employer to employ a person aged 16 years or more who has not been given permission to enter or remain in the United Kingdom, or whose permission to stay in the United Kingdom is subject to not taking up any employment.

The employer must check that a prospective employee does have the right to be employed by seeking documentation from that person. Suitable documentation includes papers issued by a previous employer (eg a P45) or a government department (eg the Benefits Agency) which shows a National Insurance number, passport which shows the right of abode in the UK, a birth certificate issued in the UK or a passport/identity card from a member state of the European Economic Area (EEA) (to clarify the differences between the European Union and the EEA, which are changing, see the European Union website (www.europa.eu.int).

If an employer is found to have employed someone who is not eligible for work it can be a defence to show a copy of these documents (hence a photocopy should be taken at the time of recruitment).

These requirements have given rise to some concern over possible race discrimination. Employers keen to avoid employing illegal workers might inadvertently treat eligible workers unfairly by rejecting an application out of concern that the workers might be illegally seeking work when they actually had full rights to be employed. As a result of the Immigration and Asylum Act 1999 the Secretary of State issued a code of practice entitled 'Code of Practice for all employers on the avoidance of race discrimination in recruitment practice while seeking to prevent illegal working'. Like all codes of practice, failure to abide by it is not illegal, but not abiding by it would be taken into account should any race discrimination claim be taken. In essence, the code of practice states that all potential employees should be treated the same at each stage of the recruitment procedure. Therefore, the checks made to ensure the person is eligible to work should be made of all potential employees.

Ex-offenders

The primary legislation relevant here is the Rehabilitation of Offenders Act 1974. The Act focuses on the issue of 'spent' convictions. An ex-offender does not have to disclose any information relating to a spent conviction when seeking employment, unless they are working in occupations such as doctors, nurses, social workers, teachers, becoming registered day-care providers or carrying out any other work with children.

When a conviction is 'spent' it means that the record has been made clean. The timing of the conviction being 'spent' is as follows:

Table 4.1

	Period of time before spent
Absolute discharges (when an individual is found guilty/admits guilt but is not punished further)	6 months after the sentencing
Probation order; conditional discharge; binding over	1 year or until the order expires (whichever is longer)
Fines; community service orders	5 years
Imprisonment for less than 6 months	7 years
Imprisonment between 6 and 30 months	10 years
Imprisonment longer than 30 months	Never spent

The Act makes it unlawful for an employer to question a prospective employee about a 'spent' conviction, and if such questioning arises the prospective employee can deny the conviction ever occurred. It is also unlawful to deny employment on the grounds of a 'spent' conviction.

Work permits

Nationals of the states of the European Economic Area have the right to seek work in the UK, and to accept offers of employment. They are also allowed to live in the UK whilst looking for suitable work. If they have not found a job within six months they can be asked to leave the UK.

Citizens of independent Commonwealth countries who have the 'right of abode' in the UK are also allowed to come into the UK and accept offers of employment. These individuals have British Citizenship that may be acquired by birth, adoption, descent, registration or naturalisation.

Some foreign nationals can also work in the UK without requiring work permits. These are people such as au pairs, seasonal farm workers, exchange students and postgraduate doctors and dentists.

Work permits are required for other foreign nationals. A work permit is applied for by the prospective employer. The permits are issued to named individuals for specific work with specific employers for a maximum period of four years. There is the possibility of an extension being allowed.

Until May 2003 work permits were issued only for jobs requiring degree-level skill, senior executives, jobs requiring administrative skills or highly qualified technicians with specialist skills. In May 2003 a new low-skilled work permit scheme was launched. The scheme operates in the food, manufacturing and hospitality sectors. Employers who have unsuccessfully tried to recruit 'resident workers' in jobs at a level lower than NVQ3 can apply for work permits, but they will be issued only for individual overseas workers aged between 18 and 30 years. Resident workers are those ordinarily resident in the UK.

In addition, specialist work permits can be sought for individuals such as top-class entertainers and sportspersons.

RELATIONSHIP BALANCE

The legislation described in this chapter is attempting to protect existing employees, employees in these special categories and employers. Do you think that there is sufficient freedom left for employers to meet particularly difficult resourcing needs (eg the recruitment of nurses, doctors and teachers from overseas – all essential due to the lack of suitably qualified people within the country)?

TASK Find out whether your organisation, or one with which you are familiar, has a policy for dealing with asylum seekers, ex-offenders and those requiring work permits. If it does, read it through and see if it meets the requirements outlined in this chapter. If it does not have a policy make an attempt at writing one!

CHAPTER REVIEW

1   Agency workers could potentially be employees of the agency, or of the organisation in which they are working. The employee tests need to be applied to each case.

2   Part-time workers have the right to be treated the same as full-time workers. To exercise this right they must be able to identify a full-time comparator in the organisation.

3   The flexible working regulations give the right to parents of children aged under 6 years, and disabled children aged under 18 years, to request flexible working. The regulations were brought into operation on 6 April 2003, and hence the impact has still not been seen.

4   The employer has a duty to check that all prospective employees have the right to work in the UK.

5   Ex-offenders are not required to reveal any details about 'spent' convictions, unless they work in certain professions.

6   An employer cannot unilaterally vary a contract of employment. If a change is needed, negotiation must take place. If that negotiation is unsuccessful the

employer can impose the change, but must be able to show it is for sound business reasons.

7   If an employee objects to a variation of the contract he can resign and claim constructive dismissal. Alternatively he can continue working, and try to seek damages for any losses the change has brought him.

WEBSITES REFERENCED IN THIS CHAPTER

www.dti.gov.uk	Department of Trade and Industry
www.europa.eu.int	European Union
www.europa.eu.int/comm	European Commission
www.europarl.org.uk	European Parliament

FURTHER READING

- *Clark* v *Oxfordshire Health Authority* [1998] IDS 605 – a temporary nurse who can refuse to work is not classified as an employee.

- *Hewlett Packard Ltd* v *O'Murphy* [2002] IRLR 4 – a case looking at the employment status of an IT specialist working for an employment agency.

- *Motorola Ltd* v *Davidson (1) and Melville Craig Group (2)* [2001] IRLR 4 – an employee–employer relationship is established.

- *Preston and others* v *Wolverhampton Healthcare NHS Trust* [2001] UKHL 5 – part-time employees excluded from an occupational pension scheme.

- *Stadt Lengerich* v *Helmich* [1995] IRLR 216 – determining whether part-timers are entitled to be paid overtime rates.

- *Turriff Construction Ltd* v *Bryant and others* [1967] ITR 292 – trade union representatives agree to a variation of working hours on behalf of employees.

- *Wickens* v *Champion Employment* [1984] ICR 365 – an attempt to show that all agency staff were working under contracts of employment.

EXAMPLES TO WORK THROUGH

1   Pam worked in your call centre for 13 months. She was provided to you by the Callit Agency, and was paid each week by that agency. Her holidays and sick pay were agreed directly by the agency. When she was unwell for four days she phoned the agency, and they sent another worker to your call centre to cover her absence. When she was at work she worked in a team with nine other people, all employed by the call centre. She did exactly the same work as them, and was allocated work by your team leader. Unfortunately Pam lost her temper with a rather difficult customer, and the conversation ended with her swearing at the customer and slamming the phone down. You asked the agency to take her away, and replace her with another worker – which they did. She has now lodged a claim for unfair dismissal with the employment tribunal. The agency is arguing that she was your employee – what is your response?

2   'Toys and Games Ltd' has a busy warehouse on the outskirts of Barchester. It operates 24 hours a day, supplying toyshops throughout the country. On each shift there are 20 staff.

They work one of three shifts – 6am–2pm, 2pm–10pm and 10pm–6am. There is a problem on the 6am–2pm shift. Of the 20 people working on this shift eight have children aged under 6 years old. Six of these are mothers, and two are fathers. There have been concerns raised about the 6am start on a number of occasions, and the staff have tried to argue for some flexibility regarding the start time. The shift is busiest at 7–11am, when most of the distribution lorries arrive. Breaks are taken after 11am, therefore. All 20 staff are busy – during holidays temporary cover is always sought, because the warehouse cannot operate with fewer staff. The supervisor knows that all the staff have become aware of the right to request flexible working, and are likely to approach the management with a request. You are asked to advise the management on how to prepare for this meeting. What are the issues you need to consider, and how will you address them?

3   The bank you work for (Bank A) has recently merged with another bank (Bank B). Over a period of time each town that has a branch of both Bank A and Bank B will have the two branches merged to form one new branch. In the town where you are personnel officer the two branches are about one mile apart. The process of a merger has now started, and you have informed your employees that their branch is to close, and they will all be relocated to the branch about one mile away. Immediately, they have claimed that this is a variation of their contract and they are not prepared to move. What can you do?

Individual Protection Rights

CHAPTER 5

The objectives of this chapter are to:

- **Examine the provisions of the Working Time Regulations;**

- **Consider various provisions relating to the payment of wages;**

- **Outline the National Minimum Wage Act 1998;**

- **Consider issues relating to payment during sickness;**

- **Overview the recent changes in maternity regulations;**

- **Explore the legislation relating to paternity leave;**

- **Examine regulations relating to parental leave;**

- **Outline the legislation relating to adoption leave;**

- **Overview situations when the employee is allowed time off work.**

WORKING TIME REGULATIONS 1998

The Working Time Regulations are the implementation of the Working Time Directive, and provisions of the Young Workers Directive. Their basis relates to health and safety – that employees are healthier, and less likely to have accidents if they have minimum levels of holidays, rest periods and maximum working hours.

The original regulations did not apply to doctors in training, the armed forces and the police. They also did not apply to the activities of air, road, sea, inland waterway and lake transport, sea fishing and other workers at sea. There were also special cases that were excluded – jobs in domestic service, managing executives, family workers and workers officiating at religious services in churches and religious communities.

The transport categories were largely excluded because workers in these sectors are covered by specific regulations relating to their work. However, this did cause some difficulty, because it is largely 'mobile' workers (eg drivers, fishermen, pilots) rather than 'non-mobile' workers (eg clerical/administration) who are covered by the specific legislation. Hence, as shown in the following case, clerical workers can be excluded from the legislation that seems to be most appropriate to their situation.

> ## *Bowden & others* v *Tuffnel Parcels Express Ltd* [2001] IRLR 838
>
> Bowden and two colleagues were part-time clerical workers in Tuffnel Parcels Express, which was a business operating in the road transport sector. They were not entitled to paid holidays under their contracts of employment. When the Working Time Regulations 1998 came into force, they asked their employer to give them the minimum holiday entitlement, as defined by those regulations. They were refused, because the road transport sector was specifically excluded from the regulations. The issue was eventually referred to the European Court of Justice to determine if 'non-mobile ' workers within the sector were covered by the regulations. The ECJ ruled that the whole sector had been excluded, and hence the clerical staff were also not covered.

However, these exclusions were amended by the Working Time (Amendment) Regulations 2003. In summary, the impact of these amendments is to apply the regulations to non-mobile workers within the transport sector. If mobile workers within the transport sector are not covered by their own specific legislation then these amendments will apply.

Outside the transport sector the amendments also affect doctors in training. The working time regulations will apply in full, but the 48-hour week will be phased in from 1 August 2004.

Who is a 'worker', under the Working Time Regulations?

The regulations (Reg 2) state that a worker includes anyone who:

> **'has entered into or works under (or where the employment has ceased, worked under) (a) a contract of employment or (b) any other contract, whether express or implied and (if it is express) whether oral or in writing, whereby the individual undertakes to do or perform personally any work or services for another party to the contract whose status is not by virtue of the contract that of a client or customer of any profession or business undertaking carried on by the individual'**

In essence the definition of a worker, therefore, covers those employed under a contract of employment and potentially many casual, freelance and self-employed workers. It excludes self-employed people who are genuinely pursuing their own business activity.

This definition is midway between the definition we had in Chapter 2 of a person employed under a contract for services and a contract of service. In the following case the EAT concluded that the regulations have created a 'hybrid' category of a protected worker.

Torith Ltd v Flynn [2002] EAT 0017/02

Flynn worked for Torith as a joiner on one of its building sites. He claimed holiday pay, under the Working Time Regulations. Torith were responsible for deducting tax and National Insurance contributions from his pay, although Flynn was still required to submit an annual tax return as a self-employed person. Flynn received limited supervision in his work. He was supplied with materials and power tools, but supplied his own hand tools. He worked exclusively for Torith, and was expected to work the normal site hours of 39 per week. He was not entitled to holiday or sick pay, and if he did take a holiday was not guaranteed any work on his return. Subject to Torith's approval, he could provide a substitute to carry out his work.

The EAT ruled that Flynn was covered by the Working Time Regulations. Flynn fell into this category of a 'hybrid' worker, because he clearly was not pursuing a business activity on his own account.

What is work?

Work is defined in Regulation 2 as:

- a period when the worker is working, at the employer's disposal and carrying out activities or duties in accordance with usual practice
- a period when the worker is receiving relevant training
- any other period which is to be treated as working time within the regulations.

The requirements of the Working Time Regulations

Annual leave

A worker is entitled to four weeks' paid leave, which includes public and any other state holidays. If there is no defined start date for the calculation of holidays (eg many organisations calculate holidays from January to December each year), the leave year runs from the date employment commenced. The entitlement is only to that holiday entitlement which has been accrued – one-twelfth of the four weeks being accrued each month.

The workers are entitled to be paid a sum equivalent to a week's pay for each week of leave. This will be the basic week's pay; non-contractual overtime (overtime which is not guaranteed) is not included in calculating the amount.

Bamsey and others v Albon Engineering Ltd [2003] EAT 365/02

Ten employees brought a claim to the Employment Tribunal that Albon Engineering had incorrectly calculated their holiday pay. Bamsey worked a basic 39-hour week, but could work up to nine hours a week in overtime – although that was not guaranteed. His holiday pay had been calculated on just the 39-hour week.

The EAT ruled that the non-contractual hours could not be included within 'normal working hours' and hence the holiday pay had not been calculated incorrectly.

Maximum working week

The number of hours worked, including overtime, must not exceed an average of 48 hours per week over a 17-week reference period. Therefore, it is not correct to state that a worker cannot work more than 48 hours in any week. He can, as long as he works less than 48 hours another week – to give an average of no more than 48 over the 17-week period.

A worker can opt out of this requirement. Any agreement to opt out must be in writing, and either relate to a specific period of time or apply indefinitely. Within the agreement there must be the right for the worker to give seven days' notice (or a greater period of notice, agreed between the two parties – but this must not be more than three months) to terminate the agreement. The employer is also required to keep up-to-date records of all the workers who have signed such an agreement.

Barber and others v RJB Mining (UK) Ltd [1999] IRLR 308

Barber and his colleagues were pit deputies working in a coalmine in Yorkshire. They were contracted to work 42 hours per week, but also worked substantial overtime. RJB approached them, asking for them to sign an 'opt out' agreement from the maximum working week regulations. Due to ongoing pay negotiations, the workers were advised by their union not to sign the proposed agreement.

The pit deputies had already worked more than the 48-hour maximum during the 17-week reference period, and hence sought a declaration that they did not need to work again until the average fell below the 48-hour maximum. This declaration was granted by the High Court.

Night work

The protection given to night workers is:

- if the work involves any special hazards or physical or mental strain, the night worker must not work for more than eight hours in any 24-hour period
- an entitlement to a free health assessment before starting night work, and at regular intervals thereafter
- an entitlement to adequate rest periods if the nature of the work is likely to cause health problems.

If the health assessment shows problems that might be connected with night work the employer should make every attempt to move the worker to work that is not night work.

In the regulations 'night work' is defined as a period that is not less than seven hours in length and includes the normal hours of 12 midnight to 5am. A 'night worker' is a worker who normally works at least three hours of working time during this period of 'night work'.

Therefore, an employee who normally works a shift from 6pm to 2am is not a 'night worker' because only two hours fall in the period defined as 'night work'. However, an employee who works from 10pm to 6am is a 'night worker' because five hours fall in the period defined as 'night work'.

It is not necessary for the worker to work these night hours each week. It is required that the hours are a *regular feature* of the pattern of work.

R v Attorney General for Northern Ireland [1999] IRLR 315

The employee changed to a shift system that involved working a night shift of 9pm to 7am, one week in every three. Clearly the shift was classified as 'night work' because there were at least three hours worked between 12midnight and 5am. Although the shift was worked only one week in three it was judged to be a regular feature of the employee's work, and hence he was judged to be a 'night worker'.

Further Exploration

Find out how the restrictions imposed on night-time working have affected shifts in various industries. Have a look at the TUC website (www.tuc.org.uk) to see if there is a general policy on how to address negotiations relating to night-time working.

Rest breaks

All adult workers are entitled to at least 11 consecutive hours rest in every 24-hour period. Young workers (those aged under 18) are entitled to a consecutive rest period of not less than 12 hours in every 24-hour period.

A worker is entitled to at least 24 hours uninterrupted rest in every seven-day period. The weekly rest period can be averaged over a period of 14 days (eg 12 hours in one seven-day period and 36 hours in the following seven-day period). If a worker's daily work lasts for more than six hours the worker is entitled to a rest period. The length of time allowed for the break can be agreed in a collective agreement, but it must be for at least 20 minutes, and the worker must be entitled to spend that period of time away from the work station. Young workers are entitled to a break of at least 30 minutes if their working time is for more than four and a half hours.

 Find out what alterations your organisation, or an organisation with which you are familiar, had to make in response to the Working Time Regulations. What difficulties did they encounter? Were there any costs involved?

RELATIONSHIP BALANCE

As stated at the start of this section, the Working Time Regulations were created in reaction to concerns relating to health and safety. Do you think that the regulations have a significant relationship to health and safety? What facts about an organisation might help to determine if there has been such an impact?

PAYMENT OF WAGES

As we noted in Chapter 3, one of the obligations on the employer is to pay wages. There are also further, more detailed rights of the employee, with regard to wages.

Right to an itemised pay statement

In accordance with the Employment Rights Act 1996 (section 8) employees have the right to receive a written pay statement with (or before) each payment of wages or salary. This statement must show the gross and net payments, and the nature of any deductions, and the purpose of those deductions.

If an employee does not receive such a pay statement he can apply to the Employment Tribunal that can declare the particulars that should have been included. If any unnotified deductions have been made during the 13 weeks prior to the application to the Tribunal being made, the Tribunal can instruct the employer to refund those deductions.

> **TASK** Look at your last pay statement. What does it include? Does it show all that is listed above?

Authorised deductions

As we noted in Chapter 1, unlawful deductions from wages is the second most common claim brought before an Employment Tribunal. The only lawful deductions that can be made are:

- those required or authorised by statute (eg PAYE and National Insurance contributions)
- those required or authorised by a provision in the contract of employment, of which the employee has been made aware (eg a payment relating to the use of company tools and equipment)
- those agreed by the employee in writing (eg a contribution to a club or society run by the organisation).

An agreement to a deduction must be made in writing, and it must be made clear that the deduction is to be made from wages – and that the employee agrees to this, as illustrated by the following case.

Potter v *Hunt Contracts* [1991] IRLR 108

Potter took an HGV driving course that was paid for by the agency he worked for. The agency placed him with Hunt Contracts, who decided to take him on as a permanent employee. As part of the deal with the agency they refunded the cost of the HGV training course. An agreement was drawn up with Potter that he would repay Hunt Contracts for the £545 cost of the course at the amount of £22 per month. One month later his employment was terminated and the outstanding money (£523) was deducted from his outstanding wages. As this was less than £523 he received nothing in his final pay. The Employment Tribunal held it was a lawful deduction. However, the EAT overturned the decision of the Tribunal because the agreement between Potter and Hunt Contracts did not make it clear that the deduction was to be made from Potter's *wages* – hence it was an unlawful deduction.

An agreement to a deduction must be made before an event leading to that deduction (for example, if an employer wants an employee to pay for a training course, this must be agreed between the employee and employer before the employee attends the course).

Discount Tobacco and Confectionery Ltd v *Williamson* [1993] IRLR 327

Williamson was a manager of the respondent's retail outlets. On a number of occasions there had been a shortfall following stocktaking. After a series of shortfalls Williamson signed an agreement that £3500 would be deducted from his wages at a rate of £20 per week, to compensate for part of the shortfalls. He was then dismissed, due to the shortfalls, and was told his outstanding wages and accrued holiday pay would not be paid to him because they were less than the £3500 he had agreed to in deductions.

The EAT supported the Tribunal in the finding that the deduction had been agreed to after the event (ie after the shortfalls) and hence was not a lawful deduction of wages. It was also noted that the respondent had a written procedure for handling shortfalls, which had not been followed and, indeed, Williamson had not been made aware of the procedures.

RELATIONSHIP BALANCE

An employee needs to know how much money he is receiving at each date of payment, because he has bills to pay. In what ways do these regulations help improve the communication between the employee and employer in relation to deductions of wages? Do you think the employee has sufficient protection to give him a reasonable expectation of what will be in each pay statement?

Definition of wages

Wages are any sum payable to a worker in connection with work done during employment.

Delaney v *Staples* [1992] IRLR 191

Delaney was dismissed from employment with Staples, and claimed that she was owed commission, holiday pay and pay in lieu of notice (money relating to the wages she would have earned if she had worked her notice period). It was ruled that the commission and holiday pay had been earned, and hence failure to pay them equated to unlawful deductions. However, the pay in lieu of notice was ruled not to be wages, because it was not money relating to work done. On this basis it was not possible for the non-payment of pay in lieu of notice to be an unlawful deduction from wages. It was ruled that pay in lieu of notice actually equates to damages to compensate the employee for being dismissed without contractual notice (wrongful dismissal – see Chapter 9). However, it was noted that if an employee had been given the correct notice but had not been required to attend work (known as 'garden leave') then that money would constitute 'wages' as a contract of employment still exists.

Further Exploration

As we saw in Chapter 2, unlawful deduction of wages is one of the most common types of claims that come before the Employment Tribunals. Do you think that the reason for this is a lack of clarity in current legislation? If so, what area of legislation needs clarification? Can you think of any other reasons for this type of claim being relatively common?

Guarantee payments

Sections 28–35 of the Employment Rights Act 1996 states that an employee with one month's continuous service is entitled to a guarantee payment if he is not provided with work throughout a day when he would normally expect to work, if the reason for the lack of work is a decrease in demand for the employer's business or for the type of work that the employee carries out, or any other event affecting the employer's normal business (eg a power cut).

The employee loses the right to a guarantee payment if:

- the failure to provide work is related to industrial action
- the employee refuses the offer of suitable alternative work
- the employee does not comply with a reasonable attendance requirement, so that the employer can keep workers together in the event that work can continue (eg vital supplies can be delivered).

Purdy v Willowbrook International Ltd [1977] IRLR 388

Purdy worked as a trimmer in Willowbrook's coach factory. There was a reduction in trimming work and Purdy was asked to move to the finishing shop – work with which he was familiar. The pay would have been similar to that which he earned as a trimmer, and definitely in excess of any guarantee payment. Purdy refused to move. Subsequently the trimmers (including Purdy) were moved to a three-day week. Purdy claimed a guarantee payment for the two days of no work, but it was ruled that he was not entitled to the payments because he had refused the opportunity of suitable alternative work.

Meadows v Faithful Overalls Ltd [1977] IRLR 330

Meadows worked at a clothing factory. On the day in question, when he arrived for work, the heating system was inoperable and the employer was waiting for a delivery of oil to fuel the heating. The employees were asked to wait in the canteen where hot tea was provided. The oil supplier informed the employer there would be a delay in the delivery, and Meadows stated he would wait only until 9.45am. At 9.45am he went home, and the oil delivery arrived just after 10.00am. Meadows claimed a guarantee payment. It was ruled that the request to wait was a reasonable request, and by refusing to do so Meadows had no entitlement to a guarantee payment.

The guarantee payment is the amount of hours normally worked on the day in question, multiplied by the hourly rate. The guarantee payment is paid for a maximum of five days in a three-month period. In 2004 this was subject to a daily maximum of £17.80 and a maximum of £89.00 for the whole five days.

NATIONAL MINIMUM WAGE ACT 1998

The National Minimum Wage (NMW) gives the right for workers to receive a minimum hourly rate of pay. In the Act, a worker is described as someone working under a contract of employment or any other contract under which the individual undertakes to perform personally any work or services for another party.

Those who are not covered by the Act include:

- workers aged under 18 years
- a worker under the age of 26 years who is employed under a contract of apprenticeship
- a worker who is on a scheme to provide training or temporary work, or a scheme designed to help him find work
- a worker who is taking part in work experience as part of a first degree course, or as part of a teacher training course
- a homeless person who is given shelter and other benefits in return for work.

The NMW is paid at two levels. From 1 October 2003 these are:

- £4.50 for those aged 22 years and over.
- £3.80 for those aged 18–21 years.

These rates are reviewed periodically – current rates can be found at the National Minumum Wage website (www.dti.gov.uk/er/nmw).

What counts as work for payment of the NMW?

An employee's pay does not always consist solely of a basic rate. There are often bonuses, tips, stand-by payments and other items that make up the total pay. A number of cases have addressed the issue of what should be taken into account when calculating the hourly rate of pay.

British Nursing Association v *Inland Revenue* [2002] IRLR 480

The BNA provides a 24-hour service, supplying nurses to nursing homes and similar establishments. During the day the bookings are made through the head office. During the night (8pm–9am) trained nurses work from home, taking calls and placing nurses accordingly. Between calls the nurses can spend their time as they wish. The Employment Tribunal was asked to determine what hours the nurses were working at night, for the purposes of calculating their wages in accordance with the NMW. The Tribunal found (and was supported by the Court of Appeal) that the nurses were working for each hour of their shift. Although they were not taking phone calls for all the time they were required to be available. In addition they noted that the process during the night was no different to the process carried out during the day. Hence, the nurses must be paid at least the NMW for each hour of their night shift.

Scottbridge Construction Ltd v *Wright* [2002] IRLR 21

Wright was a nightwatchman working from 5pm to 7am. He had to respond to telephone calls and the intruder alarm, and was sometimes given some other small tasks. Providing that he carried out these duties he was entitled to spend the rest of the time as he wished, and sleeping facilities were provided. He claimed that he should be paid the NMW for each hour of his shift. The Court of Session supported his claim, ruling that he was required to work at any time during the night, should a phone call be made or an alarm be triggered.

In determining whether the worker is working for the purposes of entitlement to the NMW it is important to consider the restrictions placed upon the worker when he is not actually carrying out a task determined by the employer (does he have to be available?). All aspects of the nature of the work must also be examined to see if it can be properly described as 'work'.

In determining if someone is being paid at least the NMW the current level of gross pay (ie the payment before tax and National Insurance is deducted) must be considered. Added to that can be the cost of accommodation provided to the employee (a formula to account for this is described in the Regulations). Amounts which are not paid through the payroll (eg tips given direct to staff by customers) are not included as part of the definition of pay.

Nerva and others v *United Kingdom* [2002] IRLR 815

The applicants were employed as waiters. If customers left cash tips they were gathered together and shared amongst the waiters. If customers left tips on a cheque or credit card payment they were also added up and paid through the payroll as 'additional pay'. For the purposes of calculating adherence to the NMW the employer claimed that the tips paid through the payroll counted as wages. The employees brought a claim, which ultimately went to the European Court of Justice. The finding of all the appeal courts was that the employer was entitled to count the tips paid through the payroll as wages. The employer held the legal title to the tips, and they were his money. He was entitled to use them to meet part of the cost of paying the waiters.

Aviation and Airport Services v *Bellfield and others* [2001] EAT 194/00

Bellfield worked as a customer care agent. She was entitled to an attendance allowance if strict attendance requirements were met. Due to the introduction of the NMW the employer sought to make alterations to the payment structure. In determining that Bellfield was being paid the NMW the employer relied on the inclusion of the attendance allowance. It was ruled that this could not be included in the calculation because it was not an allowance attributable to the performance (as opposed to being present at work) of the worker in carrying out her work.

Failure to pay the NMW

Employers are required to keep records of payments for a minimum of three years. If a worker believes he is not being paid the correct amount under the NMW regulations he can ask to see these records. If the employer refuses to let the employee see the records the employee can make a complaint to the Employment Tribunal. In addition, if the employee believes he has not been paid the NMW he can make an application to the Employment Tribunal for the situation to be assessed.

> **TASK** Find out if your organisation, or an organisation with which you are familiar, had to make any changes as a result of the introduction of the NMW? Did the organisation experience any negative impacts?

> ## RELATIONSHIP BALANCE
>
> List the reasons for and against the introduction of the National Minimum Wage. Do you think that the reasons for and against have been substantiated by evidence gained since the National Minimum Wage was introduced? Has the financial level of the National Minimum Wage been sufficient to have a real impact on the relationship between the employer and the employee?

> ## *Further Exploration*
>
> The rate at which the NMW is set has risen significantly since it was first introduced. However, many employee groups still believe that it is set too low to be of any real benefit to the employee. Read different opinions on this matter (see www.tuc.org.uk and www.cbi.co.uk as a useful starting point). Having read different opinions, draw your own conclusions on the efficacy of the current rates of the NMW.

PAYMENT AND SICKNESS

Statutory Sick Pay

There is no requirement on an employer to have a sick pay scheme. However, all employers are required to pay Statutory Sick Pay (SSP) when an employee qualifies for such payments, and cannot contract out of doing so.

Employees who are at least age 16 and under age 65 on the first day of sickness and have been continuously sick for four or more calendar days in a row and have average earnings at least equal to the lower earnings limit (the amount at which National Insurance contributions are payable) are entitled to receive statutory sick pay. Any day for which SSP is claimed must be a day on which the employee would ordinarily work. SSP is paid for a maximum of 28 weeks in any 12-month period. If the sickness absence continues once the entitlement to SSP has expired the employee can then claim incapacity benefit.

Suspension on medical grounds

If an employee is suspended from work on medical grounds (eg the employer cannot provide any work for the employee due to health and safety requirements) the employee is entitled to the normal rate of pay for the first 26 weeks of the suspension. Employees who have worked for less than one month, or who have a fixed-term contract of less than three months, are excluded from this entitlement. In addition, an employee is not entitled to the payment if he has refused suitable alternative work or has not co-operated with the employer in being available for suitable work. If the employee is incapable of working due to illness, the terms relating to suspension on medical grounds do not apply.

MATERNITY PROTECTION

Maternity protection is an area of employment law that has changed greatly over recent years. The Employment Relations Act 1999 amended the rules, and they were further amended by the Employment Act 2002. Maternity protection covers a woman through the periods of ante-natal care, care at work during her pregnancy, and maternity leave.

A pregnant woman is protected against dismissal on the grounds of her pregnancy, discrimination on the grounds of her pregnancy, or any other detrimental treatment relating to the pregnancy.

Webb v *EMO Air Cargo Ltd* [1994] IRLR 482

Webb was employed to cover another employee who was taking maternity leave. She was taken on six months before the other employee started her leave, so that she could be trained to carry out the duties of the job. Two weeks after her employment started Webb found that she was also pregnant. EMO dismissed Webb as she was not going to be available to them at the crucial time, ie to cover the whole of the period of the other employee's maternity leave. Webb appealed to the Employment Tribunal, which supported the employer's view. It held that if a man had been recruited to cover, and announced he would be on protracted leave, then EMO would also have dismissed the man. The European Court of Justice overruled this finding, ruling that any dismissal relating to pregnancy was sex discrimination, and that it was not right to make comparisons with a 'hypothetical' man. (Note: The dismissal was related to pregnancy and hence there is no requirement for the normal qualifying period of one year in order to bring a claim of unfair dismissal.)

TASK Find out if your organisation, or an organisation with which you are familiar, has a maternity policy. Read it and compare it with the statutory requirements covered in this chapter.

Ante-natal care

A pregnant woman has the right to take paid time off for ante-natal appointments during working hours. She has the right to be paid for this period of absence. If she is not allowed the time off she can complain to an Employment Tribunal, which can make a declaration that the refusal was unjustified and order the company to pay the woman an amount equal to that which she would have received for the period of time off requested. If she is allowed the time off but the company refuse to pay her, the Employment Tribunal can make a declaration to that effect, and order the company to pay her the rightful amount.

The ante-natal treatment must be recommended by a doctor, midwife or health visitor. The woman can be asked to show her employer proof of her appointment (eg an appointment card) for second and subsequent appointments.

A straightforward case showing the right to paid ante-natal appointments is given here.

Gregory v *Tudsbury Ltd* [1982] IRLR 267

Gregory took five consecutive Monday afternoons off to attend ante-natal care and relaxation classes. She produced a medical certificate signed by a doctor and mid-wife. Her employers allowed her the time off but refused to pay her for it, although they agreed it was not practical for her to arrange the classes outside of working hours. Gregory complained to the Employment Tribunal and her employer was ordered to pay her for the time spent at the ante-natal classes.

Although there is a clear right to paid time off, this right must not be abused – see the following case.

Gough v *Country Sport (Wales) Ltd* [1989] ET Case No 01075/89

Country Sport was concerned that Gough was taking off more time than was necessary for ante-natal care. On one occasion Gough had an afternoon appointment, and Country Sport refused to let her also take the morning off to go to the hairdresser. Gough took the whole day off, and was dismissed. The Employment Tribunal held that it was a fair dismissal, because the reason for the dismissal was Gough's 'flagrant disobedience' and not her pregnancy.

Maternity leave

There are three periods of maternity leave:

- *Compulsory maternity leave.* No employee may work for her employer for the two weeks immediately following the date of childbirth. This period of two weeks forms part of the period known as ordinary maternity leave.

- *Ordinary maternity leave.* All pregnant women are entitled to take 26 weeks' ordinary maternity leave, regardless of their length of service. However, in order to qualify for Statutory Maternity Pay (see later) the woman must have worked for at least 26 continuous weeks by the beginning of the 14th week before the Expected Week of Confinement (EWC – the week in which the doctors advise the baby is expected to be born).

- *Additional maternity leave.* Pregnant women with at least 26 weeks' continuous service are entitled to take a further 26 weeks' additional maternity leave at the end of the ordinary maternity leave period – in other words, giving a 52-week maximum period of leave.

Entitlement to ordinary maternity leave

Ordinary Maternity Leave (OML) can be taken only by employees (those who have entered into, or work under, a contract of employment that is defined as a contract of service). To qualify for OML the woman must inform her employer no later than the 15th week before the EWC (in writing if requested) of the following:

- that she is pregnant
- her EWC
- the date on which she wants to start her OML – this cannot be earlier than the beginning of the 11th week before the EWC.

If the employee wished to change the proposed start date of the OML, she is required to give 28 days' notice – if reasonably practical.

OML is considered to have started on the earliest of:

- the date the employee has notified to her employer of the intended start date of OML
- the day that follows the first day after the beginning of the fourth week before the EWC on which she is absent from work wholly or partly due to pregnancy
- the day that follows the day on which childbirth occurs (OML starts at this point even if the day falls before the beginning of the 11th week before the EWC).

During OML the employee is:

- entitled to the benefits of all the terms and conditions of employment that would have applied if she had not been absent
- bound by any obligations arising under those terms and conditions (unless they are inconsistent with the right to take OML, eg the requirement to attend work)
- entitled to return to the job in which she was employed before the OML, with the same seniority and rights as if she had not been absent.

Entitlement to additional maternity leave

In the same way as for OML, the entitlement is only for employees. The Additional Maternity Leave (AML) commences on the date after the OML finished. An employee is entitled to continued benefits during her period of AML, and is bound by the existing obligations of her contract of employment. There is no payment during the period of AML, (although the employer can make payments if he wishes).

Returning to work

An employee is entitled to return to exactly the same job she left and is to be treated as if she had never been absent. She should be paid the amount of pay she would have been paid if she had not been absent (ie inclusive of any pay increases awarded during her absence). If the employer does not allow the woman to return to her old job this would count as a dismissal, and would be automatically unfair because it would be a dismissal related to pregnancy.

The exceptions to this are:

- when a woman is returning after two or more consecutive periods of statutory leave, and it is not 'reasonably practicable' for the woman to return to the same job
- where a redundancy situation has arisen during the period of leave. In this situation a woman is entitled to be offered any suitable alternative work.

An example of the issues that can arise relating to redundancy can be found in the following case.

Philip Hodges & Co v *Kell* [1994] IRLR 568

Kell worked as a secretary for Philip Hodges & Co. During her maternity leave the firm decided there was no longer a requirement for her role as a personal secretary. They did not give her notice at this time. During her leave they also employed another secretary on an 'ad hoc' basis, but made her permanent and full time before Kell was due to return to work. The Employment Tribunal found that Kell worked as a legal secretary, and hence was capable of doing the other role that had originally been 'ad hoc'. On that basis, it was unfair to recruit another employee during her maternity leave, and make Kell redundant. They found, therefore, that Kell had been unfairly dismissed.

Notification of returning to work

A woman has the automatic right to return to work following her maternity leave and, unless she says otherwise, it will be assumed that she will return. A woman returning to work after having taken her full maternity leave entitlement is not required to give her employer any notice, she can simply turn up on the day after her period of leave has ended.

If a woman decides not to return to work she is required to give the notice required in accordance with her contract of employment. This cannot be less than the statutory minimum of one week.

If a woman wants to return to work before the end of her maternity leave (presuming that the period of compulsory leave has passed) she must give her employer at least 28 days' notice of her intention – specifying the date on which she intends to return.

If a woman wants to return to work, but on reduced hours, she must make her request to her employer in line with the rules regarding flexible working, which we looked at in Chapter 4.

Statutory Maternity Pay

Statutory Maternity Pay (SMP) is payable by employers, for a period of 26 weeks, to pregnant employees who have worked for that employer for at least 26 continuous weeks at the 14th week before the EWC (the 'qualifying period'). The payment of SMP cannot start until the employee has ceased working (ie started a period of maternity leave). The employee must earn at least the lower earnings limit for the payment of primary Class 1 NI contributions (£77 for the 2003/04 tax year) as an average payment over the eight weeks up to and including the qualifying period.

SMP is paid at a rate of 90 per cent of average weekly earnings for the first six weeks, and than at £100 per week for the remaining 20 weeks. The employer can pay more than this amount.

Further Exploration

Maternity legislation has changed greatly over current years. Track the changes that have occurred, and try to determine the reasons for these changes. Do you think that further changes are likely in the future? What changes are most likely to occur?

RELATIONSHIP BALANCE

Do you think that the current maternity legislation gives adequate protection to both the employer and the employee? Does the employer have adequate protection to ensure that the business can continue to run efficiently whilst accommodating women on maternity leave? Does the pregnant woman have sufficient protection to ensure her ability to continue with her employment as she wishes?

STATUTORY PATERNITY LEAVE

Statutory Paternity Leave was introduced by the Employment Act 2002. To qualify for paternity leave the employee must have worked for that employer for at least 26 continuous weeks at the 15th week before the expected week of the birth of the baby. The employee must be the father of the child, or the mother's husband or partner. The employee must expect to have responsibility for the upbringing of the child. (Note: The 'Partner' does not have to be male, it can be a female in a same-sex relationship.)

The employee must give 28 days notice to his employer of the intention to take paternity leave. The period of paternity leave will be of up to two weeks. The paternity leave will be paid at the lower rate of SMP (ie currently £100 per week). During the period of paternity leave the contract of employment continues, and the employee has the right to return to his job after the leave ends.

ADOPTION LEAVE

The Employment Act 2002 introduced a new statutory right for employees who adopt a child to take time off to build up a relationship with that child. The provisions mirror maternity leave – but either of the parents can take the leave (but not both).

Therefore, there is a period of Ordinary Adoption Leave (OAL), which lasts for 26 weeks, and can be taken by an employee who is the 'adopter' and has been continuously employed for at least 26 weeks ending with the week when s/he was notified of having been matched with the child. The payment during the period of OAL is the same as SMP.

An employee can choose to commence OAL on the day on which the child is placed with him for adoption, or at a predetermined date which is no more than 14 days before the child is expected to be placed, and no later than the day of the placement.

An employee is entitled to Additional Adoption Leave (AAL) if the child was placed with the employee for adoption, the employee took OAL in respect of the child and the OAL period did not end prematurely (for example, because of a disruption to the placement of the adopted child). AAL starts the day after OAL ends.

During adoption leave the employee's rights and obligations under the contract of employment continue. The employee is entitled to return to his old job with the same seniority and benefits that he left.

PARENTAL LEAVE

The Maternity and Parental Leave Regulations 1999 laid down a minimum framework of parental leave rights. Employers and employees have to adhere to the minimum rights, but can work out their own agreement to operate parental leave.

The minimum framework is:

- Employees with at least one year's continuous service with their employer who have responsibility for a child have the right to parental leave.
- Up to 13 weeks' leave may be taken for each child, or 18 weeks if the child is entitled to a disability living allowance.
- The leave has to be for the purpose of caring for the child.
- The right to take leave normally applies during the child's first five years, except in relation to parents of adopted children (when the leave can be taken during the first five years of the placement) and disabled children (when the leave can be taken until the child's 18th birthday).
- The employee remains employed whilst on leave, hence the contract of employment continues.
- The employee has the right to return to the same job or to another suitable job, after the period of leave ends.

The 13 weeks' leave is a total allowance, and under the statutory scheme leave must be taken in blocks of at least one week. An employee cannot take more than four weeks' leave in respect of any individual child during a particular year. Parental leave is unpaid.

If the period of intended leave is two weeks or less then at least four weeks' notice must be given. For longer periods, at least twice the length of leave requested must be given in notice (ie six weeks' notice for three weeks' leave).

RELATIONSHIP BALANCE

The regulations we have looked at here address specific aspects of the employee's family life where he might have a need to take time off. What other issues are not addressed by this legislation? Is there a situation when other employees, with other needs, could feel very unhappy with the lack of protection that current legislation offers to them?

TIME OFF FOR DEPENDANTS

The Employment Rights Act 1996 gives a right to enable an employee to take a reasonable amount of time off during working hours to take action which is necessary to:

- provide assistance when a dependant falls ill, gives birth or is injured or assaulted
- make arrangements for the care of a dependant who is ill or injured

- take actions in connection with the death of a dependant
- deal with disruption to or cancellation of arrangements for the care of a dependant
- deal with an incident involving a child at school.

A dependant is the employee's wife, husband, child, parent or someone living in the same house as the employee who is not a lodger, tenant, boarder or employee. The right is not paid, but if the employer has allowed employees paid time off in the past to deal with such issues they must continue to do so. An employee must make the employer aware of the reason for the absence as soon as is reasonably practical, but there is no requirement to give notice.

TIME OFF FOR PUBLIC DUTIES

Section 50 of the Employment Rights Act 1996 gives employees the right to take time off for certain public duties. They are not entitled to payment from their employer when taking this time off. Duties include meetings of, or work in relation to:

- membership of a local authority
- membership of a statutory tribunal
- membership of a health authority, NHS trust or health board
- membership of a relevant education body
- membership of a police authority
- membership of the Service Authority of the National Crime Squad or the National Criminal Intelligence Service
- membership of a board of prison visitors or a prison visiting committee
- membership of the Environment Agency.

In addition, the Right to Time Off for Study or Training Regulations 2001 permits employees who are aged 16 or 17 years and are not receiving full-time or further education and have not attained standards of achievement as defined in the Act (eg grades A–C in five subjects at GCSE) a reasonable time off for work for study or training. The same rights are given to employees who are aged 18 years and are undertaking training or study leading to a relevant qualification and who began that study before reaching the age of 18 years.

In Chapter 10 we shall also note the right to time off for trade union duties, and in Chapter 9 we shall note the right to time off to seek employment when faced with impending redundancy.

RELATIONSHIP BALANCE

For some employers these regulations will do little more than formalise the informal agreement to allow an employee time to deal with a family emergency. How can the employer ensure that the legislation does not allow abuse of these rights? Is the employee offered adequate protection by this legislation?

TASK Find out if there have been any requests for paternity, adoption, parental or dependant leave in your organisation, or an organisation with which you are familiar. How have these requests been addressed? Does the employer feel that the requests have been disruptive to the efficiency of the organisation?

CHAPTER REVIEW

1 The Working Time Regulations have been extended in 2003 to cover sectors previously excluded from the Regulations.

2 The Working Time Regulations set minimum standards relating to the working week, annual leave, night work and rest periods.

3 An employee is entitled to receive an itemised pay statement.

4 Deductions from wages are lawful only if they are determined by statute, are agreed within the contract of employment, or if they are agreed between the employer and employee in writing.

5 Pay in lieu of notice is not classed as wages.

6 Guarantee payments are paid to those who have at least one month's continuous employment, and are not offered work on a day when they would normally be expected to work.

7 The National Minimum Wage is paid at two levels – currently £4.50 for those aged 22 years and above, and £3.80 for those aged 18–21 years.

8 The employer has to pay statutory sick pay when the employee qualifies for such payment.

9 Maternity leave falls into three categories: compulsory leave, ordinary leave and additional leave.

10 A dismissal relating to pregnancy is automatically unfair.

11 Paternity leave is allowed up to a period of two weeks.

12 Adoption leave mirrors maternity leave, but can be claimed by only one person in relation to each child (known as the 'adopter').

13 Parental leave up to a maximum of 13 weeks can be taken in the first five years of the child's life (or in the first five years of an adoption) or a maximum of 18 weeks can be taken in the first 18 years of a disabled child's life.

14 Time off to care for dependants can be taken, with as much notice as possible being given.

15 Time off is allowed for a range of public duties.

WEBSITES REFERENCED IN THIS CHAPTER

www.cbi.org.uk	Confederation of British Industry
www.dti.gov.uk/er/nmw	Department of Trade and Industry – National Minimum Wage
www.tuc.org.uk	Trades Union Congress

FURTHER READING

- *Byrne Brothers (Formwork Ltd) v Baird & others* [2002] IRLR 96 – examining the issue of who is a 'worker' as defined by the Working Time Regulations.
- *Caledonia Bureau Investment and Property v Caffrey* [1998] IRLR 110 – if a pregnancy-related illness arises and the employee is dismissed because of that illness the dismissal will be automatically unfair.
- *Davies and others v M J Wyatt (Decorators) Ltd* [2000] IRLR 759 – the obligation to meet holiday payments cannot be met by unilaterally reducing the employees' hourly rate of pay without their consent.
- *Fairfield v Skinner* [1993] IRLR 3 – an employer claims the right to make deductions for alleged expenses accumulated by the employee.
- *Gillespie v NHSSB* [1996] IRLR 214 – a woman unsuccessfully claimed that a failure to pay her full pay whilst on maternity leave was sex discrimination.
- *Kent Management Services v Butterfield* [1982] IRLR 394 – discretionary commission is classified as wages if there is a reasonable expectation of both parties that it will be paid.
- *Kerr v The Sweater Shop* [1996] IRLR 424 – a deduction from wages must be brought to the attention of an employee.
- *MacRuary v Washington Irvine Ltd* [1994] EAT 857/93 – an employee 'working under protest' after a unilateral pay cut was entitled to recover pay which was withheld from him.

EXAMPLES TO WORK THROUGH

1 You work as a personnel manager in Organisation A, a manufacturing business. The night-shift employees have always worked four night shifts a week, from 8pm to 6am, and do not want their shifts to change. You have been asked whether these hours are allowed, in view of the Working Time Regulations. What is your advice?

2 You are a manager of a wine bar. One of your waitresses has complained that she is not being paid the National Minimum Wage. She is currently paid £4.00 per hour, and receives an average of £50 per week in tips. She works 40 hours per week. Is she being paid in accordance with the legislation?

3 Janet has informed you that she is pregnant and wishes to start her Ordinary Maternity Leave on 1 July. Her Expected Week of Confinement is 23 August. It is 15 June and she has phoned in absent with an illness related to her pregnancy. She does not want to start her OML at this time, but her manager is insisting that she does. What is your advice?

4 You have just been informed that Samantha received a phone call, during working time, and was told that her daughter had been injured during a school activity. Her husband is out of the country, and hence she said she had to go to her daughter. She went immediately. Should she be paid for the period of absence? Her manager is complaining that she gave insufficient notice. What is your advice?

Discrimination (1)

CHAPTER 6

The objectives of this chapter are to:

■ **Explore the concept of discrimination;**

■ **Analyse the difference between indirect and direct discrimination;**

■ **Explore the concept of Genuine Occupational Qualifications;**

■ **Look at specific issues of discrimination with regards to sex and race;**

■ **Explore the provisions of the Disability Discrimination Act 1995;**

■ **Outline the more recent developments in discrimination legislation: transsexuals, religion and sexual orientation.**

DISCRIMINATION

Legislation relating to discrimination has developed considerably over recent years. However, the first piece of legislation specifically focusing on issues of discrimination is over 30 years old – the Equal Pay Act 1970. That legislation started to address the issue of men and women being paid different rates for the same work – which was not an unusual practice at that time.

This legislation was followed by two major pieces of legislation: the Sex Discrimination Act 1975 and the Race Relations Act 1976. These two Acts made it illegal to treat employees differently because of their gender or their race. These Acts apply across all areas of employment, from recruitment and promotion to opportunities for training, and dismissal. As we saw in Chapter 2, a significant number of claims brought to the Employment Tribunal still relate to these two pieces of legislation.

No new areas of discrimination law were introduced for 20 more years, when the Disability Discrimination Act 1995 gave disabled employees the right not to be treated differently in all aspects of employment, in comparison to an able-bodied employee.

In 1999 transsexuals were added to the categories of employees that may not legally be discriminated against, by the Sex Discrimination (Gender Reassignment) Regulations 1999.

In December 2003 two additional pieces of legislation were introduced:

■ The Employment Equality (Sexual Orientation) Regulations 2003, making it unlawful to discriminate against employees on the grounds of their sexual orientation.
■ The Employment Equality (Religion and Belief) Regulations 2003, making it unlawful to discriminate against employees on the grounds of their religion or belief.

88

In October 2006 legislation is to be introduced making it unlawful to discriminate on the grounds of age. This legislation must be introduced by all Member States of the EU in response to the EC Equal Treatment Framework Directive (No. 2000/78).

This brief history of discrimination legislation shows how there is a move to make it essential to base all decisions relating to employment (from recruitment to dismissal) on the abilities of the employee (or to adapt the requirements of the job so that the employee can perform competently), and not on factors that do not have any bearing on how competently the employee carries out his duties. When the age discrimination legislation is added in there will be a very comprehensive range of discrimination legislation.

TASK During your studies ensure that you are aware of any further changes proposed to discrimination legislation, and of new case law as it is reported. Discrimination law is a rapidly moving area of legislation – ensure that you are always up to date. Useful websites include www.cipd.co.uk (Chartered Institute of Personnel and Development), www.eoc.org.uk (Equal Opportunities Commission) and www.dti.gov.uk (Department of Trade and Industry).

DIRECT AND INDIRECT DISCRIMINATION

Direct discrimination

This is where an employee is treated less favourably on the grounds of sex/race etc than an employee of the different sex/race etc. It is important to note that the issue is being treated less *favourably*. There are occasions when employees can be treated differently, but this does not necessarily mean the treatment is unfavourable. An example of this can be found in the following case.

Peake v *Automotive Products* [1977] IRLR 365

Automotive Products employed around 3500 men and 400 women. They had a practice that women were allowed to leave work at 4.25pm, and men at 4.30pm so that women were allowed to miss the rush at 4.30pm (on safety grounds). Peake (a man) applied to the Employment Tribunal claiming that this was unlawful sex discrimination. The EAT upheld his view, but the Court of Appeal overturned this decision. This was on the principle *de minimis non curat lex* (the law takes no account of trifles). Although the treatment was different there was no evidence that the treatment of the men was really unfavourable.

If an employee can show that their treatment is unfavourable, then they must be able to point to a comparator of the opposite gender or a different race etc and show that this comparator, who is the same as the employee in all other ways, is being treated differently. This comparator can be real or can be hypothetical.

In some cases it can be difficult to make use of a hypothetical comparator, as in the next case, which we looked at in Chapter 5.

Webb v EMO Air Cargo Ltd [1994] IRLR 482

Webb was dismissed because she found she was pregnant, and she had only been recruited to cover another employee's maternity leave. The European Court of Justice ruled that any dismissal relating to pregnancy had to be sex discrimination (because only women become pregnant). It ruled that it was not acceptable to make a comparison to a hypothetical man who had announced that he would need to take protracted leave when covering another employee's leave.

However, in the following case a hypothetical comparator was allowed.

Coleman v Skyrail Oceanic Ltd [1981] IRLR 398

Coleman worked as a booking clerk in a travel agency. Two days after her marriage to an employee who worked for a competitor she was dismissed. The two competitors had discussed the situation and had decided that she should be dismissed because 'the husband was probably the breadwinner'. The EAT accepted the employer's argument that there was no evidence that the organisation had treated Coleman less favourably than a hypothetical male in the same situation. The Court of Appeal, however, ruled that the assumption had been made that women were not breadwinners, and men were – and that was a decision based on the sex of the employee. Therefore, this was direct discrimination.

If an employee can show that there has been less favourable treatment, the next step is to show that the *reason* for the treatment related to the employee's sex/race etc. This is known as the causation question.

Bradford Hospitals NHS Trust v Al-Shabib [2002] EAT 709/01

Al-Shabib, a man of Iraqi origin, decided to join the staff gym. After signing an agreement to abide by the rules of the gym, Al-Shabib allowed his wife and child to use the gym, which was in breach of one of the rules. The gym manager reprimanded him. Following an investigation, during which Al-Shabib was not interviewed, it was decided to withdraw his gym membership. Al-Shabib brought a claim to the Employment Tribunal that he had been subjected to direct race discrimination – believing that the nature of the investigation and the withdrawal of his membership was due to his race. The Employment Tribunal upheld his claim, stating that his treatment was race discrimination, comparing Al-Shabib's treatment to a hypothetical white employee. However, the EAT overturned this decision, stating that there was no evidence that the treatment of Al-Shabib had been related to his race in any way.

Indirect discrimination

This is where the employer applies to both sexes/all races a *criterion* that adversely affects a considerably larger proportion of one sex/race etc than another (*adverse impact*) and it is to the detriment of the person that s/he cannot comply (*detriment*) and it cannot be justified, irrespective of sex/race etc (*justification*).

In summary, this is not deliberate discrimination – but discrimination that has happened indirectly because of a practice imposed by the employer. The intention of the employer is irrelevant, and it is not necessary that the employer realises that the actions are discriminatory.

Criterion
Here is an example of a criterion applied to both sexes.

Clarke v *Eley (IMI) Kynoch Ltd* [1982] IRLR 482

The employer's redundancy policy was to dismiss part-time employees first, and then use the criteria of 'last in, first out' (LIFO). A redundancy was announced and 60 part-time women, 20 full-time men and 26 full-time women were made redundant. Clarke and a colleague took a claim of indirect sex discrimination to the Employment Tribunal. It was held that the criterion of dismissing part-time employees first was indirect sex discrimination – although it was a criterion applied to all part-timers, irrespective of their sex, it had a significantly greater adverse impact on women, because more women worked part-time.

Adverse impact
Here is a case that demonstrates the concept of adverse impact.

Jones v *University of Manchester* [1993] IRLR 218

The University advertised for a Careers Adviser, specifying that the successful applicant would be between 27 and 35 years old and a graduate. Jones was aged 46 years, having started her degree as a mature student at the age of 38. In making a claim of indirect sex discrimination she had to specify the pool of people that she was comparing herself against. She sought to claim that the appropriate comparison was between male mature students and female mature students. She showed that female mature students tend to start their degrees at a later age than male mature students, and hence claimed that the age requirement for the job was indirect sex discrimination. The Court of Appeal held, however, that the correct comparison was between male and female graduates – not mature graduates – and hence there was no indirect sex discrimination, because there was no adverse impact on either men or women.

Further Exploration

The previous case also illustrates the issue of correctly defining the pool of people against which the comparison is being made. The pool must not be narrowed to a greater degree than the situation has determined. Hence, in this case the applicant had to be a graduate. To reduce the pool to mature students creates a different pool to the one specified in the original advertisement. Look at other cases of alleged indirect discrimination to see how the pools have been defined. A useful comparison would be *Price* v *Civil Service Commission* [1978] IRLR 3.

Detriment

The issue of detriment has been the subject of a number of challenges in case law. Some cases have suggested that a 'physical or economic consequence' is required for there to be a detriment. However, recent case law has shown that a disadvantage is sufficient. Here is an example of such a disadvantage.

R v *Secretary of State ex parte Equal Opportunities Commission* [1995] 1 AC 1

In this case the government was challenged by the Equal Opportunities Commission regarding the different qualifying periods (eg to claim for unfair dismissal) for full- and part-time employees. At this time a full-time employee needed to complete two years' consecutive employment, and a part-time employee had to complete five years' consecutive employment to qualify for the right. As a significantly larger proportion of women than men work part-time this rule was claimed to be indirect sex discrimination. Women suffered the detriment of having to work longer to complete a qualifying period. This claim was held and subsequent changes to legislation have introduced identical qualifying periods.

Justification

The following case demonstrates that there can be a justification for indirect discrimination.

Panesar v *The Nestlé Co Ltd* [1979] IRLR 60

Panesar was a Sikh. He applied for a job at Nestlé's factory where chocolate and coffee products were made. Nestlé had a policy of not allowing beards on the grounds of hygiene. Panesar refused to shave off his beard, and was therefore refused a job interview. Panesar took a claim of indirect race discrimination because significantly fewer Sikhs than non-Sikhs could comply with the requirement. It was agreed that the rule did indirectly discriminate against Sikhs; however, it was held to be a justifiable requirement (because of the importance of hygiene in food processing) and hence the action was not illegal.

Proof

The Respondent (typically the employer) carries the burden of proof. Hence, if the employee can show that an act has placed him at a disadvantage then the Respondent must show this can be justified as a legitimate business aim.

To help with the process of proving discrimination the legislation allows for the use of a questionnaire procedure. The applicant fills in the questionnaire explaining when he thinks the discrimination occurs and the reasons he thinks the alleged act amounted to discrimination. The employer is then asked to respond, stating whether or not he agrees that discrimination has occurred. If he does not agree then he must supply further information in response to the points that the employee has made.

Remedies for discrimination

If it is found by an Employment Tribunal that there has been an act of discrimination, the following can be awarded:

1   A declaration of the rights of the parties.

2   An order of compensation that is not subject to a maximum. The compensation should address any loss or damage that has occurred, and can include a sum relating to injured feelings.

3   A recommendation that the employer should take certain actions to ensure that the situation does not recur. If the employer does not take these actions, without reasonable justification, compensation can be increased.

The recommendation must be based on an actual adverse impact suffered by the complainant, as in the following case.

Leeds Rhinos Rugby Club & others v *Sterling* [2002] EAT 267/01

Sterling was employed by the rugby club on a succession of three contracts. He claimed that the lack of his selection for the first team was on the grounds of his race. The Employment Tribunal upheld his complaints of race discrimination and victimisation. The tribunal recognised that, as a result of the claim, Sterling was less likely to be offered another contract by other clubs because he could be seen as a 'trouble maker'. To mitigate these consequences the tribunal recommended that the Leeds Rhinos offer the player a new contract. The EAT ruled that this recommendation was not allowed by the Race Relations Act because it was based on a hypothetical outcome and not an actual adverse impact.

As we see here, the purpose of the recommendation is to reduce the adverse effect on the employee.

RELATIONSHIP BALANCE

Do you think that the definition of indirect discrimination gives adequate protection for both the employer and the employee? How can the employer ensure that he is not carrying out an act that can be interpreted as indirect discrimination? What do you think the employee's responsibilities should be if he thinks an act of indirect discrimination is being committed? Do you think there should be the same penalty for the employer for indirect discrimination as for direct discrimination? Should a deliberate act be penalised in the same way as an unintentional act?

TASK Find out if your organisation, or an organisation with which you are familiar, has a policy relating to discrimination in the workplace. Read the policy if it exists, and consider whether it meets the legal requirements. If there is no policy try drafting one.

GENUINE OCCUPATIONAL QUALIFICATIONS (GOQs)

There are occasions when it can be lawful to discriminate. This is when there is a genuine need for a particular sex or race.

Criteria relevant to sex are:

1 The job requires a certain physiology (excluding physical strength) or a certain authenticity in dramatic performances or other entertainment.

2 The job involves physical contact with people, and it would be inappropriate for this contact to be by a person of the opposite sex.

Etam plc v *Rowan* [1989] IRLR 150

Rowan, a man, was refused employment at the women's clothes shop Etam because the job would have involved measuring women who were unsure of their size, and this was inappropriate contact. The EAT held that this was a small part of the job, and could have been covered by a female colleague.

---

3 The job-holder needs to live on the premises and there are no facilities for providing separate sleeping and other facilities for each sex.

4 The job involves a special level of care, and it would be inappropriate for that care to be given by a member of the opposite sex.

5 The job is one of two jobs to be held by a married couple.

6 The job involves living in a private home and the degree of contact and intimacy involved would be inappropriate with a person of the opposite sex.

7 The job involves work outside the UK in countries where laws or customs would mean that the duties cannot be carried out by a woman.

Criteria relevant to race are:

1 The job requires authenticity in dramatic performance or other entertainment, or in modelling.

2 The job requires authenticity in the provision of food and drink to the public.

3 The job involves providing a personal welfare service that can be most effectively provided by a member of the same race.

Positive discrimination

In certain situations it might be lawful to discriminate positively in favour of a group of employees. This might be when a particular race or sex is underrepresented in a particular area or at a particular level within an organisation.

Marschall v *Land Nordrhein-Westfalen* [1998] IRLR 39

This ruling by the European Court of Justice applied to a case in Germany, but the ruling has relevance throughout the EU. Marschall was a teacher in a German school. In the area of Germany where he worked there was a rule that where there are fewer women than men in a particular grade then women are to be given priority for promotion if, on all other factors (eg suitability, performance, etc), the man and woman are equal. Marschall applied for a promotion, and was told that a woman would be getting the job, because of this rule. He claimed unfair sex discrimination. The ECJ held that if the rule was working to remove inequalities that affect women's equal opportunities, then the rule was lawful. Hence, Marschall's claim failed.

Although this claim was unsuccessful it must be possible to show that a group of employees is significantly underrepresented before making a decision to positively discriminate.

RELATIONSHIP BALANCE

Clearly there are situations in which positive discrimination might be needed to introduce a balance in the workforce that does not exist. What safeguards need to be in place to ensure that this is not used as a way to avoid discrimination claims? Can you think of situations in which both the employer and the employee might not want to proceed with a situation of positive discrimination?

ISSUES SPECIFIC TO SEX DISCRIMINATION

In examining the issues of direct and indirect discrimination we have looked at the main issues arising from the Sex Discrimination Act 1975 and Race Relations Act 1976. There are, however, some issues that are specific to just one of these acts and in this section we shall focus on issues relating specifically to sex discrimination.

Marital status

Discrimination against employees on the grounds of their married status is prohibited by Section 3 of the Sex Discrimination Act 1975. However, there is no similar protection for single people or for people who are living together.

Chief Constable of Bedfordshire Constabulary v *Graham* [2002] IRLR 239

Graham was an Inspector in the Bedfordshire force, and married a Chief Superintendent in the same force. In May 1999 Graham was appointed as Area Inspector in the same division that her husband commanded. In June 1999 she was told that her appointment had been rescinded. It was claimed that her appointment was inappropriate given the role of her husband in the division. The claims of indirect sex discrimination and direct and indirect discrimination on the grounds of marital status were all upheld. The EAT confirmed that the decision to rescind the job had clearly been on the basis of Graham's marital status.

Pregnancy

As we discovered in Chapter 5, dismissal on the grounds of pregnancy or any matter relating to pregnancy is automatically unfair. In that chapter we looked at the case of *Webb* v *EMO Air Cargo Ltd* [1994] IRLR 482. In this case the ECJ ruled that the dismissal was sex discrimination, because it was on the grounds of pregnancy – which is gender related. This does not need to fit with the requirement of the Sex Discrimination Act 1975 to have a comparator because any dismissal relating to pregnancy is automatically unfair.

ISSUES SPECIFIC TO RACE DISCRIMINATION

What is a Race?

The Race Relations Act 1976 defines 'racial grounds' as being on the grounds of 'colour, race, nationality or ethnic or national origins'. The Race Relations Act 1976 (Amendment) Regulations 2003 apply to discrimination on the grounds of 'race or ethnic or national origins'. The original definitions of the 1976 Act have, however, not been repealed.

Further Exploration

In reading new cases as they are reported in the personnel and business press, students should note any impact that the revised definition of race brings. It would also be interesting to note any overlap that occurs in bringing claims under the legislation cited above and the newly introduced legislation against discrimination on the grounds of religion or belief.

A series of cases has helped to define what is and is not a racial group. Sikhs, Jews and Gipsies have all been held to be ethnic groups; however, Rastafarians have not. In determining that Sikhs were an ethnic group (*Mandla* v *Dowell Lee* [1983] IRLR 209) it was stated that to be an ethnic group the group must regard itself, and be regarded by others, as being a distinct community with long-standing cultural traditions and a shared history. As Rastafarians have been an identifiable group for only around 60 years, they did not meet this definition.

Impact of the Race Relations Act 1976 (Amendment) Regulations 2003

The main changes brought by this Act were required by the EC Race Directive. These amendments were to:

1 Revise the definition of indirect discrimination, which has brought the definition in line with that which we have already described.

2 Insert new definitions of racial harassment, which we shall look at in the next chapter.

3 The Regulations move the burden of proof from the employee to the employer. Hence, if the employee has proved facts from which the Employment Tribunal could conclude, in the absence of an adequate explanation, that discrimination has occurred the employer is required to prove that the discrimination did not occur.

4 Post-employment discrimination is added to the legislation – where there is a close connection between the employment relationship and the discrimination complained of (eg a refusal to give a reference).

DISABILITY DISCRIMINATION

The Disability Discrimination Act 1995 (DDA) was the first piece of legislation offering comprehensive protection against discrimination for disabled people. Prior to this there was the Disabled Persons (Employment) Act 1944, which introduced a quota system whereby employers with 20 or more employees had to ensure that at least three per cent were registered disabled. However, this Act was rarely enforced, and really carried very little benefit for disabled people.

The DDA covers a wide range of protection for the disabled, but we shall concentrate only on protection in employment.

Definition of a disabled employee

In the Act a disabled person is defined as having a 'physical or mental impairment that has a substantial and long-term adverse effect on a person's ability to carry out normal day-to-day activities'.

Physical or mental impairment

In the majority of cases this is a relatively straightforward concept. However, there have been cases brought to the Employment Tribunal for a judgment on less clear illnesses. As a result of these judgments it is clearer that a mental impairment must be a 'clinically well-recognised illness'. However, the same requirement has not been imposed for physical illnesses. It is possible for a physical impairment to be classified as a disability even if a diagnosis has not been given, as in the following case.

Howden v *Capital Copiers (Edinburgh) Ltd* [1997] ET S/400005/97

Howden suffered from sharp, gripping pains, which resulted in him needing to lie down, as well as having a generally adverse effect on his well-being. He was admitted to hospital several times and had three operations. No diagnosis or cause for the pain was given. However, the Employment Tribunal held that this could be classified as a disability, because it was clearly impairing his physical well-being, and was long-term, substantial and affecting day-to-day activities.

Illnesses that have been the subject of Tribunal judgments, and have been found to be disabilities, include ME (Myalgic Encephalomyelitis), club-foot, back injury, epilepsy, diabetes and dyslexia.

Substantial and long-term adverse effect

An illness is deemed to have had a long-term effect if it has lasted, or is likely to last, at least 12 months or (in the case of a terminal illness) is expected to last for the rest of the employee's life. The definition of a substantial and adverse effect is more difficult. Clearly it is related to the latter part of the definition – the ability to carry out normal day-to-day activities. However, that is a 'yard stick', and if the employee is unable to carry out normal duties at work there is also the possibility of a disability existing.

Cruickshank v Vaw Motorcast Ltd [2001] IRLR 24

Cruickshank developed work-related asthma. He was moved away from his job to working as a fork-lift truck driver, and his symptoms went away. However, a reorganisation resulted in him needing to use his fork-lift truck near the area of the fumes that had triggered his asthma, and the symptoms returned. A medical adviser found that the asthma was triggered at work, but not at home. As there were no other jobs available it was decided to dismiss Cruickshank. The EAT found that, although Cruickshank could carry out most normal day-to-day activities he was unable to carry out normal duties at work. This could not be ignored, and hence his illness was to be classified as a disability.

Although an illness might affect some day-to-day activities, and some work activities, it is not typically classified as a disability if the extent of the impact is somewhat limited, as in the next case.

Quinlan v B&Q plc [1998] EAT 1386/97

Quinlan underwent open heart surgery. As a result of the surgery he was unable to lift the heavy loads that was required of him as a general assistant in the garden centre. He was, therefore, dismissed. The EAT supported the Employment Tribunals' view that he was not suffering from a disability because he was still able to carry smaller loads, even though he was not able to carry out the duties required of him at work.

Normal day-to-day activities
These must be normal activities carried out on a regular basis and are listed in the legislation as involving one of the following:

- mobility
- manual dexterity
- physical co-ordination
- continence
- the ability to lift, carry or move everyday objects
- speech, hearing or eyesight
- memory or ability to concentrate, learn or understand
- perception of the risk of physical danger.

As well as being part of this list, it is also required that the activity being considered is actually part of an employee's normal activities, as illustrated in the following case.

Abadeh v British Telecommunications plc [2000] IRLR 23

Abadeh worked as a telephone operator. One day, whilst at work, he received a loud screeching noise in one ear, which left him with tinnitus, hearing loss and post-traumatic stress disorder. In deciding whether Abadeh had a disability as defined by the DDA the Employment Tribunal accepted the evidence that he was unable to travel by underground or on an aeroplane because of his illness. They classified this as a 'normal day-to-day' activity. The EAT found, however, that they had erred in giving any weight to this part of the argument as Abadeh did not live in London and these forms of transport were not part of his normal daily activities.

Discriminating against a disabled employee

If an employer treats a disabled employee less favourably than a non-disabled employee, and that treatment cannot be shown to be justified, then discrimination has occurred.

In addition to this, the employer is required to make 'reasonable' adjustments to accommodate the needs of the disabled employee. These can include such things as:

1 Making physical adjustments to the workplace (eg moving a work area to the ground floor of a building).

2 Allocating some of the duties to another employee (eg in the *Quinlan* v *B&Q* case the heavy lifting could have been assigned to another employee – if that was operationally possible).

3 Moving the disabled person to another job (eg Vaw Motorcast moving Cruickshank to non-fork-lift truck driving duties).

4 Altering the hours of work (eg allowing the employee to start work at a later hour to enable him to take advantage of easier travelling arrangements).

5 Moving the employee to a different place of work (eg moving to a site/office nearer to home, and making travelling easier for the employee).

6 Allowing time off during working hours for treatment or rehabilitation.

7 Arranging training for the employee (eg to allow him to move to a more suitable job).

8 Acquiring or modifying equipment (eg purchasing a Braille machine to help a partially sighted employee).

9 Altering instructions or reference materials (eg reprinting them in larger type for a visually impaired employee).

10 Altering procedures for testing or assessment (eg allowing a longer time to complete the activity).

11 Providing a reader or an interpreter (eg to help a visually impaired employee).

12 Providing supervision (eg to help the employee avoid dangerous situations).

TASK Find out if your organisation, or an organisation with which you are familiar, has made any adjustments as a result of the Disability Discrimination Act 1995. Look at just a few of any such adjustments, and try to understand the reasons that they were necessary.

All these possible modifications have a potential impact on the employer. There is clearly a financial impact in most cases, and some adjustments (although highly desirable) might be impossible for logistical reasons. In determining whether the employer has acted reasonably the Employment Tribunal will take all these issues into consideration.

Beart v HM Prison Service [2003] EWCA Civ 119

Beart worked as an administrative officer. She had relationship difficulties with her line manager. She discussed the possibility of working part-time, and her line manager took this as meaning she wanted to resign, and advertised her job. This left Beart facing demotion and a substantial drop in salary. She went on sick leave suffering from clinical depression. During her sick leave HM Prison believed she was working in a clothes shop that she owned and hence dismissed her on grounds of gross misconduct. She claimed unfair dismissal and disability discrimination.

In considering her claim for disability discrimination the Employment Tribunal held that the employer should have considered making the reasonable adjustment of moving her to a different workplace. In not doing so disability discrimination had occurred. This finding was supported by the Court of Appeal.

Further Exploration

The range of adjustments that might need to be made to accommodate the needs of a disabled person are wide ranging. To gain further understanding of the range of adjustments students should read recent cases, such as the following:

- *Archibald* v *Fife Council* [2002] EAT 0025/02 – a process of competitive interviewing for upgraded posts did not place a disabled employee at a substantial disadvantage.
- *Hutchison 3G UK Ltd* v *Mason* [2003] EAT 0369/03 – not allowing an employee depressed and suffering from drug addiction to be absent for rehabilitation, assessment or treatment amounted to discrimination.
- *Mid Staffordshire General Hospitals NHS Trust* v *Cambridge* [2003] IRLR 566 – the need to make a full assessment of reasonable adjustments is explored.

The issue of whether an employer cannot be held responsible for making adjustments if he does not know that the employee is disabled is unclear – see the following case.

O'Neill v Sym & Co [1998] ICR 481

O'Neill worked as an accounts clerk. Three months after starting work with Sym & Co she was dismissed for sickness absence. At her interview she had told them that she had previously suffered from viral pneumonia, but had since recovered. During her period of employment she was diagnosed as suffering from ME but she did not tell her employers. When she was dismissed she claimed disability discrimination, but it was found that the employer could not have discriminated if he did not know that there was a disability.

Further Exploration

Further to the above case, the judgment in the case of *H J Heinz Co Ltd* v *Kenrick* [2000] ICR 491 found that it was not necessary for an employer to know that an employee had a disability in order for them to be liable for discrimination. Read this case and compare the judgment with the O'Neill case.

Proving discrimination

The Disability Discrimination Act 1995 (Amendment) Regulations 2003 reversed the burden of proof. Once the employee has produced facts from which the Employment Tribunal could deduce that discrimination has occurred, then the complaint is upheld unless the employer can prove that he did not commit the act of alleged discrimination, or is not responsible for it.

Remedies

The remedies are the same as for sex and race discrimination. Again, there is no limit on the amount of compensation that can potentially be awarded.

RELATIONSHIP BALANCE

As we have noted in examining this legislation, the requirement on the employer is to make 'reasonable' adjustments. How much do you think this qualification of the extent of adjustments protects the employee? Alternatively, do you think that the lack of clear definition of what constitutes a reasonable adjustment could result in an employer refusing to make any adjustments?

GENDER REASSIGNMENT

The Sex Discrimination (Gender Reassignment) Regulations 1999 make discrimination against a transsexual for reasons relating to the gender reassignment unlawful. Although this legislation has not been reported on in much detail (probably due to the relatively small number of employees who could potentially be affected) there are two interesting cases to consider.

A v *Chief Constable of West Yorkshire Police* [2002] EWCA Civ 1584

A was born male, but underwent gender reassignment surgery in May 1996. Since that time she has dressed and presented herself as a woman. In 1997 she applied to join the West Yorkshire Police Force but was told that that the Force had decided not to employ transsexuals because they were unable to perform all the necessary duties. In particular, they would not be able to carry out searches of individuals. A brought a claim of discrimination. The Court of Appeal upheld A's claim, stating that the Force could sensibly have avoided the problem by exempting her from the requirement to carry out searches.

Croft v Consignia plc [2002] EAT 1160/00

Croft started work with Consignia in March 1987, as a man. In April 1998 Croft started the process of gender reassignment by taking feminising hormones. At this stage she announced that she would adopt a female role. The way of announcing this to the workforce was discussed, and in particular there was discussion about which toilet Croft should use. It was agreed that she would start by using the gender-neutral disabled toilet, but would eventually move to using the female toilet. Croft was concerned about this, because she wanted to live fully as a female and that included using the relevant toilets. However, the female staff (who had known Croft as a man for many years) were not happy with her using their toilets. Her claim of discrimination was unsuccessful because it was found that Consignia were not refusing to allow her ever to use the toilet, but were trying to deal with a difficult employment relations issue as well as waiting for medical advice.

RELATIONSHIP BALANCE

This aspect of discrimination legislation can be difficult for both the employer and the employee to manage. How should an employer act if employees are expressing concerns? Consider the Consignia case above in drawing your conclusions.

SEXUAL ORIENTATION

The Employment Equality (Sexual Orientation) Regulations 2003 made it unlawful for employers to discriminate against or harass a person on the grounds of sexual orientation. The regulations cover those in employment, those completing vocational training, job applicants and any discrimination or harassment relating to the employment relationship after it has ended.

Sexual orientation is defined as 'a sexual orientation towards persons of the same sex, persons of the opposite sex or persons of the same sex and the opposite sex'. Therefore, the regulations cover all aspects of sexual orientation. It does not cover discrimination relating to any particular fetishes (eg sado-masochism) and it cannot be argued that 'orientation' covers orientation towards children (ie paedophilia is not covered by the Act).

Direct and indirect discrimination is defined in the same way as the legislation relating to sex and race discrimination. There is a clause within the Act allowing for 'genuine occupational requirements' – allowing for the situation where it is a genuine need to employ someone of a particular sexual orientation. In practice this is likely to be limited to specific counselling or support issues, but it is too early to provide any case law to explain this further.

There is potential for claims of indirect discrimination if a job is advertised requiring a married couple. In this situation homosexual couples would be at an immediate disadvantage because, of course, they cannot marry. Again, there is not yet any case law to explore this issue further.

In the next section we shall look at the regulations relating to discrimination on the grounds of religion. There could be potential conflict here. If a particular religious group objects to homosexuality on religious grounds would the refusal to employ a homosexual be discrimination on the grounds of sexual orientation, or a reasonable requirement under the religious discrimination legislation? Again, as yet there is no case law to help us to answer this question.

RELIGION

The Employment Equality (Religion or Belief) Regulations 2003 made it unlawful to discriminate against workers on the grounds of religion or belief. 'Religion or belief' is defined as 'any religion, religious belief or similar philosophical belief'. It is clear that people who belong to established religions (eg Christians, Jews, Muslims) are covered. What is unclear is whether those who belong to non-conventional 'religions' such as Druidism, or those who have 'beliefs' such as animal rights activists, are covered. It is also not clear to what extent an employee has to follow a religion in order to be covered by the Act, or the evidence they need to give to show that they are a member of a religion. Again, we need case law to give guidance on these issues.

The regulations state that direct discrimination will occur when an employee is treated less favourably than other employees on the grounds of his religion or belief. This covers discrimination on the grounds of:

■ the employee's religion or belief
■ the discriminator's perception of the employee's religion or belief (even if that perception is wrong)
■ the association of the employee with someone of a particular religion or belief
■ a refusal by the employee to carry out an act that is discriminatory.

The definition of indirect discrimination is the same as for sex and race discrimination. Although the regulations do not require an employer to provide facilities and time for religious activities, it is possible that requiring employees to work at times or days when the employee's religion require him to be at prayer could be indirect discrimination. In the same way, having a certain dress code that clashes with that required by a person's religion could also be seen to be indirect discrimination. At present, there is no case law to help us explore this further.

There are genuine occupational requirements allowed within the legislation. For example, it could be a requirement for a Christian school to employ Christian teachers. However, there must be a genuine need for this requirement. The Acas draft guidance notes suggest that it could be a genuine requirement for a teacher to promote a Christian ethos, but questions whether the same requirement could be applied to a maintenance worker employed by the school.

The remedies for discrimination on the grounds of religion are the same as those for sex and race discrimination, including unlimited compensation.

CHAPTER REVIEW

1 Discrimination legislation has grown rapidly over the past 30 years.

2 Direct discrimination is where an employee is treated less favourably on the grounds of race/sex etc than employees of a different race/sex.

3 Indirect discrimination is where an employer applies a criterion that adversely affects a considerably larger proportion of one group than another and it is to that group's detriment that it cannot apply and the criterion cannot be justified.

4 There are occasions when the employment of someone of a particular race or sex is essential because of the nature of the job – this is known as a Genuine Occupational Qualification (GOQ).

5 Discrimination on the grounds of being married is prohibited within the Sex Discrimination Act 1975.

6 The Race Relations Act 1976 defines 'racial grounds' as being on the grounds of 'colour, race, nationality or ethnic or national origins'. The Race Relations Act 1976 (Amendment) Regulations 2003 apply to discrimination on the grounds of 'race or ethnic or national origins'.

7 A disability is defined in the Disability Discrimination Act 1995 as a 'physical or mental impairment that has a substantial and long-term adverse effect on a person's ability to carry out normal day-to-day activities'.

8 It is illegal to discriminate against an employee on the grounds of gender reassignment.

9 It is illegal to discriminate against an employee on the grounds of his sexual orientation.

10 It is illegal to discriminate against an employee on the grounds of his religion or belief.

WEBSITES REFERENCED IN THIS CHAPTER

www.cipd.co.uk   Chartered Institute of Personnel and Development
www.dti.gov.uk   Department of Trade and Industry
www.eoc.org.uk   Equal Opportunities Commission

FURTHER READING

■ *Board of Governors of St Matthias Church of England School* v *Crizzle* [1993] ICR 401 – a school was justified in requiring its head teacher to be a communicant Christian because of the religious focus of the school.

■ *British Gas Services Ltd* v *McCaull* [2000] IRLR 60 – an employer is unaware of the duty to make reasonable adjustments under the Disability Discrimination Act 1995.

■ *Bullock* v *Alice Ottley School* [1992] IRLR 564 – different retiring ages for men and women are justified because of specific recruitment difficulties.

■ *Horsey* v *Dyfed CC* [1982] IRLR 395 – it is not lawful to refuse a woman an opportunity to attend a training course because of a belief that she will then return to the area of the country where her husband is working.

- *Leonard* v *Southern Derbyshire Chamber of Commerce* [2001] IRLR 19 – a complaint of disability discrimination is upheld following a dismissal of an employee with clinical depression.

- *Ministry of Defence* v *Jeremiah* [1980] QB 87 – the requirement that men, and not women, should carry out dirty and unpleasant work was a detriment, because there was a deprivation of choice.

- *P* v *S & another* [1996] ECJ 13/94 – the ECJ ruled that it was contrary to the Equal Treatment Directive to dismiss a transsexual for reasons related to gender reassignment.

- *Perera* v *Civil Service Commission* [1983] ICR 428 – a Sri Lankan was denied a post as legal assistant because of the nationality and language abilities that were requested – this was indirect discrimination because these were not essential requirements.

- *Price* v *Civil Service Commission* [1978] IRLR 3 – a restricted age entry for job opportunities indirectly discriminates against women.

EXAMPLES TO WORK THROUGH

1 *Sex discrimination*. Susan is a teacher within a large secondary school. She has always trained the school choir after the school day has finished. She has now been asked to start a further choir for the younger children, again rehearsing after school hours. She has refused to do this because she has her own young children, and stopping late on two days causes her child-care difficulties. The head teacher has stated that she is Head of the Music Department, and hence these duties are part of her job. She is threatening to resign and claim sex discrimination. What is your advice to the head teacher?

2 *Disability discrimination*. Peter has worked in the welding department of a car factory for three years. He has recently been involved in a car accident, and as a result of his injuries can no longer stand for lengthy periods of time. Due to the size of the items being welded the welders always stand to carry out their work. He wants to return to work and the production manager has asked for your advice. What would you tell him?

3 *Gender reassignment*. Mark, who has worked in the call centre for five years, has informed you that he now wants to be known as Mary and is starting the process of gender reassignment. His team leader is very disturbed by the change, and has asked that Mark be moved to another team. Mark says he likes his work and does not want to move. What would you advise?

4 *Religious discrimination*. The production manager has asked the whole department to work overtime for four consecutive Fridays to cover a backlog of work. Three members of the department are Muslims, and they state they are unable to work later on Fridays because they need to attend a prayer time. The production manager has stated that if they refuse to work the overtime they will be excluded from a payment under the monthly bonus scheme. They are claiming that this is discrimination on the grounds of their religion. What do you advise?

Discrimination (2)

CHAPTER 7

The objectives of this chapter are to:

- **Consider the legislation relating to discrimination on the grounds of trade union membership;**
- **Consider issues relating to harassment, victimisation and vicarious liability;**
- **Look at issues associated with equal pay and work of equal value;**
- **Examine the proposed legislation relating to age discrimination.**

TRADE UNION MEMBERSHIP

Refusal of employment

It is unlawful to refuse employment to people because they are, or are not, members of a trade union, or they refuse to accept a requirement that they either become a member of a trade union, or they cease to be a member of a trade union, or they refuse to make payments to the trade union if they fail to join – Section 137(1) of the Trade Union and Labour Relations (Consolidation) Act 1992 (TULRCA).

It is important to note that this legislation makes the concept of the 'closed shop' illegal. This used to exist in many organisations where, upon starting employment, it was a requirement to join the relevant trade union.

 Try to find someone who was at work in the 1970s who is willing to discuss their experiences with you. Ask them about the 'Closed Shop'. How did it work? What were the advantages and disadvantages associated with it?

'Refusing employment' covers all of the following:

- Refusing to consider a job application or enquiry.
- Asking the applicant to withdraw an application.
- Refusing to offer employment.
- Making an offer of employment that includes terms that no reasonable employee would agree to, thereby making it difficult for the person to accept the offer.
- Withdrawing an offer of employment after having made it, or causing the applicant to refuse the offer.
- Including a requirement that goes against that listed above (S137 [1]).

An example of 'refusing employment' can be found in the following case.

Harrison v Kent County Council [1995] ICR 434

Harrison was a Social Worker working for Kent County Council. He was an active trade union member with a reputation for being a 'strong and forthright' negotiator. He resigned from his job for family reasons, but later reapplied to the Council. He was refused re-employment on the account of his 'confrontational and anti-management approach' in his previous post. The Employment Tribunal held that this was a fair refusal because it related to previous activities as a trade union member, rather than specifically to trade union membership. The EAT overturned that view, stating that the trade union membership could not be separated from activities carried out because of that membership. Hence, the refusal to re-employ Harrison had been unfair.

Detriment

Section 146 (1) of TULRCA provides for employees not to suffer any detriment by an act (or omission of an act) by the employer if this takes place for the purpose of:

- preventing or deterring him from becoming a member of an independent trade union, or penalising him for doing so
- preventing or deterring him from taking part in the activities of an independent trade union, or penalising him for doing so
- compelling him to become a member of a trade union.

Here is an example of such a detriment.

British Airways Engine Overhaul Ltd v Francis [1981] ICR 278

Francis was a shop steward. She made a statement to the press criticising her trade union for taking so much time to pursue an equal pay complaint by her members. She made this statement during her lunch break. When the article was published she received a formal warning from British Airways, stating that unauthorised statements to the press were forbidden. Francis challenged the warning in the Employment Tribunal, stating that it was a detriment based on trade union activities. The employer argued that the statement came about after an informal meeting of union members, and was too remote from Francis's union duties to be classed as trade union activity. The tribunal found, however, that the statement was linked to trade union activity and hence the warning was unfair because it was a detriment related to such activity.

Dismissal

Section 152 (1) of TULRCA 1992 defines a dismissal as being unfair for the following principal reasons:

- The employee was, or proposed to become, a member of an independent trade union.

- The employee had taken part, or proposed to take part, in the activities of an independent trade union.
- The employee was not a member of a trade union, and had refused to become a member.

> ## *Port of London Authority* v *Payne and others* [1992] IRLR 447
>
> The Port of London Authority derecognised the TGWU trade union, and also carried out a redundancy process. Employees were selected for redundancy based on a number of criteria, including attitude. Seventeen shop stewards were amongst those selected for redundancy, and they claimed they had been selected on the grounds of their trade union activities, and hence their dismissal was unfair. The tribunal held, and the EAT supported this view, that the shop stewards had been selected by the employer because there was concern that they would become involved in a campaign by the TGWU to restore negotiation rights. As this campaign was authorised and run by the TGWU it was held that it must be classified as trade union activity, and hence the dismissal was unfair.

There is no statutory definition of trade union activity, therefore in supporting this conclusion, the EAT spelt out the process that must be followed to determine if there has been an unfair dismissal relating to trade union activity:

'An industrial tribunal must determine the following: the belief held by the employers which formed the basis of the decision to dismiss; whether that belief was genuinely held; and whether the facts upon which that belief was based, judged objectively, fell within the phrase "the activities of an independent trade union".'

RELATIONSHIP BALANCE

Do you think that there are any potential benefits to an employee in being forced to join a trade union? Examine the reasons why the 'closed shop' was abolished. Do you think that this abolition was beneficial to both the employer and the employee?

VICTIMISATION

Victimisation is the act of penalising employees in some way for exercising their rights under discrimination legislation. Victimisation is unlawful if the employer knows, or suspects, that the person being victimised intends to, or has:

- brought proceedings relating to alleged discrimination
- given evidence or information in relation to a claim of discrimination
- done anything else in reference to discrimination legislation
- alleged that a person has committed an act which would be a contravention of discrimination legislation.

These are all known as 'protected acts'.

In determining whether someone has suffered victimisation, their treatment needs to be compared to the treatment of someone who has not carried out a protected act and it needs to be judged whether that treatment was less favourable.

McGuigan v *T G Baynes and Sons* [1998] EAT 1114/97

During an appraisal meeting McGuigan criticised the firm's attitude towards employing women. Due to a downturn in work T G Baynes announced a redundancy. All employees were scored according to selection criteria, and McGuigan was selected for redundancy using this process. She had two points deducted from her score due to her comments at her appraisal. The EAT found that the criticism of the firm's attitude to employing women counted as a protected act (because it was referring to potential sex discrimination) and hence the reduction of points and subsequent selection for redundancy had been an act of victimisation.

Victimisation can also occur after the employment relationship has ended. This was determined by the following case that was referred to the European Court of Justice for a ruling.

Coote v *Granada Hospitality Ltd* [1998] IRLR 656

Coote was employed by Granada from December 1992 to September 1993. In 1993 she brought a claim of sex discrimination against the employer that was settled. She left the organisation in September 1993 and was unable to find alternative employment. She considered that this was because Granada refused to supply her with a reference. She challenged this decision in the Employment Tribunal, which ruled that it could not be classified as victimisation because the employment had ended (although the issue at the centre of the argument was a protected act). The case was eventually referred to the ECJ, which ruled that the employer should be required to give a reference once the relationship had ended and failure to do so had resulted in victimisation.

RELATIONSHIP BALANCE

As we have seen, victimisation relates only to protected acts. Given this, and the range of other discrimination legislation covered in both this chapter and in Chapter 6, do you think the employee has adequate protection?

TASK Find out if your organisation, or an organisation with which you are familiar, has a policy relating to victimisation. What training do managers have in this policy?

HARASSMENT

In response to the EC Equal Treatment Directive (amended in 2000) the UK has introduced specific provisions into discrimination legislation protecting workers from harassment across all areas of possible discrimination. Within these provisions a common definition of harassment is given:

> **'unwanted conduct related to race/sex/disability etc takes place with the purpose or effect of violating the dignity of a person and of creating an intimidating, hostile, degrading, humiliating or offensive environment'**

Prior to this definition it had been established by UK courts that acts of sexual and race discrimination could constitute direct discrimination.

Harassment can relate to a series of events that add up to an unbearable situation, as in the following case.

Strathclyde Regional Council v *Porcelli* [1986] IRLR 134

Porcelli was employed as a Laboratory Technician working in a school. Two male colleagues subjected her to a series of degrading treatments that included making suggestive remarks, deliberately brushing against her, removing her personal belongings, storing equipment where she could not reach it and withholding information from her. They were eventually successful in their aim of forcing her to leave. The tribunal found that this was direct sex discrimination and harassment because the male employees would not have acted in the same way to a fellow male colleague.

And harassment can also relate to one single incident, providing that it is deemed to be sufficiently serious.

Bracebridge Engineering Ltd v *Darby* [1989] IRLR 3

Darby had been criticised on a number of occasions for leaving work early. On one occasion two male supervisors stopped her as she went to wash her hands, thinking that she was attempting to leave early. She denied this, but they carried her forcefully into a darkened room where they made lewd remarks to her and sexually assaulted her. She immediately complained to a superior, but the general manager decided that no action should be taken against the supervisors. She resigned and claimed sexual discrimination and harassment. The employer argued that harassment had to relate to a series of acts, and not one incident. However, the EAT found that a single incident, if sufficiently serious, can constitute harassment. As it was judged that the treatment given to Darby would not have been given to a man it was found that this was an incident of sexual discrimination and harassment.

Harassment can come from a third party.

Burton and another v *De Vere Hotels* [1996] IRLR 596

Burton and her colleague were occasional waitresses serving, on this occasion, at a function at the hotel. They were of black ethnic origin. The after-dinner speaker was a comedian who was expected to make sexually explicit jokes, but it was known he would also be racially abusive. When the comedian started his act he saw the two waitresses and started to make racially and sexually offensive comments directed specifically at them. This encouraged an atmosphere where other guests joined in with the abuse. The next day the waitresses complained and their manager apologised to them. However, they also took a claim of race discrimination against the hotel, claiming they had been subjected to racial harassment.

The EAT found that the employer was responsible for racial discrimination because they should have warned the assistant manager who was on duty in the hotel to monitor the act and to withdraw the waitresses if there were any concerns. If the employer had withdrawn the waitresses then the incident would not have occurred and hence the employer could have prevented racial discrimination occurring.

However, the House of Lords ruled that it was not sufficient for the employees to state that the conduct to which they were exposed was racist. They would have to show that they were exposed to it because they were black, and that white waitresses would not have been exposed to something they found objectionable (eg the sexist jokes).

These cases all date prior to the changes brought to the definition of harassment in 2003. However, they are all useful illustrations of acts that can be deemed to be harassment – new case law will help us to see any changes that the revised definition brings. One important change brought in 2003 is making harassment a specific act of unlawful discrimination, separate from direct or indirect discrimination.

Another important aspect of the definition is the requirement for the conduct claimed of to have the purpose or *effect* of violating the dignity of a person. Existing case law has shown that in determining whether an act violates the dignity of a person it has to be considered from the perception of the complainant. The EC Code of Practice on dignity at work stresses that the individual determines what is, and is not, offensive.

This need to consider the matter from the view of the claimant is illustrated in the following case.

Driskel v *Peninsula Business Services* [2000] IRLR 151

Driskel worked as an advice line consultant. In 1995 Huss was appointed as the department head, and over a period of time the relationship between Huss and Driskel deteriorated, partly due to the sexual repartee in which Huss indulged. In June 1996 a vacancy for senior advice line consultant arose and Driskel applied. On the evening before the interview (which Huss was to conduct) he told Driskel to attend the interview in a short skirt and a see-through blouse showing plenty of cleavage to make an attempt to impress him. Driskel did not comment on this at the time, but the next day pointed out that she had ignored his instructions. She subsequently complained of sex discrimination. There was an investigation which the EAT described as involving much 'toing and froing' and eventually Driskel informed the employer that she refused to work unless Huss was moved elsewhere. This was deemed to be impractical and Driskel was told she would be dismissed if she refused to work with her department head. This happened, and Driskel claimed unfair dismissal and sex discrimination.

The Employment Tribunal dismissed her complaints finding that as she had not complained about the behaviour at the time, and the other various incidents were trivial, the events did not amount to sex discrimination.

The EAT overturned this ruling. It held that the incidents should not have been looked at individually, but considered as an overall pattern of treatment. It also held that the tribunal should have considered whether the remarks made undermined Driskel's dignity as a woman. The banter could not be compared to banter between two men, as the perception of the banter by a woman could be totally different.

It should also be noted that employees who resign from employment as a result of harassment could potentially bring an additional claim of constructive dismissal. We shall explore this in more detail in the next chapter.

The Protection from Harassment Act 1997 makes harassment, of whatever nature, a criminal offence. In this Act, harassment is defined as pursuing a course of conduct that the harasser knows, or ought to know, amounts to harassment, or conduct that causes fear of violence in another person. Conduct includes speech. Note also that 'course of conduct' suggests that the conduct has occurred on more than one occasion. Injunctions can be brought, under this Act, against those causing or likely to cause harassment. The Act also allows for the person who has been harassed to seek damages for financial loss and anxiety caused by the harassment.

FURTHER EXPLORATION

Consider the definition of harassment given in the Protection from Harassment Act 1997 and given within discrimination legislation. Does workplace harassment necessarily equate to criminal harassment?

Find out what policy your organisation, or an organisation with which you are familiar, has for dealing with alleged incidents of harassment. Do you think the policy addresses all the potential issues sufficiently?

VICARIOUS LIABILITY

Vicarious liability means that the employer is held liable for wrongs committed by employees in the course of their employment. An example to explain this is found in the following case.

Jones v *Tower Boot Company* [1996] IRLR 168

Jones, a 16-year-old of mixed race origin, started work at Tower Boot Company. He was immediately subjected to a campaign of physical and verbal assaults from two of his colleagues. This included him being burnt with a hot screwdriver and having metal bolts thrown at his head. He resigned after one month and brought a claim of racial discrimination. The Employment Tribunal found that the employees had been acting within the course of their employment, and hence Tower Boot Company was vicariously liable for the actions of the employees. The EAT disagreed that the actions were in the 'course of employment' but the tribunal's findings were supported by the Court of Appeal. Therefore, it was found that Tower Boot Company was vicariously liable for the claim of race discrimination.

The potential defence of the employer is to show that he had taken every reasonable precaution against the event in question occurring. However, as shown in the following case, if an employer is aware of unpleasant actions being taken by its employees and does nothing to prevent them from continuing the employer becomes *directly* responsible for the discrimination.

Chessington World of Adventures v Reed [1997] IRLR 556

Reed, a biological male, announced four years after joining the organisation that she was going to start the process of gender reassignment. Following this announcement a small minority of male colleagues subjected her to a campaign of harassment and ostracism. A series of unpleasant acts took place. Reed attempted suicide and, despite asking for a transfer on her return to work, her employer did nothing to help her. Reed eventually resigned. The EAT found that Chessington World of Adventures was directly liable for the actions of the group of colleagues who had subjected Reed to abuse. The employers argued that they were only vicariously liable for what had occurred, but the EAT found that they were aware of what was happening and had done nothing to stop it. This resulted in direct liability.

RELATIONSHIP BALANCE

To what extent do you think the employer can realistically be expected to know all that is happening in the organisation? As we have already noted, a defence is to show that the employer has done everything this is reasonably practicable to ensure that the harassment has not occurred. How can the employer do this? Is it more difficult to achieve in different types of organisation?

EQUAL PAY ACT 1970

The Equal Pay Act 1970 (EqPA) legislates against discrimination between men and women in relation to their terms and conditions of employment. Although its name suggests it focuses only on pay, it does actually legislate across all terms and conditions of the contract of employment. It is important to emphasise that the Act is looking at comparisons between men and women. It is not relevant in addressing grievances of men complaining against their conditions in comparison to other male colleagues, or of women complaining against their conditions in comparison to other female colleagues. Note: This does not mean that discrimination relating to terms and conditions of employment is allowed on the grounds of race. Such discrimination is specifically cited as unlawful in the Race Relations Act 1976.

Although the EqPA is dated earlier than the Sex Discrimination Act 1975 (SDA) they actually came into force at the same time. They are seen as complementary pieces of legislation – the SDA dealing with such issues as recruitment, dismissal, promotion and non-contractual benefits; the EqPA dealing with contractual terms. The legislation relating to equal pay is greatly influenced by the relevant contents of Article 141 of the Treaty of Rome (1957), and also by the EC Equal Pay Directive (75/117).

The EqPA allows a woman to bring a claim if her terms and conditions of employment are less favourable than a man (and vice versa) if they are employed on:

- like work
- work rated as equivalent
- work of equal value.

Like work

In the legislation this is defined as 'work of the same or a broadly similar nature'. Generally, the Employment Tribunals take quite a broad view of this concept. They are not looking for identical work, but an overall similarity in the work that is done. It is important that the total work is looked at, and not too much emphasis is placed on small tasks that rarely occur. It is also important that the focus is on what actually happens regularly in the job, rather than a narrow focus on what the contract suggests will happen.

The comparison focuses on the jobs in question, and not on the individuals carrying out the jobs. The need to take this broad approach is shown in the following case.

Capper Pass v *Lawton* [1977] ICR 83

Lawton was employed as a cook working a 40-hour week and being in sole charge of preparing daily lunches for 10–20 directors and their guests. She brought an equal pay claim, comparing her jobs with that of two male assistant chefs. They worked a basic 40-hour week with 5.5 hours of regular weekly overtime, and they worked one weekend in three. They prepared 350 meals each day in two sittings of breakfast, lunch and tea. The Tribunal held that the cook and assistant chefs did 'like work' and hence the equal pay claim was upheld. In supporting this decision the EAT emphasised that a broad consideration of the skill and experiences required to do the job and a general consideration of the type of work required was essential. Although there were clearly differences between the jobs, these were largely trivial.

If there are genuine differences between the jobs, and they are compensated for separately, this does not mean that basic terms and conditions should also vary, as illustrated by the following case.

Dugdale and others v *Kraft Foods Ltd* [1977] ICR 48

Women quality controllers, working with a food processing company, were paid at a lower rate than the male quality inspectors. The men and women all worked shifts, but only the men were expected to work nights and Sundays. The men were paid an additional shift allowance for Sundays and nights. The Employment Tribunal found that the differences in shifts were 'differences of practical importance' and hence this was not a case of like work. However, the EAT overturned this finding, stating that the work of the men and women was broadly similar. They found that the hours when the work was carried out should be discounted, especially because the men were compensated for the different shift patterns.

However, if there are genuine differences in the work being carried out, the differences cannot be separated from the main duties and ignored in making a claim of like work – see the following case.

Maidment and Hardacre v *Cooper and Co* [1978] IRLR 462

Maidment was a packer who also carried out some clerical duties. She compared her job with a male packer who also carried out some storeman duties. The Tribunal found that there were significant practical differences in the job, and hence there could not be a claim of equal pay.

Hardacre was a machine operator who compared her job with a male machine operator. They did the same job, apart from the fact that he could set his own machine, whereas she could not. Again, the Tribunal found that there were significant practical differences that meant there could be no claim for equal pay.

Both women appealed to the EAT, which supported the tribunal's decision. The women noted that the packer/storeman was paid an additional £2 per week for his store duties, and that the store duties could be seen as a separate activity. They claimed that this activity could be set aside and the remainder of the two jobs could be compared. The EAT did not support this view, and emphasised that the total job must be compared to consider whether like work existed.

Work rated as equivalent

This can be used only where an analytical, non-discriminatory job evaluation scheme is in place. An analytical scheme is one that breaks jobs down into component parts, whereas a non-analytical scheme simply compares whole jobs and does not consider the individual tasks and components that make up the job. There are many ways in which a job evaluation scheme can become discriminatory; main pitfalls include relying too heavily on subjective judgments rather than objective data, and basing schemes on existing internal benchmark jobs that could perpetuate existing discrimination.

If the points allocated in a job evaluation scheme are directly related to a job grade within the company then the employee should receive the terms and conditions of employment relating to the grade in which they are placed, as in the following case.

Springboard Sunderland Trust v *Robson* [1992] IRLR 261

Mrs R was a team leader, and she compared her terms and conditions to Mr R, an induction officer. Following a job evaluation process carried out by the employer, Mrs R's job was evaluated at 410 points, and Mr R's job at 428 points. The company grading scheme stated that jobs with between 360 and 409 points were grade three, and jobs with between 410 and 439 points were grade four. However, the company continued to treat Mrs R as a grade three. The Tribunal found, supported by the EAT, that Mrs R had to be treated as a grade four, in accordance with the job evaluation scheme and hence Mrs R and Mr R were carrying out work 'rated as equivalent'.

TASK Find out if your organisation, or an organisation with which you are familiar, has a job evaluation scheme. Is it analytical and non-discriminatory? Could it be used to defend a claim for equal pay?

Work of equal value

The Equal Pay (Amendment) Regulations 1983 added the concept of 'work of equal value'. This amendment was introduced because the existing legislation did not allow for claims of equal value and hence infringed the requirements of the EC Equal Pay Directive.

This category of equal pay claims adds in the opportunity to make a claim when there is no like work, or work formally rated as equivalent. It is a complicated and lengthy process to prove a case of equal value. An Employment Tribunal often appoints an independent expert to investigate the claim, and the investigation and writing of the report takes a considerable amount of time.

The Employment Act 2002 has tried to address this issue by reviewing the process of Equal Pay Questionnaires that can be used by the employee to obtain information from the employer. One of the difficulties that many employees face in bringing an equal pay claim is obtaining data about pay within the organisation. Prior to 6 April 2003 employees could issue a questionnaire seeking relevant information from the employer only once a tribunal application had been made. Now a questionnaire can be issued before proceedings are started, and it is hoped that this might reduce the number of equal pay claims that are made. A sample questionnaire has been provided by the Women and Equality Unit (www.womenandequalityunit.gov.uk), which employees may use if they wish. The employer must respond to the questions within eight weeks. The Tribunal may draw inferences from a refusal to respond, or from evasive answers.

The employee was successful in showing work of equal value in the following case.

Hayward v *Cammell Laird* [1984] IRLR 463

Hayward was a cook employed in the shipyard. She claimed her work was of equal value to painters, insulations engineers and joiners working on the same site. The Tribunal appointed an independent expert who carried out an investigation into the claim. He supported Hayward and the claim for equal pay was allowed.

One of the difficulties that the Tribunal has in determining whether there is a situation of work of equal value is in deciding how to make this judgment – see the following case.

William Ball Ltd v *Wood and others* [2002] EAT 89/01

Nine female employees (one supervisor and eight cleaner/packers) claimed work of equal value in comparison to work being carried out by picker/packers. The female employees appointed their own expert who carried out a system called 'Value Check' to determine if the jobs were of equal value. He concluded that they were. This was presented to the Tribunal, with the employers not bringing any alternative evidence. The Tribunal worked through the 'Value Check' system, after hearing all the evidence, and altered any scores that they disagreed with, based on what they had heard. They concluded that the jobs were of equal value. The EAT supported their finding, concluding that they had acted fairly on the only constructive approach available to them.

What defence can the employer give?

In some cases it might be possible for the employer to argue that there is a reason for the differences in the terms and conditions of employment. This is known as a 'genuine material difference'. If there is a genuine (significant and relevant) factor, other than sex, which is the reason for the difference then the claim of equal pay will fail. The Tribunal must be convinced that the reason given is genuine, and not an excuse. There have been a number of cases relating to this point, covering a wide range of different factors, discussed below.

Different negotiating groups

Enderby v *Frenchay Health Authority* [1993] IRLR 591

Enderby, an NHS senior speech therapist, claimed she was employed on work of equal value to that of male principal grade pharmacists and clinical psychologists, also employed in the NHS. The NHS claimed that the differences related to the fact that the two groups of employees were represented by different negotiating groups. The case was referred to the ECJ. They ruled that there was a clear difference in pay between the groups, which gave a prima facie case of sex discrimination. They ruled that it was insufficient to rely on the defence that the pay rates were arrived at through separate negotiations. Justification for the actual differences in pay had to be given.

FURTHER EXPLORATION

This is an interesting case, and somewhat complicated to follow because of the number of stages of appeal involved. Students wanting to explore this issue further are recommended to read the whole judgment in the case – particularly the ruling of the ECJ. It is particularly interesting to note the reasons that each stage of the court process give for reaching their conclusions.

Collective bargaining

Returning to the case of *William Ball Ltd* v *Wood and others* [2002] EAT 89/01, part of the defence of the employer was that the rates of pay had been agreed through a process of collective bargaining. The relevant collective agreement categorised workers in the furniture-making industry. It was noted that the agreement pre-dated any equal pay legislation, and the Tribunal concluded that it was 'tainted' because for historical reasons it maintained higher pay rates to picker/packers, a job traditionally reserved for men. Hence, the collective bargaining process (resulting in the collective agreement) was not allowed as a material defence.

Experience

Arw Transformers Ltd v *Cupples* [1977] IRLR 228

Cupples and a male colleague were both employed as work study engineers. She was paid £40.75 a week and he was paid £60 a week. He was aged 53 and she was aged 27, and he had considerably more experience than Cupples (although he had joined the employer after her). It was found that they were doing like work, and that the differing level of experience was not a material defence because the important issue is the work being carried out, not the person doing it.

Red circling

Red circling is where an employee, or group of employees, have his/their pay protected either for a specific period of time or for the full duration of the remaining period of employment. For example, an employee might need to move to a lighter job for medical reasons, and the employer could decide not to reduce his pay accordingly. Alternatively, following a restructuring, there might be a group of employees who are demoted, but again the decision is made not to reduce the pay accordingly. There have been a number of cases examining whether this is a fair defence for a difference in terms and conditions. An interesting ruling is in the following case.

Outlook Supplies v *Parry* [1978] IRLR 12

Parry was an accounts supervisor and claimed equal pay with a male colleague who was also an accounts supervisor. The colleague had previously been both a supervisor and an assistant accountant. However, due to ill-health he was relieved of some duties and reverted to being an accounts supervisor only. The employer 'red circled' his pay. This situation had continued for two and a half years. The Tribunal concluded it had gone on too long, and allowed the claim. However, the EAT overruled this finding stating that the period of time was actually reasonable. However, it did note that a prolonged period of red circling could be unreasonable, and it might not be possible to rely on this as a material defence.

Location

> ## Navy, Army and Air Force Institutes v Varley [1976] IRLR 408
>
> Nottingham office staff worked a 37-hour week, whereas London staff worked a 36.5-hour week. Varley, a female clerk in Nottingham, claimed her hours should be brought in line with a male clerk in London. This claim was not allowed because it was held that the difference was due to location, and not to sex.

TASK Find out if your organisation, or one with which you are familiar, has significant differences in pay relating to any of the genuine material defences outlined above. Do you think they are genuine defences?

Enforcement of claims

A claim can be brought to the Tribunal at any time during the period of employment when the comparator is also working, or within six months of leaving employment. The remedy is arrears of pay or damages, limited to a maximum of two years before the proceedings were instigated.

FURTHER EXPLORATION

Despite the equal pay legislation there is still clear evidence that the average salary paid to a man is greater than the average paid to a woman. There are factors that influence this (such as women taking career breaks to have children) but overall there still seems to be an underlying difference. Students wishing to explore this issue further would be well advised to read the Kingsmill Report on Women's Pay and Employment (www.kingsmillreview.gov.uk).

AGE DISCRIMINATION

In July 2003 the Government published the consultation document 'Equality and Diversity: Age Matters', which outlined the proposals for outlawing age discrimination in employment and vocational training. It is expected that, following a consultation period, the legislation will be brought before Parliament by the end of 2004. Legislation will come into force on 1 October 2006.

The proposed legal framework will make both direct and indirect age discrimination illegal. It is proposed to allow a limited defence to direct age discrimination in exceptional circumstances, which meet a list of specific aims. These are:

- health, welfare and safety
- to allow employment planning (eg succession planning)
- particular training requirements
- encouraging or rewarding loyalty
- the need for a reasonable period of time before retirement (if the cost of training would be excessive given the amount of time the person would be in the job).

If a policy or practice disadvantages a certain group of people because of their age it is possible that this will amount to indirect age discrimination. Particular issues to consider under this heading are:

■ *Retirement.* Employers will need to take a much more flexible view about retirement ages.

■ *Unfair dismissal.* The current age limit of 65 years for making a claim will go. In addition, the calculation for the basic award (and redundancy payments) will be linked only to service and not to age.

■ *Recruitment.* Any decisions based on age will be unlawful (this includes promotions). Advertisements specifying age ranges will not be allowed.

■ *Pay and benefits.* Pay made with relation to age will not be lawful. Pay relating to length of service is likely to be a possible defence, to allow employers to continue to reward loyalty.

As with the other discrimination legislation we have looked at, the focus is on selecting and rewarding the right person for the right job, and not basing decisions on irrelevant factors. Between now and 2006 there is time for employers to learn more about the requirements and to ensure they have implemented the correct procedures and policies.

TASK Find out if your employer, or one with which you are familiar, has taken steps to prepare for this new legislation. Have they done enough? What else do they need to do?

FURTHER EXPLORATION

Students wishing to understand the reasoning behind the forthcoming age discrimination legislation in more detail should refer to the DTI website for updates to the draft legislation (www.dti.gov.uk). In addition it is important to read the personnel and business press for reports of legislative developments.

CHAPTER REVIEW

1   Employees are protected against discrimination on the grounds of trade union membership in recruitment, dismissal and suffering other detriments.

2   Employees are protected against victimisation for carrying out a protected act as defined under discrimination legislation.

3   Harassment is unwanted conduct related to race/sex/disability, etc that takes place with the purpose or effect of violating the dignity of a person and of creating an intimidating, hostile, degrading, humiliating or offensive environment.

4   Vicarious liability means that the employer is held liable for wrongs committed by the employee during the course of his employment.

5   Equal pay claims focus on a comparator carrying out like work, work rated as equivalent, or work of equal value.

6 An employer can defend the difference in pay between a man and woman doing equal work if it can prove a genuine material difference other than sex.

7 Legislation related to age discrimination is to be introduced on 1 October 2006. It will encompass direct and indirect discrimination.

WEBSITES REFERENCED IN THIS CHAPTER

www.dti.gov.uk	Department of Trade and Industry
www.kingsmillreview.gov.uk	Kingsmill Report on Women's Pay and Employment
www.womenandequalityunit.gov.uk	Women and Equality Unit

FURTHER READING

■ *Beneviste* v *University of Southampton* [1989] IRLR 122 – an employee appointed on less favourable terms because of financial difficulties could claim equal pay once those restraints were lifted.

■ *Bromley* v *Quick Ltd* [1988] IRLR 249 – the jobs of the applicant and comparators must be subjected to job evaluation, not just the use of benchmark jobs.

■ *Discount Tobacco & Confectionery Ltd* v *Armitage* [1995] ICR 431 – an employee claims that she has been dismissed on grounds of her trade union membership.

■ *Irving and another* v *The Post Office* [1987] IRLR 289 – the employer was not vicariously liable for the independent action of an employee.

■ *Pickstone* v *Freemans plc* [1988] IRLR 357 – an equal value claim can be pursued as long as the comparator is doing like work or work rated as equivalent.

■ *Rainey* v *Greater Glasgow Health Board* [1987] IRLR 26 – market forces and the method of entering employment can be a material defence in an equal pay claim.

■ *Reed and another* v *Stedman* [1999] IRLR 299 – sexual harassment consists of words or conduct that are unwelcome to the recipient.

■ *Robb* v *Leon Motor Services Ltd* [1978] ICR 506 – a shop steward suffers the detriment of moving to a job in which he had much less contact with fellow employees.

■ *Scott* v *London Borough of Hillingdon* [2001] EWCA Civ 2005 – an unsuccessful job applicant had not been victimised for bringing a complaint against a former employer.

EXAMPLES TO WORK THROUGH

1 Fred is a shop steward within the trade union recognised by your organisation. A number of people who work with him have complained about his confrontational attitude. They complain that he brings grievances to the head of the department on a regular basis, claiming

that they all support his arguments. They very rarely do. They have approached you, the personnel manager, asking if Fred can be moved to another department. What response would you give?

2   Mary claims that she is being sexually harassed at work. She works within a team of six, and is the only woman. She claims there is a constant sexual banter, and she is asked a lot of personal questions about her own sex life. The men in the team deny any harassment. They agree that a certain amount of banter takes place, but say that Mary often joins in. They are offended at her claims. What should you do?

3   Peter is a waiter within the restaurant of your large hotel. He is claiming that his work is of equal value to the female receptionists. What process must you follow to examine this claim?

4   You have been asked to draft out a policy for your organisation in light of proposed discrimination legislation. What key points must you include?

Termination of Employment (1)

The objectives of this chapter are to:

- **Understand the circumstances in which a dismissal might occur;**
- **Examine the five potentially fair reasons for dismissal;**
- **Evaluate the process of ensuring that a fair dismissal takes place;**
- **Understand the concept of constructive dismissal;**
- **Outline the automatically unfair reasons for dismissal;**
- **Examine the potential remedies for unfair dismissal.**

WHEN DOES A DISMISSAL OCCUR?

Section 95 of the Employment Rights Act 1996 states that an employee is to be treated as dismissed if:

- the contract under which he is employed is terminated by the employer (this can be with or without notice)
- the employee is working under a fixed-term contract and the same contract is not renewed
- the employer terminates the contract of employment (with or without notice) in circumstances when he is entitled to terminate the contract without notice due to the employee's conduct.

There are circumstances in which a contract of employment can be terminated but no dismissal has occurred:

Resignation of the employee

If an employee states that he wishes to terminate the contract of employment this is not a dismissal. However, if the employee considers that he has been forced into the resignation by the actions of the employer there is the potential for a claim of constructive dismissal. We shall examine this in more detail later in the chapter.

Mutual agreement

If the employer and employee mutually agree to terminate the contract, a dismissal will not be deemed to have taken place. There is the possibility of an employee feeling forced into reaching a mutual agreement, and again this could lead to a potential claim for constructive dismissal.

If the employer gives an indication that the employment will terminate at 'some time' but gives no precise details about when then it is unlikely that a dismissal will have taken place. This was determined in the following case.

Morton Sundour Fabrics Ltd v Shaw [1966] ITR 84

Shaw worked in the velvet department of the employer. He was told that the velvet department would close at some time in the future, although no precise details of dates were given. The employer offered to put him in contact with another employer. Shaw met this other employer, was offered a job, resigned from Morton Sundour and started with the new employer. He then claimed a redundancy payment from Morton Sundour. They refused to make the payment, claiming that he had resigned and had not been dismissed. The Employment Tribunal stated that a redundancy had taken place and instructed Morton Sundour to make the payment. However, the EAT overruled this decision stating that the employee had only been given a warning about a possible dismissal at some time – but no actual dismissal had taken place.

This definition of dismissal was supported by the judgment in the following case.

Haseltine Lake & Co v Dowler [1980] IRLR 25

Dowler was warned that there would be no long-term role for him in the organisation, and in February 1979 was advised to start to look for alternative employment. In May he received an offer of employment elsewhere and told Haseltine Lake & Co about this. He was told that if he was not happy with this new offer of employment he did not need to leave straight away, but it was confirmed that he would need to leave eventually. It was agreed that he would leave in June 1979. Dowler claimed unfair dismissal. The Employment Tribunal supported Dowler's claim, but this was overturned by the EAT because the ruling of Morton Sundour Fabrics had not been applied. As there had been no precise indication of when the employment was going to terminate there could be no dismissal.

RELATIONSHIP BALANCE

Is there ever a situation when an employee and an employer can make an equal contribution to a decision to terminate employment (ie by mutual agreement)? Will the employer, in reality, always have that bit more power in making this decision? Try to determine a situation in which such a decision really would be mutual.

Frustration

A contract of employment is held to be frustrated when circumstances have prevented one or both of the parties from performing the contract. Examples of potential frustration include long-term sickness and the employee being sentenced to a term of imprisonment.

If applying the concept of frustration to a long-term sickness absence, care must be taken to determine whether the employee is suffering from a disability as defined by the Disability Discrimination Act (see Chapter 6). If there is a disability it is highly possible that pursuing the route of frustration will lead to a claim for disability discrimination.

Here is a case relating to frustration caused by imprisonment.

Harrington v *Kent CC* [1980] IRLR 353

Harrington was a primary school teacher who was convicted of indecency offences and sentenced to 12 months' imprisonment. Kent CC informed Harrington that his contract of employment had ended due to his inability to carry out the duties for which he was employed, for a substantial period of time. When Harrington was released from prison he wrote to Kent CC and requested his job back; they refused. He made a claim of unfair dismissal. However, both the Employment Tribunal and the EAT agreed that the contract had been automatically terminated by the prison sentence and hence no longer existed.

TASK Find out if your organisation, or an organisation with which you are familiar, has had a situation where the contract of employment appeared to be frustrated. How was this dealt with?

Further Exploration

In *Marshall* v *Harland and Wolff Ltd* [1972] WLR 899 a series of requirements were set out that should be used to determine whether a contract of employment has been frustrated. To gain a further understanding of frustration of contract read through this judgment, and the judgment in *Egg Stores* v *Leibovici* [1976] ICR 260. Having read the judgments, evaluate why the courts are usually reluctant to apply the approach of frustration of contract.

ELIGIBILITY TO MAKE A CLAIM OF UNFAIR DISMISSAL

Section 94 of the Employment Rights Act 1996 states that an employee has the right not to be unfairly dismissed by his employer.

There are cases where a dismissal can be judged to have occurred, but the person in question cannot make a claim of unfair dismissal to the Employment Tribunal. These situations include:

- non-employees
- those with less than one year's continuous service of employment (unless the reason for dismissal was one of those that are automatically unfair – see later in this chapter)
- where the employee is employed under an illegal contract
- persons employed in the police service.

In addition, Section 109 (1) of the Employment Rights Act 1996 states that the right to make a claim of unfair dismissal does not apply to the dismissal of an employee who has reached the normal retiring age for an employee holding that position, or is aged 65 years or more. This is currently under review through the case of *Harvest Town Circle Ltd* v *Rutherford* [2001] IRLR 59. In this case the Employment Tribunal has confirmed its decision that the application of a compulsory retirement age of 65 years is discriminatory under European Law. This will result in an age bar being ignored for any claims of unfair dismissal. However, at the time of writing this case is currently under appeal so no clear direction can be given on this issue.

Despite the ruling in this case, the age discrimination legislation coming in 2006 is expected to result in the removal of the upper age limit for claiming unfair dismissal. If it is allowed to let employers operate mandatory retirement ages (which could be the age of 70, or could be allowed only in exceptional circumstances which can be clearly justified) then dismissal at such an age would be a fair reason. However, the current age limit of 65 years for making unfair dismissal claims is very unlikely to remain once this legislation is in place.

TASK	Keep abreast of developments in this area by reading the personnel and business press. Look out for a ruling on the appeal against the judgment in the case mentioned above.

Further Exploration

The issue of an upper limit on the age for bringing a claim for unfair dismissal has been the subject of a number of cases. Contrast and compare the rulings in the cases of *Nothman* v *Barnet LBC* [1979] WLR 67, *Hughes* v *DHSS* [1985] AC 776 and *Taylor* v *Secretary of State for Scotland* [1999] SC 372. Contrast them with the case identified above that is currently the subject of an appeal. What guidance can be gained from these cases?

POTENTIALLY FAIR REASONS FOR DISMISSAL

Section 98 of the Employment Rights Act 1996 lists five potentially fair reasons for dismissal. They are:

- capability or qualifications
- conduct
- redundancy
- statutory ban
- some other substantial reason.

Capability or qualifications

The Employment Rights Act 1996 defines capability as 'skill, aptitude, health or any other physical or mental quality'. Qualifications is defined as 'any degree, diploma or other academic, technical or professional qualification relevant to the position which the employee holds'.

The employer should, at the recruitment stage and in the subsequent period of induction, make sure that the employee understands the requirements of the job. The employer should determine any training needs that exist and act upon them. The employer should also make clear to the employee the likely penalty of failing to meet the required standards. If the employee does not meet the required standards of performance the employer would be expected to try to assist that employee through further training and education before taking disciplinary action.

If the capability issue relates to ill-health the employer must consider the nature of the illness, the actual and potential length of the absence and the employer's situation (eg the size of the business and the impact that the absence is having on the organisation). The need to act reasonably is illustrated by the following case.

Rolls Royce Ltd v Walpole [1980] IRLR 343

Despite having a good attendance record for his first four years of his employment, during the next three years prior to his dismissal Walpole's attendance record averaged 50 per cent. There was no pattern to the attendance. Rolls Royce followed their procedures in making Walpole aware of their concerns, and could not foresee any improvement of the situation. They dismissed Walpole. He took a claim of unfair dismissal, which was supported by the Employment Tribunal. The EAT overruled the Employment Tribunal's decision, stating that it was perverse. Dismissal was a reasonable response to an attendance record as poor as that of Walpole.

It is important that the employer's response is reasonable in the particular circumstances of each situation. Although an absence record may be poor, the employer must consider the reasons for this in deciding how to react.

Kerr v Atkinson Vehicles (Scotland) Ltd [1973] IRLR 36

Kerr was severely disabled. He was moved from a role where his absence was interfering with his work, to another role in the organisation. Although his work was satisfactory he was dismissed due to his absences. Kerr successfully claimed unfair dismissal because his employer should have anticipated the absence pattern, and taken steps to accommodate it.

In the same way, the employer must act reasonably in addressing capability issues that relate to performance in the job. The following case illustrates the need to ensure that adequate training and supervision is provided.

Mansfield Hosiery Mills Ltd v Bromley [1977] IRLR 301

Bromley responded successfully to an advertisement for a boiler service fitter. Although the advertisement stated that training would be given, he received none. He performed well and was promoted to maintenance supervisor. In this role a number of issues occurred and he was eventually dismissed. The Employment Tribunal found that he had been given inadequate supervision, insufficient direction and encouragement, and hence the dismissal was unfair. The EAT supported this finding.

If the employer has taken action to try to help the employee improve the standard of performance, but capability remains an issue then the dismissal can be potentially fair.

Gozdzik & Scopigno v *Chlidema Carpet Co Ltd* [1979] EAT 598/78

The two employees were employed as winders. Due to the effects of the recession the employer introduced a new bonus system aimed at improving the productivity of the winders. The two employees did not meet the new standards and were given further training by the employer. They still did not meet the new standards and they were dismissed. Their claim for unfair dismissal failed because the employer had acted reasonably in providing them with additional training before taking the decision to dismiss.

TASK Find out what procedures your organisation, or an organisation with which you are familiar, has for addressing capability issues. Do you think they are adequate in defending potential claims of unfair dismissal?

RELATIONSHIP BALANCE

How much is the responsibility for capability held by the employer, and how much by the employee? If the employer has recruited or promoted someone who is not able to do the job, what action should the employer be reasonably expected to take? What approaches can the employer take to determine the reason for the lack of capability, and how much effort do you think the employer should reasonably be expected to take to determine this?

Conduct

Conduct is typically divided into two categories:

- *Gross misconduct*, which can result in summary dismissal (dismissal without notice). Examples of gross misconduct include theft, assault, vandalism, falsification of records.

- *Misconduct*, which are less serious offences and are usually dealt with through disciplinary warnings. If the behaviour does not cease then there is the possibility that the employee will be dismissed. Examples of this include bad language, poor time-keeping, improper wearing of uniform.

A dismissal for misconduct is potentially fair, but the employer must show that he has acted reasonably in reaching the decision to dismiss. The role of the Employment Tribunal is not to determine whether the employee committed the act of misconduct, but whether the employer investigated the situation thoroughly, had a reasonable belief that the employee committed the act and then took a reasonable course of action. This is referred to as acting within the 'range of reasonable responses'.

This test of reasonableness is illustrated in the following cases. The following is an important case that demonstrates the need for the employer to have a reasonable belief in the guilt of the employee.

British Home Stores v *Burchell* [1978] IRLR 379

Burchell was dismissed because of irregularities in staff purchases. Evidence was obtained from dockets relating to purchases of Burchell and other staff, and a statement from another employee. Burchell took a claim of unfair dismissal to the Employment Tribunal, which supported her claim stating that BHS had not clearly established Burchell's guilt. The EAT overturned this decision, stating that the Employment Tribunal had tried to apply tests more fitting to a criminal investigation. This strict standard of proof was not required – what was required was that the employer had a reasonable belief based on a reasonable investigation. The EAT identified three key elements to this process:

1   The fact underlying the belief must be established.

2   The belief must be held on reasonable grounds, after an appropriate investigation.

3   The investigation must be reasonable, in the circumstances.

It is important to note that the level of investigation and belief required in order to proceed with a dismissal is not the same level as that required in a criminal prosecution.

The reasonableness of a dismissal can also relate to the previous disciplinary record of an employee.

Bartholomew v *Post Office Telecommunications* [1981] EAT 53/81

Bartholemew was dismissed for making a 20-minute private overseas telephone call. His employers investigated, but Bartholomew could not give an explanation for the call. As Bartholomew had already been given a number of warnings for misconduct, the decision was taken to dismiss him. Both the Employment Tribunal and the EAT supported the decision to dismiss, in the light of Bartholomew's employment history. However, making the decision to dismiss an employee who had made such a telephone call, and had no record of any past disciplinary issues would probably be seen as unreasonable.

If an employee is charged with a criminal offence it can be reasonable to proceed with a dismissal, even if that employee will not co-operate with any dismissal hearings. The tests established by *British Home Stores* v *Burchell* [1978] IRLR 379 are relevant here. This is demonstrated in the next case.

Harris & another v Courage (Eastern) Ltd [1982] IRLR 509

Courage believed that Harris and another had stolen some beer, and the police charged them both. Courage also started disciplinary proceedings. On legal advice the two employees did not attend the disciplinary hearings, and were not prepared to co-operate with any investigation by Courage. Courage carried out an investigation to the best of their ability – including the taking of witness statements. On the basis of the evidence they had gained they dismissed the two employees. The claim for unfair dismissal was rejected because Courage had carried out a reasonable investigation, and had a reasonable belief that the employees had stolen the beer. It was found that there was no requirement to wait until after a criminal trial. (In the actual criminal trial the employees were acquitted.)

TASK Cases of unfair dismissal are regularly reported in the personnel press. Read some recent cases and apply the 'Burchell test' to them. Try to develop an understanding of what the Employment Tribunal sees as a 'reasonable response' from an employer.

RELATIONSHIP BALANCE

The issue of acting reasonably is central to the relationship between the employer and the employee when addressing alleged actions of misconduct. Do you think that there is a sufficiently clear definition of reasonableness to give guidelines to both the employer and the employee? Do you think there is a fair balance in the way that the test of reasonableness is applied?

Redundancy

We shall explore this issue in detail in the next chapter.

Statutory ban

This is when it is unlawful to continue working because of a legal restriction or duty. An example of this is an employee who has the job of a driver within an organisation who then loses his driving licence because of motoring offences that he has committed. Clearly, he cannot continue to work in the role of driver whilst this ban is in place.

Again, the concept of reasonableness is central to the reaction of the employer. The employer should consider the length of time that the restriction is likely to be in place. If, to continue the use of our example, the driver has lost his licence for three months it might be possible to find him alternative duties during this period. If, however, he has lost his licence for five years, it would be necessary to completely redeploy him, which might be more difficult.

This issue is illustrated in the following case:

Roberts v *Toyota* (GB) Ltd [1981] EAT 614/80

Roberts was an area sales manager, and there was an implied term in his contract that he would have a driving licence. He was convicted of driving whilst over the legal alcohol limit, and lost his licence for 12 months. He offered to purchase a company car and provide a driver during this 12-month period, but the employer went ahead and dismissed him, viewing the option of using a driver as impractical. His claim of unfair dismissal was rejected, because there was clear evidence that the requirement to have a driving licence was an implied term of his contract of employment.

The need to act reasonably in reaching the decision to dismiss was demonstrated in the next case.

Sutcliffe and Eaton Ltd v *Pinney* [1977] IRLR 349

Pinney was a hearing aid dispenser, and it was a requirement of the profession that he passed a series of examinations within a five-year period. He repeatedly failed the examinations, although he did pass the oral examination just before the five years expired. He was dismissed by the employer because they believed that he would never pass the examinations, and continuing to employ him would breach the professional requirements. The day after his dismissal he applied for an extension to the examination period, and was informed nearly three months later that an extension had been granted. He claimed unfair dismissal and this claim was supported by the Employment Tribunal.

The employer, in this situation, had acted too quickly. If Pinney had not been granted the extension we can presume that there would have been a fair dismissal. However, in not seeking an extension and waiting to hear the response to the request, the employer had acted unreasonably.

Some other substantial reason

This category allows the Employment Tribunal to consider any dismissal that does not fall under one of the other four headings, and to consider the reason and its fairness. Examples under this heading are as follows.

Pressure from an external source to dismiss

Consider the following case.

Scott Packing and Warehousing Co Ltd v Paterson [1978] IRLR 166

The US Naval Authorities refused to have Paterson working on their contract due to alleged incidents of misconduct. This was a major part of Scott Packing's business. The Employment Tribunal found that Paterson had been unfairly dismissed because the employer had not investigated the issue of misconduct and established a reasonable belief in Paterson's guilt. However, the EAT overturned this decision, stating that the issue here was not one of conduct but of 'some other substantial reason'. In this case the employer had not acted unreasonably because he had acted in accordance with the wishes of his major customer.

Although a customer might refuse to have an employee working for them, the requirement on the employer to act reasonably remains. The above case was referred back to the Employment Tribunal for them to consider whether there was other work to which Paterson could have been moved. Even if there is pressure from a customer to remove an employee, the employer cannot dismiss without exploring all the options for continued employment.

Reorganisation of the business

If an employer needs to reorganise a business and can show that it is essential to make alterations to an employee's working pattern there is a potentially fair reason. Again, the employer must show that all the options have been considered and that the conclusion that dismissal is the solution has been reached after reasonable consideration. This occurred in the following case.

Davey v Daybern Co Ltd [1982] EAT 710/81

Davey worked in a sweet kiosk. Business was poor, and it was decided to reorganise the working hours in order to cut wage costs. The reorganisation meant that Davey would be required to work two evenings, which she was unable to do because of family commitments. A temporary arrangement was put in place, but eventually Davey was dismissed. Her claim of unfair dismissal was unsuccessful because the Employment Tribunal found that the employer had acted fairly. They were able to demonstrate the commercial needs for the reorganisation, and hence the reason for the dismissal was reasonable under the heading of 'some other substantial reason'.

Mistaken belief

If an employer has a genuine belief that the reason he has for dismissing an employee is fair, the dismissal could come under the heading of 'some other substantial reason' if it is later shown that the belief was actually mistaken. This categorisation refers back to the need for an employer to carry out a reasonable investigation, which leads to a reasonable belief.

This is demonstrated in the following case.

Bouchaala v *Trust House Forte Hotels Ltd* [1980] ICR 721

Bouchaala was a Tunisian student who was given limited leave to enter and remain in the UK. Trust House Forte employed him as a trainee manager, but was then informed by the Department of Employment that he did not qualify for a work permit and continuing to employ him would be illegal. He was dismissed. The Department of Employment then informed the employer that Bouchaala had been given indefinite leave to remain in the UK and hence a work permit was not required. Bouchaala took a claim of unfair dismissal. This claim was not supported because the employer had a genuine belief that there was a substantial reason for the dismissal of Bouchaala. Although that belief was later shown to be mistaken, the dismissal, at the time, was still fair.

Further Exploration

Read through the judgments in a variety of unfair dismissal cases (for some ideas of where to find these, see Further Reading at the end of this chapter). In each one, identify the test of reasonableness and how it is being applied. Build up a clear picture of what the courts consider to be reasonable behaviour on the part of both the employer and the employee. Do some clear guidelines develop? Are there cases that do not fit in with these guidelines? How can any such anomalies be explained?

DISCIPLINARY PROCEDURE

In showing that he has acted reasonably the employer must be able to show that he has followed an appropriate dismissal procedure. Many organisations have their own procedures, but those that do not would be expected to follow the guidelines given in the Acas Disciplinary and Dismissals Procedure (copies available from Acas or on their website – www.acas.org.uk).

However, the Employment Act 2002 outlined the implementation of new statutory discipline, dismissal and grievance procedures. These new rules take effect from 1 October 2004.

The main purpose of the statutory procedures is to encourage employers and employees to resolve disputes internally, rather than resort to the Employment Tribunal. Although, at the time of writing (early 2004), the details of the requirements are not known, it is expected that the following will be included in the provisions.

- All employers will be obliged to follow statutory dismissal and disciplinary procedures.
- All employers will be obliged to follow statutory grievance procedures. Employees will not be allowed to apply to an Employment Tribunal until they have raised their grievance with their employer, in writing.
- There will be an implied term in every contract of employment that will require both the employer and the employee to comply with the minimum procedures.

There are also some important changes to existing law and practice:

- An extension to the current three-month limit for bringing a claim of unfair dismissal (see Chapter 2) will be allowed if the employee has reasonable grounds for believing that a disciplinary or grievance procedure is still ongoing when the three-month limit expires.

- There will be a requirement that the disciplinary and dismissals procedures are set out in the employee's written particulars of employment.

- Employees cannot bring claims to the Employment Tribunal if they have not followed the internal grievance procedures. The purpose of this is to try to resolve more disputes before they escalate into Employment Tribunal claims. Another aim is to eliminate the situation of the first the employer knowing about a grievance is when he receives a copy of the employee's application to the Employment Tribunal. However, there is concern that this might stop an employee expressing a grievance, because of the fear of the reaction of the employer. A formal definition of a grievance will be added: 'a complaint by an employee about action which his employer has or is contemplating taking in relation to him'.

- If an employer has not followed the statutory disciplinary and dismissals procedure the dismissal will be deemed to be automatically unfair.

This provision overturns the widely applied ruling in the following case.

Polkey v *A E Dayton* [1987] AC 344

Polkey was one of four van drivers working for A E Dayton. There was a need to cut costs for commercial reasons, and it was decided that the four van drivers would be replaced by three van salesmen. A E Dayton decided that Polkey was unsuitable for the role of van salesman and accordingly decided to make him redundant. The first Polkey knew about this was when he was given a letter setting out his redundancy payments and was dismissed.

On hearing his claim of unfair dismissal it was determined that the employers had not acted correctly because they had not consulted with Polkey or warned him of the possible redundancy (we shall explore this procedure more in the next chapter). However, they also concluded that even if the procedure had been followed Polkey would still have been made redundant. On that basis his dismissal was found to be fair. The case was eventually referred to the House of Lords, which found that the Employment Tribunal had taken the wrong approach. The key issue was whether the employer had acted *reasonably* in not giving any warning of the possible redundancy. This case has become a key part of determining the fairness of a dismissal. It can be fair to dismiss without following a correct procedure if the actions can be shown to be reasonable.

However, this key ruling seems no longer to be valid given the expected requirements to follow the statutory disciplinary and dismissals procedures.

It is inevitable that there will be much more discussion about this issue in the personnel press. Be sure that you follow the challenge to the Polkey ruling – particularly taking note of any developments in case law.

Further Exploration

Students wanting to know more about the proposed procedures should read the consultation document (www.dti.gov.uk/er/individual/dis_res_consdoc.htm).

RELATIONSHIP BALANCE

In what way does the introduction of statutory procedures improve the protection of the employee? Is the requirement to adhere to these procedures a fair burden on the employer? What are the possible difficulties that might be encountered by both parties?

THE RIGHT TO BE ACCOMPANIED

Sections 10–15 of the Employment Relations Act 1999 gave workers the right to be accompanied by a fellow worker or trade union representative to any disciplinary or grievance hearing that falls within the following definitions:

- the giving of a formal warning to a worker by the employer
- the taking of some other action to a worker in relation to a disciplinary matter
- the confirmation of a warning or other action that has been taken.

If the hearing is informal there is no statutory right to be accompanied. It must also be emphasised that the right is to be accompanied by a fellow worker or a trade union representative – not a solicitor, member of the family or any other person who does not fall within the given definition.

CONSTRUCTIVE DISMISSAL

If the employer's conduct is such that it breaches the contract of employment, and that breach goes to the very root of the contract, the employee can terminate the contract of employment and claim constructive dismissal.

In order to show that there has been a constructive dismissal the employee must demonstrate that:

- there was a fundamental breach of the contract on the part of the employer
- the breach of the contract caused him to resign
- there was no significant delay in resigning.

In the next case the Court of Appeal ruled that the employer's conduct that gave rise to the claim of constructive dismissal must involve a breach of contract.

Western Excavating (ECC) Ltd v *Sharp* [1978] QB 761

Sharp asked for an afternoon off, and was refused. Nevertheless, he still took the afternoon off. He was dismissed, but successfully appealed. The appeal reduced the punishment to five days' suspension without payment. However, this led him into financial difficulties so he asked the employer to pay him five days accrued holiday pay. This was refused because it was against company policy. He then asked for a loan that was also refused. He then resigned claiming constructive dismissal.

The Employment Tribunal upheld his complaint. This finding was overturned by the Court of Appeal. They found that the Employment Tribunal had focused on whether the conduct of the employer was unreasonable. However, the test in a case of constructive dismissal is whether the contract of employment has been breached. In this case, they found no evidence of a breach of contract and hence the complaint was dismissed.

It can be difficult to determine whether the behaviour of the employer has actually breached the employment contract. It is not important to consider what the employer *intended* to do. The Employment Tribunal will focus on the actual behaviour of the employer, and whether an employee cannot reasonably have been expected to tolerate such behaviour.

This is illustrated in the following case.

Stanley Cole (Wainfleet) Ltd v *Sheridan* [2003] IRLR 52

Sheridan had been an employee for more than five years, and had no record of disciplinary action. She had a heated discussion with a colleague that upset her, and she then left the office for one and a half hours (which included her half-hour lunch break). She returned, and her line manager suggested that she go home because she was clearly still upset. She then went absent on the grounds of ill-health. Disciplinary action was taken against her for leaving the office without permission and she was issued with a final written warning (the last stage of the disciplinary procedure before dismissal). Her appeal against the decision was rejected. She resigned and claimed constructive dismissal.

The Employment Tribunal found that the severe penalty of a final written warning for a first (and relatively minor) offence amounted to a breach of the contract of employment because it breached the implied term of trust and confidence or/and the implied term that the disciplinary procedure would be used fairly. Her claim for constructive dismissal was upheld.

In this case it was judged that the behaviour of the employer, in giving such a severe penalty, was not behaviour that Sheridan could be expected to tolerate, and hence there was a breach of contract.

A potential breach of employment can also relate to an employer's lack of action. This was demonstrated in the following case.

Thanet District Council v *Websper* [2002] EAT 1090/01

Websper went on long-term sick leave claiming his illness was to do with work-related stress. The Council took advice from its medical officer who concluded that Websper would not be able to return to his old job, but might be able to return to different work in a different department. The Council told Websper they would try to find him work in the same department, but in a different section. Websper refused this and resigned, claiming constructive dismissal.

The Employment Tribunal found that the lack of an offer of work in a different department had breached the implied contractual duty to provide the employee with a safe place of work. Therefore, this was a case of constructive dismissal.

The important factor in determining whether constructive dismissal has taken place is whether the actions (or inaction) of the employer have amounted to a breach of the contract. The specific part of the contract that has been breached must be identified, and it must then be possible to show that the breach is fundamental.

RELATIONSHIP BALANCE

If the employer acts in a way that breaches the contract of employment, the employee can resign and make a claim of constructive dismissal. Do you think that this gives the employee sufficient protection? It must be noted that the employee will need to leave employment to make such a claim – therefore potentially sustaining significant loss. Does this give a fair balance of protection to both the employer and the employee?

AUTOMATICALLY UNFAIR REASONS FOR DISMISSAL

There are situations in which a dismissal is automatically unfair. This means that the one-year qualifying period required to bring a claim of unfair dismissal is not required. This includes situations where the reason for a dismissal relates to:

- the employee's membership (or non-membership) of a trade union
- the employee's pregnancy or any maternity-related issue
- a transfer of employment (see the next chapter for further explanation)
- the refusal of a retail employee to work on a Sunday
- a conviction that is, according to law, deemed to be 'spent' (see Chapter 3)
- activities carried out in the role of health and safety representative
- asserting a statutory right
- making a protected disclosure under the Public Disclosure Act (see Chapter 10)
- asserting the right to be paid in accordance with the National Minimum Wage Act 1998
- disclosing fraud or corruption.

REMEDIES FOR UNFAIR DISMISSAL

If the Employment Tribunal finds that an employee has been unfairly dismissed it has to decide on the remedy. As explained in Chapter 2, there are three possible remedies:

- reinstatement
- re-engagement
- compensation.

Although reinstatement and re-engagement are by far the least common remedies, the Employment Tribunal has a duty to explain these options and to ask the employee whether he wants the Tribunal to make such an order. In reality, the employee rarely wants such an order, either because he has already obtained alternative employment or because the relationship with the employer is sufficiently poor after bringing the claim that future employment would seem to be untenable.

If the employee is reinstated he returns to the job he previously held and the employer must treat the employee as if he had not been dismissed. This means that all monies that would have been paid to the employee (salary and any benefits) during the time between the dismissal and the order to reinstate must be paid. All rights and privileges that the employee previously enjoyed must be reinstated.

If the employee is re-engaged, he returns to the employer but in a different role. The Employment Tribunal must state the nature of the employment, and the benefits that accompany the role. Again, the employee must be treated as if he had not been dismissed, and any monies he would have earned during the period between dismissal and the order to re-engage must be paid.

If the Employment Tribunal makes an order for reinstatement or re-engagement and that is not carried out by the employer the tribunal will then award compensation to the employee in the way we shall outline later in this section. In addition, there will be an additional award of not less than 26 weeks', and not more than 52 weeks', pay.

If compensation is awarded it will consist of two parts (according to Section 118 of the Employment Rights Act 1996). These two parts are the basic award and the compensatory award.

The basic award is calculated by determining the employee's period of continuous service with the employer (up to a maximum of 20 years). The following amounts are awarded:

- 1.5 weeks' pay for each year when the employee was between the ages of 41 and 64 years.
- 1 week's pay for each year when the employee was between the ages of 22 and 40.
- 0.5 week's pay for each year of employment between the ages of 18 and 21.

If the date of termination is after the employee's 64th birthday the basic award is reduced for 1/12 for each whole month that elapses after the birthday. (As previously noted, the restrictions relating to an upper age limit of 65 are currently under challenge, and hence this process of reducing the basic award could be removed.)

The statutory definition of the maximum limit on a week's pay is reviewed each year by the government. It is currently £270 (February 2004). If an employee is paid more than this, the figure of £270 will be used for all calculations.

If the employee has been unfairly dismissed for a reason relating to health and safety, being a trustee of an occupational pension scheme, or an elected employee representative there is a minimum basic award of £3600.

If an employee is judged to have unreasonably refused an offer of reinstatement by the employer the amount of the basic award can be reduced. An Employment Tribunal can also decide to reduce the basic award on the basis of conduct before the dismissal that makes such a reduction fair.

The compensatory award is that which the Employment Tribunal sees as fair given all of the circumstances, and the loss that the employee has suffered. The aim is to compensate the employee for the loss he has suffered, not to punish the employer. The items that are taken into consideration when determining the compensatory award are:

- loss of earnings from the date of dismissal to the date of the Employment Tribunal hearing
- potential future loss of earnings (the tribunal will give consideration to the degree of difficulty the employee might encounter in getting alternative employment, and the likelihood of obtaining employment at a similar level of remuneration to the role from which he was dismissed)
- loss of statutory industrial rights (the employee has lost the continuous service he had accrued with the previous employer, and will need to start the process of accrual anew with a new employer. This item aims to compensate the employee for that loss).
- loss of pension rights
- loss of benefits (eg health insurance, company car)
- expenses incurred in seeking alternative employment
- damages for injury to feelings.

The issue of damages for injury to feelings has been contentious. In Section 123 of the Employment Rights Act 1996 the compensatory award in unfair dismissal cases is defined as that which is 'such amount as the tribunal considers just and equitable in all the circumstances having regard to the loss sustained by the complainant in consequence of the dismissal'.

In determining the amount of compensation in the case of *Norton Tool Co Ltd* v *Tewson* [1972] ICR 501 a clear statement was made that the compensatory award for unfair dismissal could reflect only economic loss.

Johnson v *Unisys Ltd* [2001] ICR 480.

This interpretation of Section 123 of the ERA 1996 remained unchallenged until a ruling in the case of *Johnson* v *Unisys Ltd* [2001] ICR 480. In this case Johnson claimed he had suffered psychological problems due to the nature of his dismissal. He won a claim for unfair dismissal, but the compensatory award did not include any damages for injury to feelings. He tried to pursue a claim for breach of contract in the County Court, on the basis that the nature of the dismissal had breached the term of mutual trust and confidence. However, it was ruled that such a claim could not be made because the term of mutual trust and confidence applied to preserving the relationship, and not terminating it.

In making the House of Lords judgment, specific reference was made by one of the judges to the Norton Tool case. It was commented that the interpretation of the compensatory award was too narrow, and the definition of compensatory award should include damages for distress, humiliation, damage to reputation or family life and psychiatric injury when appropriate. (Note: In the Johnson case the House of Lords did not go on to review the unfair dismissal compensatory award as they were hearing an appeal relating to a breach of contract claim.)

This judgment was then tested in the following case.

Dunnachie v *Kingston upon Hull City Council* [2004] EWCA Civ 84

Dunnachie worked for the Council and had been subjected to a long campaign of bullying and undermining by his colleague and former line manager. The Council failed to resolve the situation and eventually Dunnachie resigned and successfully claimed constructive dismissal.

Although there was no evidence of Dunnachie suffering from a recognised psychiatric disorder, he had been reduced to a 'state of overt despair'. In light of the ruling in the *Johnson* v *Unisys* case the Employment Tribunal included a £10,000 award within the compensatory award for injury to feelings flowing from the dismissal.

Although the EAT overturned the Tribunal's decision the Court of Appeal supported the £10,000 award, and hence supported the Tribunal's calculation of the compensatory award.

The Court of Appeal issued some guidance in determining whether an amount should be added to the compensatory award for injury to feelings. First they determined that the definition of the compensatory award in Section 123 of the ERA 1996 was sufficiently wide to allow for non-financial losses to be considered. Second, not every upset caused by an unfair dismissal should attract a compensatory award. There must be a real injury to the employee's self-respect.

The maximum amount of compensation that can be awarded is reviewed by the government each year. At present (February 2004) it is £55,000.

The amount of compensation can be reduced due to the employee's contribution to the dismissal.

Parker Foundry Ltd v *Slack* [1991] IRLR 11

Slack was dismissed following a fight with a fellow employee. The Employment Tribunal found that Slack had been unfairly dismissed because of procedural irregularities relating to the way that the claim had been handled. However, they reduced his compensation by 50 per cent, because they believed that his conduct resulted in him being 50 per cent to blame for the dismissal.

There is also the possibility to make a reduction to the compensatory award when the procedure for dismissal had not been followed fairly, but the Employment Tribunal judges that (even if the procedure had been followed) the employee would still have been dismissed. This approach refers back to the case of *Polkey* v *A E Dayton* [1988] AC 344, which we examined earlier in this chapter.

The Employment Tribunal can apply the 'Polkey' reduction when the employer can show that there was a potentially fair reason for dismissal but a correct procedure was not followed. The tribunal can then assess what chance the employee would have had of keeping his job if a correct procedure had been followed, and that percentage chance can be applied to reduce the compensation awarded. However, we must note that the Polkey rule has been challenged by the Employment Act 2002 and this approach will no longer apply when statutory disciplinary and dismissals procedures are introduced.

The employee also has a duty to take reasonable steps to mitigate his loss (by making serious efforts to find alternative employment). The basic rule of mitigation is that the employee must take all reasonable steps to mitigate the loss to him resulting from the employer's actions, and he cannot recover compensation for any such loss that he could have avoided but failed to avoid through unreasonable action or inaction. The duty is to act reasonably, although the level of requirement on the employee is not high – given that the employer is the wrongdoer.

The level of mitigation expected is illustrated in the next case.

Fyfe v *Scientific Furnishings Ltd* [1989] IRLR 331

Fyfe was dismissed on the grounds of redundancy, but was offered the alternative of taking early retirement. Although the financial package offered as part of the early retirement was more advantageous than the redundancy payment, Fyfe chose not to take early retirement. He claimed unfair dismissal, and his claim was upheld by the Employment Tribunal. However, they determined that he had failed to mitigate his loss by not taking the offer of early retirement, and hence reduced his compensation by 100 per cent. The EAT overruled this decision. They found that the circumstances in which Fyfe had been made the offer of early retirement, and the time he was given to consider the option, were not adequate. Given the relatively low level of expectation on the employee to mitigate the loss, the EAT found that he had not failed in the requirement to act reasonably, and should be entitled to the full amount of compensation.

RELATIONSHIP BALANCE

As we have seen, it is possible for an employee to win a claim of unfair dismissal but to have any compensation significantly reduced. Do you think this is fair for the employee? Do you think it is fair for the employer to have to compensate an employee who has committed an offence, when the employer has erred only on procedural issues?

CHAPTER REVIEW

1 A contract of employment can be terminated without a dismissal taking place.

2 There are five potentially fair reasons for dismissal – capability, conduct, redundancy, statutory ban, and some other substantial reason.

3 Some employees, including those with less than one year's continuous service of employment, are unable to take a claim of unfair dismissal.

4 The restriction on employees over the age of 65 bringing a claim of unfair dismissal is currently under review.

5 For a dismissal to be fair a correct procedure must be followed. Following the Employment Act 2002 statutory disciplinary and dismissals procedures are to be introduced.

6 Employees have the right to be accompanied at a disciplinary hearing.

7 Constructive dismissal is where the conduct of the employer breaches the contract of employment, making it intolerable for the employee to continue working according to that contract.

8 There are a number of situations in which it will be automatically unfair to dismiss an employee.

9 The remedy for unfair dismissal is reinstatement, re-engagement or compensation.

10 Compensation consists of a basic award and a compensatory award.

11 Compensation can be reduced on the basis of the employee's contribution to the dismissal, or the failure of the employee to mitigate his loss.

WEBSITES REFERENCED IN THIS CHAPTER

www.acas.org.uk	Advisory, Conciliation and Arbitration Service
www.dti.gov.uk/er/individual/dis_res_consdoc.htm	DTI dispute resolution consultation document

FURTHER READING

- *East Lindsay DC* v *Daubney* [1977] IRLR 181 – a case outlining the issues to be considered before proceeding with a dismissal for ill-health incapability.
- *Hare* v *Murphy Brothers Ltd* [1974] ICR 603 – a significant period of imprisonment resulted in the frustration of the contract of employment.
- *Horkulak* v *Cantor Fitzgerald International* [2003] EWHC 1918 (QB) – an employee who resigns in response to his manager's conduct was constructively dismissed.
- *James* v *Waltham Holy Cross UDC* [1973] IRLR 202 – in this case the overlap between issues of capability and conduct is shown.
- *Ogilvie* v *Neyrfor-Weir Ltd* [2003] EAT 0054/02 – an employee who resigns in response to his manager's abusive language had been constructively dismissed.
- *Peara* v *Enderlin Ltd* [1982] ICR 804 – determining the basis that reductions should be made for the failure to mitigate loss.

There are many cases relating to conduct that you might want to read. All the following cases are of potential interest:

- *Carr* v *Alexandra Russell Ltd* [1976] IRLR 220.
- *John Lewis plc* v *Coyne* [2000] IRLR 139.
- *Lock* v *Cardiff Railway Company Ltd* [1998] IRLR 358.
- *McDonagh* v *Johnson & Nephew (Manchester) Ltd* [1978] EAT 140/78.
- *Morgan* v *Electrolux Ltd* [1990] IRLR 89.
- *Panama* v *London Borough of Hackney* [2003] IRLR 278.

EXAMPLES TO WORK THROUGH

1 Fred, a supervisor in your call centre, has complained that Joanne's performance is inadequate. He wants her to be dismissed. What issues must you consider before making any decision about Joanne's future?

2 Bill and Eddie have been fighting in the office. What steps must you take to ensure that any resulting action by the employer is fair?

3 Mary has resigned, having accepted an offer of employment with a new employer. She has now told you that her line manager has been subjecting her to humiliating and abusive comments for the past year. She is claiming constructive dismissal. You are asked to advise on the issues that will determine whether her claim is successful – what advice will you give?

4 Peter was caught stealing company property. The managing director was so angry that he told Peter to leave immediately, and did not carry out any investigation or ask Peter to explain his actions. Although you accept that the dismissal will be found to be procedurally unfair, your managing director is determined not to pay Peter a penny! What advice can you give?

Termination of Employment (2)

The objectives of this chapter are to:

■ **Understand the concept of wrongful dismissal and the associated remedies;**

■ **Outline the differences between wrongful and unfair dismissal;**

■ **Evaluate the concept of termination by summary dismissal;**

■ **Outline the procedures required to ensure that a redundancy is a fair dismissal;**

■ **Explain the Transfer of Undertaking Regulations.**

WRONGFUL DISMISSAL

Wrongful dismissal occurs when the employer terminates the contract of employment, and in doing so breaches the contract of employment. The breach of contract can be:

■ giving no notice of termination, or insufficient notice (presuming that a summary dismissal was not justified – see next section)

■ where the dismissal is in breach of a contractual disciplinary procedure

■ where the dismissal is in breach of a contractual redundancy procedure

■ the termination of a fixed-term contract before the date it is due to expire.

If the employee is claiming that a wrongful dismissal has taken place he must be able to show that the employer has terminated the contract of employment, and that such termination has been a breach of the contract. To defend the action of termination the employer must demonstrate that the employee had conducted himself in such a way as to show no intention to be bound by the contract of employment.

If an employee successfully shows that wrongful dismissal has taken place he is entitled to compensation for the breach of the contract. This will usually be equal to the loss of salary between the date of the termination and the date of the hearing when wrongful dismissal is determined. Alternatively, the employee can ask for an injunction against the dismissal being carried out, or a declaration by the court that the dismissal is invalid. In most cases the remedy given is that of damages.

Although injunctions are not common, the granting of one was allowed in the following case.

Irani v *Southampton and SW Hampshire Health Authority* [1984] IRLR 203

In this case Irani was a part-time ophthalmologist working in a clinic within the health authority. Irreconcilable differences developed between Irani and the consultant in charge of the clinic. The health authority decided that the only solution was for one of the employees to leave the clinic. As Irani was the more junior employee, and worked part-time, he was dismissed. The health authority did not determine that there was any particular fault with Irani.

Irani successfully obtained an injunction against the dismissal because the correct procedures had not been followed. The injunction meant that the dismissal was suspended until the issues had been correctly considered. Irani did not work during this period.

The salary lost during the period between the termination and the hearing determining wrongful dismissal will include any pay awards agreed during that period, or agreed at a later date and backdated. However, any discretionary increases or discretionary bonuses will not automatically be included in the calculation of losses. This is shown in the next case.

Lavarack v *Woods of Colchester* [1967] QB 278

In this case Lavarack was successful in a claim of wrongful dismissal. At the time of his dismissal Woods of Colchester operated a discretionary bonus scheme. Some time after the dismissal the employer decided to end the bonus scheme, and in doing so gave most of the employees previously covered by the scheme an increase in pay. Lavarack claimed that his damages should reflect this increase because he would have received it if he had still been employed. The Court of Appeal ruled, however, that the bonus scheme was discretionary and hence there was no contractual obligation to continue paying bonus amounts. Therefore, he was not allowed to make any claim relating to the bonus scheme.

If an employee is wrongfully dismissed due to the employer not following the correct disciplinary procedure the employee will be entitled to damages reflecting the time that it would have taken for the procedure to operate. This is illustrated in the following case.

Gunton v *London Borough of Richmond upon Thames* [1980] IRLR 321

Gunton was dismissed and given one month's notice. The dismissal did not follow the correct procedure, and hence Gunton claimed wrongful dismissal. He was successful in his claim and, on outlining his damages, claimed loss of earnings up to retirement age stating that he would have remained with the employer until that time unless he were made redundant or dismissed in accordance with the disciplinary procedure. The employers appealed against this assessment of the damages.

The Court of Appeal supported the finding that he had been wrongfully dismissed, but stated that the damages should be limited to the period from when the dismissal took place until the contract could have been properly brought to an end. In this case it would have been when the disciplinary procedure had been properly carried out plus the one-month notice period.

If an employee has lost the right to claim unfair dismissal because of the wrongful dismissal there is the possibility that extra damages can be received. This could occur, for example, when an employee with 10 months' service with a three-month contractual notice period is wrongfully dismissed by reason that the contract was terminated without notice. If the correct notice period had been given the employee would have had 13 months' service at the time of termination, and hence would have been eligible to bring a claim of unfair dismissal. This was shown in the following case.

Raspin v *United News Shops* [1998] IRLR 9

Raspin was dismissed because her employers suspected that she had stolen money from them. Raspin successfully claimed wrongful dismissal because she was dismissed without notice, and the Employment Tribunal found no evidence that she had been stealing the money. In awarding compensation for the wrongful dismissal an additional three weeks' pay was awarded to reflect the time it would have taken to reach the decision to dismiss if the correct procedure had been followed. This additional three weeks would have increased Raspin's service to an extent that she would have been eligible to make a claim for unfair dismissal.

The Employment Tribunal rejected this claim, relying on case law that suggested that a tribunal must restrict its deliberations to what has happened, and not consider what might have happened. However, this decision was overturned by the EAT and the claim for damages relating to the lost opportunity of claiming unfair dismissal was allowed.

It should be noted that if there is a clause in the contract of employment allowing the employer to pay in lieu of notice (see Chapter 5) then such a claim would not be allowed. This would be because the ending of the contract without the employee working their period of notice is expressly allowed by the contract.

It should also be noted that the damages allowed for wrongful dismissal do not include an amount for injury to feelings, as was ruled in the next case, which has not been since overruled.

Addis v *Gramaphone Company Ltd* [1909] AC 488

In this particular case Addis was wrongfully dismissed. In assessing his damages Addis claimed loss of earnings, and also sought damages for injury to feelings, distress caused by the manner of his dismissal and the difficulty in finding alternative employment. The additional damages were not allowed, and similar claims since this case have also failed.

RELATIONSHIP BALANCE

The ability to claim wrongful dismissal protects the employee against the employer terminating the contract by breaching that contract. Can you think of any situations in which the employer would be entitled to breach a contract of employment? In such a case would it be fair for the employee to make a claim of wrongful dismissal?

Further Exploration

If an issue of public law is involved an employee can seek a judicial review. Public law deals with matters that affect the whole community, or significant parts of it. Read the case of *R* v *Liverpool City Council ex parte Ferguson* [1985] IRLR 501 as a good example of a review under public law. Claims under public law are not commonly allowed, because there are a limited number of employees who can make such claims. Other cases that might be of interest to explore this issue further are *McLaren* v *Home Office* [1990] ICR 824 and *R* v *East Berkshire Health Authority ex parte Walsh* [1984] QB 152.

THE DIFFERENCES BETWEEN UNFAIR AND WRONGFUL DISMISSAL

In studying both unfair and wrongful dismissal many of the differences will have already become apparent. A summary of the main differences is:

Table **9.1**

	Wrongful dismissal	Unfair dismissal
Basis	On breach of contract	On statute and the concept of fairness
Right to claim	No qualifying period	One year's continuous service, unless the reason for the unfair dismissal is automatically unfair
Time limit	Within six years of the dismissal	Within three months of the dismissal
Damages	No limit	Maximum award is £55,000 (February 2004)
Court	Claims are heard in the Employment Tribunal (only if the amount of damages claimed is under £25,000). Alternatively they are heard in the High Court or County Court	Claims are heard in the Employment Tribunal
Future loss	Not considered	Considered
Remedy	Damages	Reinstatement, re-engagement, compensation

147

TERMINATION BY SUMMARY DISMISSAL

If your organisation, or an organisation with which you are familiar, has a dismissal procedure look to see if it has a procedure dealing with summary dismissal. Read this and then read this section to gain a better understanding of the legal requirements of such a procedure.

A termination by summary dismissal is where the employer terminates the contract of employment without giving the employee a period of notice. The contract is terminated because the employee has breached the contract of employment. This is not the same as an instant dismissal where the employer has acted unlawfully because he has chosen not to follow a correct procedure. If the employer can show that the employee has breached the contract of employment then the act of summary dismissal can be lawful.

The nature of the behaviour that causes the breach of contract can be varied. As a general principle, the behaviour must be shown to have disregard for the essential conditions of the contract. For example, if the employee has stolen from the employer there is a potential breach of mutual trust and confidence (the employer can no longer trust the employee because of his actions).

In determining whether the employee has breached the contract of employment the Employment Tribunal will consider whether the act is one isolated incident, or indicative of a pattern of behaviour. This is illustrated in the following case.

Pepper v *Webb* [1969] WLR 514

Pepper was employed as the head gardener by the Webbs. After a period of time both his standard of work and his attitude deteriorated. One day he refused to carry out their instructions, and used foul language to them. He was summarily dismissed. In considering his claim for wrongful dismissal the Court of Appeal found that his manner and his standard of work showed that he had no intention to be bound by the fundamental aspect of service within a contract of employment. By taking such a stance he had breached the contract of employment and hence summary dismissal was justified.

In another case of a gardener, considered next, the courts found that an isolated incidence of foul language and not obeying an instruction did not amount to a breach of contract and hence summary dismissal was unfair.

Wilson v *Racher* [1974] ICR 428

Wilson was the head gardener employed by Racher. One afternoon he was cutting the hedges using an electric hedge cutter when it started to rain. He stopped the hedge cutting and busied himself with other jobs. Two days later Racher accused him of stopping work early when he stopped cutting the hedge. There followed a heated exchange, when Wilson used a range of foul language. He was summarily dismissed.

Although the summary dismissal of Wilson was unfair, there can be occasions where an isolated incident is sufficient to be classed as a breach of contract. Consideration must be given to the nature of the incident, and the impact it has. This is shown in the next case.

Jupiter General Insurance Company Ltd v *Shroff* [1937] ER 67

Shroff worked in insurance and recommended that an endowment policy be issued upon a life that a senior employee had refused to reinsure a few days earlier. The Privy Council concluded that the seriousness of making such an error in the insurance business could lead to a serious loss. Hence, the summary dismissal was justified.

RELATIONSHIP BALANCE

If the employee breaches the contract of employment it can be argued that he has shown no intention to be bound by that contract. If that has been shown can it be unfair for the employer to terminate the contract of employment? Do you think there are sufficient safeguards for the employee in being dismissed without notice?

Further Exploration

Students wishing to explore this area in more detail should consider the relationship of wrongful and summary dismissal. In one the employer breaches the contract of employment; in the other the breach is by the employee. Compare and contrast the cases cited here, and referenced in the further reading section. In each case identify which part of the contract of employment has been breached. Are there any cases where the breach of the contract seems to be carried out by both the employer and the employee?

REDUNDANCY

Definition of redundancy

As we saw in the last chapter, redundancy is one of the five potentially unfair reasons for dismissal – as listed in the Employment Rights Act 1996. According to Section 139(1) of this Act employees are regarded as redundant if their dismissals are attributed, primarily or partially, to the following facts.

The fact that the employer has ceased, or intends to cease, to carry on the business for the purposes for which the employee was employed

Hindle v *Percival Boats* [1969] WLR 174

Hindle was employed as a boat builder. Percival Boats moved from their traditional methods of making boats from wood to making them from fibreglass. Hindle was unable to adapt to the new methods of working, and was made redundant on the grounds that the employer had ceased to carry on the business for which Percival had been employed.

However, it was ruled that Hindle was not in fact redundant. He was employed to make boats, and Percival Boats were continuing as boat builders. Hence, there was no redundancy.

TASK If Hindle was unable to make boats out of fibreglass and could not be lawfully made redundant what action could Percival Boats take? Would a dismissal on the grounds of capability be potentially fair?

The fact that the employer has ceased, or intends to cease, to carry on that business in the place where the employees were employed
If the employee has a clause in his contract of employment requiring him to be 'mobile' then it is possible that a redundancy will not occur if the location at which the employee works is closed, but other locations remain open. The mobility clause may allow the employer to move the employee to a different location. The employer would need to show that such a request was reasonable.

Bass Leisure Ltd v *Thomas* [1994] IRLR 104

Thomas worked at the employer's Coventry depot, which it closed. She was asked to move to another depot that was 20 miles away, and refused because of family commitments. There was a mobility clause in her contract, which the employer relied on in requesting her to make the move. After a trial period she left employment and claimed a redundancy payment. The EAT ruled that she should be paid a redundancy payment because, given her family commitments, travelling 20 miles was an unreasonable request.

The fact that the requirement of that business for employees to carry out work of a particular kind, or for employees to carry out work of a particular kind in the place where they were employed, has ceased or diminished or is expected to cease or diminish
In the following case the EAT gave a clear approach to follow in determining whether there has been a reduction in the need for employees.

Safeway Stores plc v Burrell [1997] IRLR 200

Burrell was employed as a petrol station manager. Following a reorganisation the role of manager disappeared and was replaced with the role of filling station controller, at a lower salary and lower level of status. Burrell decided that he did not want this role and he was dismissed with a redundancy payment. He claimed the dismissal was unfair, because there was no diminution in the duties that he had been carrying out – they were being carried out by someone else. The Employment Tribunal supported his claim.

In considering the appeal made by Safeway against the decision, the EAT laid out the following approach to determining whether someone has been dismissed for redundancy:

1   Has the employee been dismissed?

2   Had the requirements of the employer's business ceased or diminished, or were they expected to do so?

3   If so, was the dismissal the whole or primary result of the cessation or diminution?

In applying this test the EAT found that the dismissal of Burrell was due to redundancy and was fair. His duties as a manager had diminished, because not all the duties would be carried out by someone of a lower status; hence this is a redundancy situation.

Selection for redundancy

TASK   Try to find an example of selection criteria that have been used by an organisation for the selection of employees for redundancy. Do they meet the requirements laid out in this section?

Although an employer might have a situation that classifies as a redundancy under the definition we have just considered, it is still possible for the dismissal to be unfair if the selection of the redundant employee(s) is unfair.

It is important to emphasise that it is the job that is made redundant. Therefore, if there is more than one person carrying out similar jobs and only some of those jobs are to be made redundant, there must be a fair way of determining who is to be selected for redundancy.

The first step is to determine the selection 'pool'. These are the employees who all carry out a similar job, and hence are all potentially at risk from the redundancy. In some cases this is quite straightforward. For example, presume that a company operating a call centre needs, for economic reasons, to make 10 call centre operators redundant. The call centre has 50 call centre operators who all do broadly similar work. The call centre has no other operations. In this case the selection of 10 redundant employees must be made from the 50 call centre operators.

However, consider the example of another call centre that handles three separate contracts. One is for a car breakdown company, one is for a home shopping company and one is for a tourism information company. The home shopping company's business has reduced and hence there is a need to make five employees redundant. Should the selection be made from only those call centre operators working on the home shopping company? Would your decision change if you were told that the employees working on each contract do move around when necessary to cover absence?

The general rule gleaned from case law is that the employer should err on the side of including employees in a pool. This is illustrated in the next case.

Bristow and Roberts v *Pinewood Studios Ltd* [1982] EAT 600/81–601/81

Bristow and Roberts were two of 14 drivers employed by Pinewood. The drivers were employed in four different sections of the business. Bristow and Roberts were employed in the commercial section, along with two other drivers. Pinewood announced the need to make two drivers redundant, and following consultation with the trade union it was agreed that the selection would be made solely from the commercial section. As a result Bristow and Roberts were selected for redundancy. The EAT ruled that the redundancy had been an unfair dismissal, because no good reason had been given for the restriction of the selection pool.

Having determined the correct selection pool, the method of selection must then be agreed. The process of selection must be fair and must be as objective as possible.

In the past the most common method of selection has been LIFO (Last in, first out). This is totally objective, because the employees with the shortest period of service are those selected for redundancy. However, many employers have moved away from this approach to selection because of the impact it can have on the balance of the skills mix in the organisation.

The approach of LIFO was challenged in the next case.

Blatchfords Solicitors v *Berger and others* [2001] EAT 25.4.01

Blatchfords announced that it was going to close two of its three offices. The cashier at one of the offices that was to close was put in a selection pool for redundancy with two other cashiers working in the other offices. The selection of the cashier to be made redundant was made solely on the length of service.

The Employment Tribunal found that the employer was unable to give any reason for LIFO being the only criterion that was considered in the selection process and the selection pool was also unexplained. The tribunal's view was that no reasonable employer would use LIFO as the sole reason for selection. The EAT rejected that opinion because the tribunal was imposing its own view of the best selection criteria to be used, and it was a perverse finding that LIFO could never be a reasonable criterion.

However, in looking wider than length of a service as a selection tool the employer must choose appropriate criteria. Guidelines for this were laid down in the following case.

Williams v Compair Maxam [1982] IRLR 83

In this case employees were selected for redundancy by the three departmental managers listing those they felt should be retained for the best long-term viability of their departments and the company. The employer justified this approach because the reasons for the redundancy were that business was struggling, and long-term viability was a real issue.

However, the EAT found that the selection criteria were completely subjective. There had been no attempt to agree objective criteria with the trade union representatives, and hence the selection was unfair. In making the ruling on this case a number of points were made that should be followed to ensure a fair redundancy:

- As much warning as possible should be given of any impending redundancies
- Consultation must take place over the selection criteria, with a view to agreeing those criteria
- The criteria chosen must be able to be checked objectively (eg against attendance records or records of performance)
- The criteria must be applied fairly in carrying out the selection
- If possible, alternative employment must be offered in preference to making an employee redundant.

Any selection that is carried out must be completed by assessors who know all the employees in the selection pool, and are able to assess each of the criteria correctly.

There have been various challenges relating to the right to see a selection assessment that has been made. The ruling in the following case is of relevance here.

British Aerospace v Green and others [1995] IRLR 433

British Aerospace announced the need to make 530 of its 7000 employees redundant. They used agreed selection criteria in identifying the employees to be made redundant. Two hundred and thirty five of the employees made redundant claimed unfair dismissal. In preparing for their claims at the Employment Tribunal the employees asked for sight of their own assessments (which were provided) and the assessments of those employees who had not been made redundant – so the reason for selecting the redundant employees could be examined. This disclosure was refused.

There are occasions, however, when a ruling has been made that such assessments should be revealed for specific reasons.

- *Eaton Ltd* v *King and others* [1996] EAT 1353/96 – because the employer was unable to explain how the selection criteria had been applied.
- *British Sugar plc* v *Kirker* [1998] IRLR 624 – because the employee alleged that a disability had been taken into account when making the assessment, and it was important to see how the criteria had been applied to employees who were not disabled.

It should be noted that any employee wanting to see their own assessment criteria would have the right to do so under the Data Protection Act 1998. Similarly, the employer might fall foul of the Act if they allow employees to see assessments made of other employees (see Chapter 11).

In devising selection criteria it is important to note that no criteria must be directly or indirectly discriminatory (see Chapters 6 and 7).

RELATIONSHIP BALANCE

If selection criteria are agreed for the selection of employees for redundancy what safeguards need to be in place for the employee – to ensure a fair selection? Will it be possible for the employer to 'target' specific employees for redundancy? Should long-serving employees be more protected than those with shorter service? What protections need to be in place against unfair dismissal claims for the employer who operates the selection criteria correctly?

Further Exploration

Consider the impact of discrimination legislation on redundancy selection criteria. Think broadly about the type of criteria that an employer might want to use. Consider whether there are any circumstances in which indirect discrimination might possibly occur. How can the need to make a fair selection be balanced with the requirements of this legislation?

Consultation

If no consultation takes place prior to employees being made redundant the redundancy will usually be unfair. If the employer can show that any consultation would have been a futile exercise then it could be found that consultation was not necessary – however, this is an unusual finding.

The length of time that must be spent in consultation is laid down in the Trade Union and Labour Relations (Consolidation) Act 1992 (TULRCA):

- If the proposed redundancies involve more than 100 employees then the consultation must take place over at least 90 days.
- If the proposed redundancies involve more than 20, but fewer than 100 employees, then the consultation must take place over at least 30 days.
- If fewer than 20 employees are to be made redundant, the redundancy is not covered by the above legislation relating to collective redundancies. However, case law has demonstrated a clear requirement on the employer to consult with the individual who

is potentially affected by the proposed redundancy. This consultation must take place over a 'reasonable' period of time.

It should be noted that any employer intending to make more than 20 employees redundant at one establishment is required to inform the Secretary of State for Trade and Industry in writing at the time that the intention is announced, using the form HR1.

Some key requirements of the consultation period were laid down in the Court of Session's ruling in the following case.

King and others v Eaton Ltd [1995] IRLR 199

Eaton Ltd announced redundancies, and consultation took place with the trade union representatives. During this consultation period the issues relating to selection were not addressed. The Employment Tribunal found that the redundancies were unfair because there had been insufficient consultation. The EAT disagreed with this view, but it was supported by the Court of Session. In making the decision they laid down the following guidelines:

- The consultation must take place when the proposals are still at a formative stage (ie starting the consultation when all decisions have already been made does not lead to a meaningful consultation).
- The employer must give adequate information and give adequate time for a response to be given.
- The employer must give 'conscientious consideration' to the points made during the consultation process.

Section 188 (4) of TULRCA 1992 also determines that certain information must be given in writing by the employer at the start of the consultation:

- The reason for the proposed redundancies.
- The number and description (ie the types of jobs involved) of the employees it proposes to make redundant.
- The total number of employees at the establishment who will be affected.
- The proposed method of selection.
- The procedure to be followed in dealing with the redundancies.
- The method of calculating the redundancy payment, if it differs from the statutory payment.

A meaningful period of consultation cannot start until the employees (or employee representatives) have been supplied with all the required information regarding the redundancy. In *Green and Son (Castings) Ltd and others v ASTMS and AUEW* [1983] IRLR 135 a redundancy was announced, but details of the proposed selection methods were only given to the trade unions eight days before the dismissals took effect. In this case it was ruled that there was insufficient time for meaningful consultation to take place regarding the selection criteria.

If the employer fails to consult, the dismissal will not be automatically unfair, although that is a possible conclusion. However, a protective award will be made when the appropriate length of consultation has not been observed. The protective award is the wages that the employee would have earned during either the 30- or 90-day consultation period, if that period of consultation had taken place.

Redundancy compensation

An employee is entitled to a statutory redundancy payment if he has been employed for more than one continuous year at the time of the dismissal, and if he is aged over 18 years. If the employee is aged over 65 years no redundancy payment will be made (although this will be challenged when the age discrimination legislation is introduced).

The statutory redundancy payment is calculated in the same way as the basic award (see the previous chapter).

If an employee is offered suitable alternative employment and refuses this unjustifiably then they lose their entitlement to a redundancy payment.

Suitable alternative employment

Section 141 of the Employment Rights Act 1996 provides that:

- If the employer makes an offer to renew the contract of employment, or to re-engage the redundant employee under a new contract that is to take place when the old contract expires, or within four weeks of the contract expiring THEN
- If the capacity and place of employment, and the other terms and conditions of employment do not differ from the previous contract OR
- The terms and conditions of the proposed contract differ, but the proposal constitutes an offer of suitable employment AND
- In either case the employee unreasonably refuses that offer THEN
- The employee will not be entitled to a redundancy payment.

The employer has the burden of showing that the offer of employment was a suitable alternative, and that the refusal of it was unreasonable. In assessing these points consideration needs to be given to the extent that any terms and conditions might vary, and the impact that this might have upon the individual employees concerned, as illustrated in the following cases.

> ## *Universal Fisher Engineering Ltd* v *Stratton* [1971] ITR 66
>
> When Stratton was recruited it was agreed that he would work only four night shifts per week. The employer then told him he would need to work five nights a week. He refused and was dismissed. The employer claimed that the job working five shifts was a reasonable alternative, but this was not supported because it had been clearly agreed that no more than four shifts would be worked when Stratton was recruited.

Allied Ironfounders Ltd v *Macken* [1971] ITR 109

Macken was made redundant and was offered an alternative that involved working double day shifts. He refused this because he had a sick wife whom he looked after. His claim that this, and the drop in salary, made the alternative unsuitable was supported by the Employment Tribunal.

Little v *Beare and Son Ltd* [1980] EAT 130/1980

Little was employed at Rathbone Place, when his job was moved to Barnet (an additional 30 miles). Beare and Son bought him a van to assist in the travelling. There was then a further move to Hemel Hempstead that involved an additional 70 miles of travel – the cost of which his employers agreed to pay. He refused the second move, but the Employment Tribunal found he had refused a suitable offer of alternative employment.

It should be noted that, in considering such issues, consideration will normally be given to the mode of transport available to the employee and any impact that the extra travelling time might have.

If the employee accepts an offer of alternative employment he is entitled to a statutory minimum trial period of four weeks. If, during that period, the employee finds the job to be unsuitable he can resign and claim a redundancy payment.

Further Exploration

The proposed statutory disciplinary and dismissal procedures include one procedure that will cover discipline, sickness and redundancy. How might this affect current redundancy procedures and practices? Refer back to the requirements of these procedures and consider whether there will be an impact on any of the cases discussed in this section.

RELATIONSHIP BALANCE

Does the trial period give similar levels of protection to both the employer and the employee? How can the employer and employee ensure that the alternative employment is fairly assessed during the trial period?

TRANSFER OF UNDERTAKING

The Transfer of Undertakings (Protection of Employment) Regulations 1981 (known as TUPE) were introduced as a result of the Acquired Rights Directive No 77/187/EEC. The rights protect employees who work in an organisation that is transferred to a new owner. When a transfer of undertaking takes place all the contractual rights of an employee are transferred from the old owner to the new owner. This includes continuity of service and all benefits (apart from pensions).

Definition of a transfer

The Acquired Rights Directive and the TUPE Regulations give unclear definitions of a transfer. Hence, there has been much case law building up a picture of what defines a transfer of undertaking. Inevitably there have been rulings that have seemed to be contradictory and a significant amount of confusion has arisen. The government is currently consulting (early 2004) about amendments to the TUPE regulations, and part of these amendments will be to give a clearer definition of a transfer. Implementation of the amendments is expected in 2004, although no clear details are yet known.

TASK Read the personnel press carefully to keep up to date with any amendments to the TUPE Regulations. In particular, read any guidelines that are given on the definition of a transfer.

The first guideline given is that a change in the legal ownership of the organisation will constitute a transfer of undertaking. This was ruled in the next case.

Berg and Busschers v Besselsen [1988] IRLR 447

This case is a ruling by the ECJ. Berg was the manager of a bar/disco in the Netherlands. His employer decided to transfer the ownership of the bar/disco to a commercial partnership under a lease-purchase agreement. The new ownership was ultimately unsuccessful and the business was transferred back to the original owner. Berg claimed for loss of wages during the period of the transfer. In making its ruling the ECJ referred back to the Acquired Rights Directive that states that the TUPE Regulations apply when there is a change in the legal or natural owner of the entity. In this case there had been a clear change of ownership, and hence there was a transfer.

It is important to note that the transfer takes place when there is a change in legal ownership. If there is simply a change in the shareholders of an organisation a transfer will not occur. This was ruled in the following case.

Brookes and others v Borough Care Services Ltd and others [1998] IRLR 636

The running of a number of care homes for the elderly was to be transferred to the voluntary sector. This was achieved by the directors of the voluntary company becoming directors of Borough Care Services and the shares being transferred – there was no change in legal ownership.

An important ruling in determining the actual nature of a transfer was made in the following case.

Spijkers v *Gebroeders Benedik Abattoir CV and another* [1986] CMLR 296

In this case a slaughterhouse was sold to a new owner, who kept all the existing employees apart from Spijkers and one other. At the time of the sale the existing owner had ceased trading. The buildings and equipment were transferred to the new owner, but the question posed to the ECJ was whether the transfer of assets was sufficient to determine that a transfer had taken place, and whether the fact that the business had ceased trading before the change of ownership precluded a transfer from taking place.

Because a clearly defined economic entity had not been transferred there was not a transfer of undertaking. In making this judgment the ECJ determined that all the factors of the situation needed to be considered in deciding whether a transfer had taken place. These included such things as the transfer of tangible assets (eg buildings and equipment), the similarity of activities before and after the transfer, the period of time for which the business is interrupted (if it is) before and after the transfer, and the value of any intangible assets.

A further important case that addressed the issue of defining a transfer is illustrated next.

Süzen v *Zehnacker Gebäudereinigung GMBH Krankenhaus Service and Lefarth GMBH* [1997] IRLR 255

Süzen was a cleaner employed by a contract cleaning company to work in a school. The contract ended and one month later was taken over by a new contractor. Süzen was not offered work with the new contractor. Süzen claimed her employment should have been protected by the transfer of undertaking regulations. The ECJ ruled that, in this case, a transfer of an entity did not take place. There was no transfer of assets or taking over of the majority of the workforce; all that happened was a transfer of an activity.

The judgment in Süzen has led to a period of confusion in judgments in the UK courts regarding transfers of undertaking. In general, the strict interpretation that a transfer cannot take place of labour-intensive activities where there are no significant tangible activities has not been applied by the UK courts although there are contradictory judgments. This confusion should be solved by a proposed amendment to the TUPE Regulations that is expected to state that a transfer does take place if there is a change in service provision. This will include the contracting out of a service or a change of contractors who provide a service (for example, as a result of a contract being put out to tender and a new contractor being selected to provide a service). If there is a clear organised group of employees providing the service then they will transfer to the new employer.

TASK Try to find an example of a transfer of undertaking in an organisation with which you are familiar. Take time to understand why the events that took place were defined as a transfer.

Further Exploration

Students wanting to explore the issue of definition further would benefit from reading recent judgments of the courts in this area. From this some of the current confusion will become evident. Recommended cases include:

- *McLeod and another* v *(1) Ingram t/a Phoenix Taxis (2) Rainbow Cars Ltd t/a Rainbow Taxis* [2001] EAT 1344/01.

- *Ministry of Defence* v *(1) Carvey and others (2) Rentokil Initial Security Ltd* (2000) EAT 202/00.

- *Pinnacle AIC Ltd* v *(1) Honeyman and others (2) Cape Industrial Service Ltd* [2001] EAT 411/01.

- *RCO Support Services Ltd* v *Unison and others* [2002] ICR 751.

- *Temco Service Industries SA* v *Imzilyen and others* [2002] IRLR 214.

Protection by the TUPE Regulations

The Regulations give protection to employees of the company being transferred at the time of the transfer. If employees are unfairly dismissed immediately prior to the transfer they will still be covered by the transfer regulations.

An employee can refuse to transfer to the new employer. In this case the employee will be treated as having resigned, and not as having been dismissed.

Any dismissal relating to the transfer of undertaking will potentially be unfair. Any employee with one year's continuous service will be able to take a claim of unfair dismissal. As already stated, the new employer is not entitled to make any changes to the employee's contract of employment.

The only exception to these rules is where the employer can show an economic, technical or organisational (ETO) reason for his actions. An example of the use of the ETO defence is found in the following case.

Whitehouse v *Chas A Blatchford and Sons Ltd* [1999] IRLR 492

The supply of certain hospital supplies was transferred to the new employer. A condition of the contract was that the costs of running the contract would be reduced, in line with the reduction of the hospital's budget. In order to make the required cost savings the new employer had to make an employee redundant. The employee claimed that this redundancy was an unfair dismissal because it resulted from a transfer of undertaking. The employer successfully argued the ETO defence, showing that the dismissal was essential in order to fulfil the economic requirements of the contract.

> ## RELATIONSHIP BALANCE
>
> Employees working in sectors where tendering for services is common (eg the catering, cleaning and security industries) could encounter changes of employer reasonably frequently. Do the regulations give them sufficient employment protection? The preservation of contractual agreements can cause anomalies with existing employees – are the restrictions on the employer too strict?

Consultation

The Regulations specify that consultation must take place with the relevant employee representatives. The following information must be supplied to the representatives:

- the reason for the transfer and when it is expected to take place
- the implications for the employees (legal, social and economic)
- the measures the employer expects to take in relation to the employees
- the measures the transferee expects to take in relation to the employees.

CHAPTER REVIEW

1 Wrongful dismissal is when the employer terminates the contract of employment, and in doing so breaches that contract.

2 A wrongful dismissal can relate to a dismissal that does not follow the correct procedure, a dismissal without appropriate notice being given, or the termination of a fixed-term contract before the agreed date.

3 Summary dismissal is where the employee breaches the contract of employment and as a result the contract is terminated without notice.

4 Redundancy is one of the five potentially fair reasons for dismissal.

5 If an employer is proposing to make more than 20 employees redundant he must follow clear guidelines on the length of the consultation period.

6 The consultation period must be meaningful, and employees must be supplied with certain minimum information in writing.

7 Statutory redundancy payments are calculated in accordance with the basic award.

8 An employee who refuses an offer of suitable alternative employment forgoes the right to a redundancy payment.

9 A transfer of undertaking takes place when there is a change in legal ownership of the organisation.

10 An employee transfers to a new organisation with no change to his contract of employment.

11 Any changes to the contract, or dismissals associated with the transfer, can be allowed only if they can be supported by the ETO defence.

FURTHER READING

- *Bakers' Union* v *Clark's of Hove Ltd* [1978] ICR 366 – a case where the issue of defining an establishment for the purposes of redundancy is considered.
- *Laws* v *London Chronicle Ltd* [1959] WLR 698 – a case considering when summary dismissal can be deemed to be justifiable.
- *Lovett* v *Biotrace International Ltd* [1999] IRLR 375 – looking at the entitlement to exercise share options when a wrongful dismissal has been successfully claimed.
- *Mugford* v *Midland Bank plc* [1997] IRLR 208 – the requirement to consult individually as well as collectively when a redundancy is proposed.
- *Murray* v *Foyle Meats* [1999] IRLR 562 – a redundancy which was attributable to the diminution of the employer's business.
- *Silvey* v *Pendragon plc* [2001] IRLR 685 – a case considering damages relating to loss of pension when a wrongful dismissal has been successfully claimed.
- *Taylor* v *Kent CC* [1969] QB 560 – a case defining suitable alternative employment.

For additional cases relating to transfers of undertaking see the relevant Further Exploration section in the main text.

EXAMPLES TO WORK THROUGH

1 Mary has taken a claim of wrongful dismissal against your organisation. She was summarily dismissed when it was alleged that she had been stealing company property. The managing director stated that she had breached the term of mutual trust and confidence within her contract of employment. Might she have any grounds for a wrongful dismissal claim? What will be considered when assessing her claim?

2 You are in the process of consultation relating to a proposed redundancy of 40 employees. The trade union representatives have argued that they want LIFO to be used as a selection criterion. You are not happy to use LIFO and would like to use a broad range of selection criteria. Why might the trade union representatives prefer LIFO and not want to use the selection criteria you propose? What arguments might you use to try to convince them to agree to your approach?

3 You work for a catering company. Your managing director is currently in the process of tendering for a contract that is currently being run by a competitor of yours. You have been asked to write a section of the tender relating to potential transfer of undertaking issues. What points will you include in this section?

Trade Union Legislation

CHAPTER 10

The objectives of this chapter are to:

■ Define a trade union;

■ Understand the role of the Certification Officer and the Central Arbitration Committee;

■ Outline the legislation relating to the recognition and derecognition of a trade union;

■ Explore the legislation relating to collective bargaining;

■ Understand the legislation relating to industrial action;

■ Explore legislation relating to consultation.

TRADE UNIONS

TASK Before studying this chapter about trade union legislation find out if your organisation, or an organisation with which you are familiar, recognises a trade union. Try to understand the reasons behind the recognition or lack of it and the impact it has on the relationships between the employer and employees.

Section one of the Trade Union and Labour Relations (Consolidation) Act 1992 (TULRCA) defines a trade union as:

'an organisation consisting wholly or mainly of workers of one or more descriptions and whose principal purposes include the regulation of relations between workers of that description or those descriptions and employers or employee associations.'

This definition shows us that the group of people wishing to be defined as a trade union must be workers who are concerned with relations with employers. This was demonstrated in the following case.

Midland Cold Storage v *Turner* [1972] ICR 230

In this case the employees took industrial action against the employer, instructed by the 'Joint Shop Stewards Committee' (JSSC – the employee representative body within the organisation). The company tried to sue the JSCC because of its actions in threatening drivers who attempted to cross picket lines set up to deter anyone from working during the industrial action. Section 10 of TULRCA allows for a trade union to be sued. The courts held that the JSSC was not a trade union, rather it was a pressure group, because it was not primarily concerned with the relationships between workers and employers – hence it could not be sued.

A list of trade unions is kept by the Certification Officer. The post of Certification Officer was established under Section 7 of the Employment Protection Act 1975. The Certification Officer is an independent statutory authority appointed by the President of the Board of Trade.

A trade union can be included on this list by paying the appropriate fee and submitting a copy of its rules, officers, address and the name under which it is known. The list of trade unions is available for public inspection. If a trade union wants to apply for a certificate of independence it must be on this list held by the Certification Officer.

There are clear advantages to a trade union in receiving a certificate of independence. If they are successful they can:

■ appoint safety representatives (see Chapter 12)
■ receive information for bargaining purposes (see later in this chapter)
■ be consulted in the situation of redundancies and transfers of undertaking (see Chapter 9)
■ take time off for trade union activities (see later in this chapter).

In addition, their members cannot have action taken against them because of their membership or trade union activities.

The Certification Officer determines whether the trade union is independent or not. In making that decision the Certification Officer must consider the definition of independence given in Section 5 of TULRCA:

■ The trade union is not controlled or dominated by an employer or a group of employers.
■ The trade union cannot be interfered with by an employer or group as a result of the giving of financial or material support or by any other means which could tend towards control.

The process of determining whether a trade union is truly independent was laid down by the EAT in the next case

Blue Circle Staff Association v *Certification Officer* [1977] ICR 224

The Blue Circle group of companies formed a staff consultative organisation. Initially it was under the control of the management, and received financial support from the company. The organisation wanted to move away from this control and instituted a new set of rules, and agreed a negotiating procedure with the management in a bid to achieve this independence. Five months after agreeing the rules it applied to the Certification Officer for a certificate of independence. This was refused on the grounds that there had been no clear move away from the former dependence on the employer.

In giving its judgment the EAT gave some clear guidelines on what issues should be considered when assessing independence. These were:

- *Finance* – if the organisation is getting any financial help from an employer it is clearly not independent.

- *Other assistance* – giving assistance such as free premises from which to operate is likely to rule out independence, although the extent of the support needs to be considered.

- *Employer interference* – if the organisation gets considerable help from the employer it is unlikely to be independent.

- *History* – it is quite possible for an organisation to start as dependent, and then to grow into independence. However, the recency of this will be relevant. In the case of Blue Circle the dependence was still very recent.

- *Rules* – is there anything in the rule book of the organisation that allows the employer to interfere or control it. If so, this is likely to contradict independence.

- *Single company unions* – although it is possible to have an independent trade union that is single company, they are more likely to be interfered with than a trade union that represents workers across a range of organisations.

- *Organisation* – who is in charge of the group that wants to be recognised as an independent trade union? If it is senior management of the employer it is likely to have more interference.

- *Attitude* – is there a record of a robust attitude to negotiation, giving a sign of genuine independence?

Further Exploration

In considering the important issue of independence, students should examine the status of a range of trade unions. Start by looking at some of the larger and well-known trade unions and understand why they are clearly independent (eg Amicus, USDAW, Unison). Then look at some smaller trade unions, perhaps those that are specifically focused on an industry. Do these have a certificate of independence? Why/why not?

> ## RELATIONSHIP BALANCE
>
> So far in this book almost all of the relationship issues we have considered have been between the employer and the individual employee. In this chapter we are concerned with collective relationships (ie the relationship between the employer and a group of employees). In what ways does this collective approach alter the way we think about the relationship between the employer and the employee?

RECOGNITION AND DERECOGNITION

Recognition of a trade union means that the employer is required to negotiate with the trade union on matters covered by collective bargaining such as redundancies or pay negotiations. It is possible for an employer to agree to negotiate on a limited range of issues (maybe just disciplinary and grievance matters). In such a case the trade union is not defined as a recognised trade union.

There are four routes to recognition:

- Voluntary – when the agreement is made voluntarily between the employer and the trade union.
- Semi-voluntary – when the trade union makes a formal approach to the employer in writing, which the employer then agrees to.
- Automatic recognition.
- Recognition by ballot.

The last two routes can be a result of the statutory recognition procedure. This applies only when the employer has at least 21 employees (although the employees potentially represented by the trade union can be of a smaller number). For the statutory recognition procedure to be invoked the trade union making the request must have a certificate of independence.

The statutory recognition process is as follows:

1 The trade union seeking recognition makes a written request to the employer for recognition. This must identify the trade union and the bargaining unit.
2 The bargaining unit is the group of workers that the trade union is seeking to represent. This might be all employees, or it could be a specific group.
3 If the employer and the trade union cannot agree on the definition of the bargaining group the Central Arbitration Committee (CAC) will decide. The CAC can become involved in the discussions only if there are at least 10 per cent of trade union members in the proposed unit and the majority of workers in the unit are likely to favour recognition.

The CAC is an independent body that has statutory powers, the main one being the adjudication on decisions relating to recognition or derecognition of trade unions. Although the body is independent, the committee members are appointed by the Department for Trade and Industry following discussions with Acas.

Further Exploration

Students wanting to know more about the work of the CAC and recent judgments it has made should look at its website (www.cac.gov.uk).

In determining the bargaining unit the CAC will consider the need for the unit to work within current management and bargaining arrangements. It will also try to avoid small fragmented units within an organisation. It should be noted that clarification of procedures for establishing what is an appropriate bargaining unit are contained within the Employment Relations Bill introduced to parliament in 2003. As this has yet to receive royal assent at the time of writing it is not possible to determine exactly what these procedures might be. However, students should be alert to any changes that might be announced.

Once the bargaining unit has been decided, the next question is whether the trade union should be recognised as representing the workers. If the CAC is satisfied that at least 50 per cent of the workers in the unit are union members the CAC will issue a declaration that the trade union is recognised for the purpose of collective bargaining. This is the route of automatic recognition.

However, the CAC can decide to proceed with the route of a ballot if one of three qualifying conditions are fulfilled. These are:

- The CAC determines that a ballot is the best way of proceeding for the purpose of good employee relations.
- A significant number of the members of the trade union within the bargaining unit tell the CAC that they do not want the trade union to carry out collective bargaining on their behalf.
- The CAC has evidence that leads to doubts that a significant number of trade union members do want the union to represent them.

In addition, if less than 50 per cent of the workers are union members then a ballot of the workers in the bargaining unit will be held.

If the CAC decides to proceed with a ballot it will appoint an independent person to carry this out. The ballot must take place within 20 days of the appointment unless there are good reasons for an extension to that period of time.

If the result of the ballot is such that a majority of those who voted supported recognition and at least 40 per cent of the workers within the bargaining unit supported recognition, the CAC will issue a declaration that the union is recognised.

Once the declaration of recognition has been given, the two parties have 30 days to agree a process for conducting collective bargaining. They can agree an extension to this period of time if required. If the two parties are unable to reach an agreement the CAC may be asked to assist. The CAC has 20 days in which to help the parties reach agreement, although this period of time may be extended by agreement. If the parties are unable to reach agreement, the CAC will specify the method of collective bargaining that is to be used.

Once an agreement is reached it is a legally enforceable contract.

If there are significant changes to the original bargaining unit, either party may apply to the CAC asking for a decision on the appropriate bargaining unit. If the CAC accepts that the bargaining unit has changed it can issue a declaration ending the current bargaining arrangements or making a declaration on a more appropriate bargaining unit.

RELATIONSHIP BALANCE

We have noted that there are four potential routes to recognition of a trade union. Do you think that the routes of automatic and ballot recognition are more likely to cause ongoing difficulties in relationships between employees and the employer? Why? What are likely to be the manifestations of any difficulties that do occur?

An application for derecognition of the trade union can be made only after a minimum of three years after the declaration of recognition. The application can be made only if:

- the size of the workforce is now less than 21
- there is no longer majority support for the collective bargaining arrangements
- the original declaration was made on the basis of 50 per cent union membership and the rate of membership has now fallen below this level.

Further Exploration

Students wanting to explore the issue of recognition further would be well advised to look at some recent cases in which the CAC have been involved. Recommended reading is:

- *Amicus and Solent & Pratt* [2002] TUR 1/168 – union membership amounted to 68 per cent, but the employers wanted a ballot due to concerns about union recognition that had been expressed by one worker (who stated that many of his colleagues felt similarly). There was also concern about some level of misrepresentation of the company's position on a range of issues. The CAC ruled that a ballot was not in the best interests of employee relations because of the high level of union membership.
- *TGWU and Economic Skips Ltd* [2002] TUR 1/121 – the CAC ordered that a ballot be carried out although 55 per cent of the bargaining unit were union members. The union and the company had carried out their own surveys that gave greatly differing figures of support for recognition (73% and 10%).
- *UNIFI and Bank Tejerat* [2002] TUR 1/144 – 54 per cent of the bargaining unit were union members. The employer argued that it was inappropriate to proceed with the recognition process because of an impending merger. The CAC ruled that the process could continue and, indeed, no ballot was necessary. If the bargaining unit changed significantly as a result of the merger there could be an application for a review.

TIME OFF FOR TRADE UNION DUTIES

Employers must allow official representatives of independent trade unions that they recognise a reasonable amount of paid time off during working hours. The allowed time should be for the purpose of:

- carrying out duties relating to negotiations with the employer
- carrying out duties connected with their role – specifically listed in section 178 (2) of TULRCA 1992 – and duties that the employer has agreed they may carry out. The most likely examples are representing their members at disciplinary and grievance hearings
- receiving information from the employer
- undergoing training relevant to their trade union duties, which is approved by their trade union or the TUC (Trades Unions Congress).

The trade union representative is not required to have a minimum length of service before these entitlements apply.

COLLECTIVE BARGAINING – DISCLOSURE OF INFORMATION

As we have seen in the previous section, a recognised trade union negotiates with the employer on issues covered by collective bargaining. Examples of such issues are terms and conditions of employment, disciplinary matters, and grievances. Sections 181–185 of TULRCA give the regulations relating to information that the employer is required to disclose in order for the bargaining process to proceed effectively.

The information that should be disclosed is:

- information without which the union would be impeded to a material degree in carrying out collective bargaining with the employer
- information that it would be good industrial relations practice to disclose.

Clearly there could be a range of interpretations of these two definitions. The Code of Practice produced by Acas ('Disclosure of Information by Trade Unions for Collective Bargaining Purposes') gives useful additional guidance. Some important guidelines to consider are:

- Any information requested must be relevant to the issue being addressed through the collective bargaining.
- The information must be of importance to the negotiations.
- The level at which the negotiations are taking place must be considered.
- The relevance of the type and size of the organisation must be taken into account.

TASK Students are recommended to read the Acas code of practice to gain a fuller outline of the disclosure process. This can be accessed from the Acas website (www.acas.org.uk).

The need for the requested information to relate to the matters being discussed in the collective bargaining is illustrated in the following case.

> ### R v Central Arbitration Committee ex parte BTP Tioxide Ltd [1981] IRLR 60
>
> In this case BTP Tioxide entered into a limited bargaining agreement with ASTMS. ASTMS subsequently asked the employer to disclose information regarding a job evaluation process that was not part of the area covered by the bargaining agreement. BTP Tioxide refused to disclose the information and ASTMS took a complaint to the CAC. The CAC ordered BTP Tioxide to disclose the information, and they appealed to the High Court. The appeal was upheld – the High Court stated that the CAC had been misdirected because the information did not relate to the representational function of the trade union.

There are certain classifications of information that the employer is not required to disclose. These include:

■ information that might affect national security
■ information that can be disclosed only by contravening other legislation (perhaps the Data Protection Act 1998 – see the next chapter)
■ information that has been given to the employer in confidence
■ information relating specifically to an individual, unless he gives consent
■ information that could significantly damage the employer's undertaking
■ information obtained by the employer for the purpose of defending or bringing legal proceedings.

Any information that is disclosed by the employer may be used only for the purposes of collective bargaining.

If the trade union considers that the employer is failing to comply with the requirement to disclose information it can make a complaint to the CAC.

RELATIONSHIP BALANCE

Do you think that the disclosure of information regulations protect both the employer and the employee fairly? To what extent might the employee be impeded by not knowing what information exists, and hence not knowing what he can ask to see? To what extent might the employer be forced to reveal information that it does not want to be common knowledge amongst employees?

INDUSTRIAL CONFLICT

TASK In understanding the legislation relating to industrial conflict it would be useful to consider occurrences within recent employment disputes. Find articles relating to disputes in newspapers, magazines or relevant websites to broaden your understanding of the processes of such disputes.

Within the law there is a right to organise strikes and other industrial action. This right is supported by giving statutory immunity from liability at common law for civil wrongs or torts providing that certain conditions are met.

Whenever workers strike, or take some other form of industrial action, they are acting in breach of their contract of employment. Therefore, when a trade union calls for organised industrial action they are inducing their members to take action in breach of their contracts.

Under common law it is unlawful to induce people to act in breach of a contract, and hence trade union officials would face legal action each time they called for strike action if there were not special immunities granted. The immunity from legal action applies only to actions that are in preparation for or in the activities of a trade dispute. The immunities relate to:

- inducing a breach of contract
- intimidation
- conspiracy
- interference with a business by unlawful means
- inducing a breach of a statutory duty.

A trade union's immunity from any legal action will only apply to actions that are in contemplation or furtherance of a trade dispute. This immunity is known as the 'golden formula'. To understand the immunity in more detail we will look at the first three of those listed above as they are most commonly encountered.

Inducing a breach of contract

Direct inducement is when pressure is put on a person to break a contract. A tort (wrong) is committed if the person putting the pressure on knows that the result of the pressure will be a breach of the contract.

Indirect inducement is where pressure is put on a person to do an unlawful act to another body, which then results in that other body breaching a contract.

Section 219 of TULRCA gives immunity from any legal action in relation to the tort of inducing a breach of contract, presuming that the inducement related to the contemplation of furtherance of a trade dispute.

The issue of inducement is illustrated in the following case.

Timeplan Education Group Ltd v *National Union of Teachers* [1997] IRLR 457

Timeplan (a recruitment agency for teachers) had agreed to place a series of advertisements in a magazine run by a teachers' union in New Zealand (NZEI). However, the NUT was in dispute with Timeplan at this time, regarding terms and conditions of the teachers that it supplied. As the NZEI was a sister organisation of the NUT, the NUT contacted it to inform it of the ongoing dispute with Timeplan and to request that the advertisements cease. After some correspondence NZEI agreed to withdraw the advertisements. Timeplan then took action against the NUT claiming that it had unlawfully interfered with the contract between Timeplan and NZEI.

The Court of Appeal held that the NUT had not been aware of any contract that existed between NZEI and Timeplan and hence could not be found guilty of persuading, procuring or inducing the NZEI to breach a contract. Therefore the NUT had not committed the tort of inducement to breach a contract.

Intimidation

This tort is committed when a person is threatened. For example, Fred is convicted of stealing the funds of the local football club. He is also an employee at Bloggs Ltd. A number of the employees at Bloggs Ltd are also members of the football club. They are no longer prepared to work with Fred and their trade union representative tells the management of Bloggs Ltd that the employees will take industrial action unless Fred is dismissed. If such a threat is made in contemplation or furtherance of a trade dispute, Section 219 of TULRCA gives immunity from any legal action.

Conspiracy

This occurs when two or more people combine to damage the employer by unlawful means with intent to damage the employer (for example, gathering together to take industrial action to protect jobs). Any industrial action is likely to damage the employer. Alternatively it, can be when two or more people combine together to harm the employer by using unlawful means.

Section 219 of TULRCA gives immunity if the action is taken in contemplation or furtherance of a trade dispute, unless the act would be subject to legal action if it had been carried out by one person (eg criminal action).

If a trade union is involved in action without the support of a ballot, unlawful picketing, secondary action, or action to enforce union membership it will forfeit statutory immunity.

RELATIONSHIP BALANCE

As already noted, if the trade union did not have some level of immunity when planning or taking industrial action such action could never take place. Do you think the range of immunities is fair to both the employer and the employee? Can you think of any circumstances in which it might seem unfair?

Lawful industrial action

Sections 226–235 of TULRCA 1992 explain the process that must take place for any industrial action to be lawful.

At least seven days before any ballot is held the trade unions must inform the employers (in writing) of all employees involved in the ballot. They must tell the employers that a ballot is to be held, when the ballot will take place, and give the employer information that the trade union holds which will help the employer to make plans and bring information to the attention of those employees who are to be balloted. This requirement does not mean that the trade union must supply the names of all those who are to be involved in the ballot, but the numbers, categories of employees and workplaces are to be disclosed. If the trade union intends to organise industrial action at more than one place of work it must carry out separate ballots at each of those places of work. An independent scrutineer must be appointed to oversee the ballot process, and the counting of the votes.

It has been shown that a trade union is not deprived of its immunity from the tort of inducing a breach of contract if additional members join the trade union after the ballot has taken place.

London Underground v National Union of Rail, Maritime and Transport Workers [1995] IRLR 636

The RMT Union held a ballot of members, receiving a clear majority in favour of strike action (over a number of one- and two-day periods). After the ballot a further 20 members joined the trade union, which the London Underground was prepared to accept.

However, around one month later notice was given of further industrial action and this time a further 672 new members had joined the RMT. London Underground claimed that the action could no longer be supported by the original ballot, and a further ballot was required. However, the RMT argued that the original ballot still held as a clear majority had voted for industrial action.

The Court of Appeal ruled that the industrial action was supported by the view of the majority of those who were eligible to vote in a ballot, and that this ballot was not rendered invalid if new members joined the trade union, because the ballot was still relevant to the dispute in question. Therefore, the industrial action was still lawful and the RMT still had immunity from the tort of inducing breach of contract.

All those who are entitled to vote must be given a reasonable opportunity to vote. This includes giving the opportunity for a postal vote when this is appropriate. The voting paper must clearly state the name of the independent scrutineer, the address to which the ballot paper is to be returned (presuming there is the option of a postal vote) and the date by which it must be returned, be marked with a number that is one of a series of consecutive numbering, must allow the voter to clearly indicate a 'yes' or 'no' response to the willingness to participate in strike action, and identify the person authorised to call industrial action.

In the next case the issue of the definition of a strike was addressed.

Connex South Eastern Ltd v National Union of Rail, Maritime and Transport Workers [1998] IRLR 249

The members of the RMT were balloted for industrial action that was to include an overtime ban and refusal to work on rest days. On the ballot paper they were asked to vote 'yes' or 'no' for strike action, with no mention of action short of a strike. Following a majority vote, the RMT informed Connex of a subsequent overtime ban

---

and refusal to work on rest days. Connex immediately applied for an injunction, claiming that such action had not been addressed by the ballot paper.

The Court of Appeal refused the injunction. It agreed that the definition of a strike used by the RMT in this situation was not the usual definition. However, 'strike' is defined in TULRCA 1992 as any concerted stoppage of work. Clearly the proposed action of the RMT fell into this definition, and hence lawful industrial action was being proposed.

The voting paper must also contain a clear statement as follows:

'If you take part in a strike or other industrial action you may be in breach of your contract of employment. However, if you are dismissed for taking part in a strike or other industrial action which is called officially and is otherwise lawful, the dismissal will be unfair if it takes place fewer than eight weeks after you started taking part in the action, and depending on the circumstances may be unfair if it takes place later.'

The voting must be secret and the ballot papers must be fairly and accurately counted. As soon as reasonably possible the trade union must inform all those concerned of the result of the ballot. If the result is in favour of industrial action the trade union must give the employer seven days' notice of the industrial action. Any industrial action must commence within an agreed period. This is usually four weeks, but could be longer if agreed between the employer and the trade union. If the industrial action does not commence within the agreed period a new ballot must take place.

The notice to take industrial action must give the employer sufficient information to make plans and to bring information to the attention of those who are likely to be involved in the action. The trade union must explain whether the industrial action is intended to be continuous or on specific days or at specific times (and explain what days and times those are to be). If the action is to be continuous the date it will start must be given.

If this procedure is not followed in any significant way the ballot can be declared void.

RELATIONSHIP BALANCE

The somewhat lengthy procedure for ensuring lawful industrial action, introduced by TULRCA 1992, was criticised for weakening the employee's strength in an industrial dispute. Some believe that, by the time the balloting process is completed, some of the initial 'passion' has gone out of the situation and employees are less likely to vote in favour of industrial action. Others would argue that this is the very point of the legislation – making sure that any action taken has been thought about, rather than being an emotional reaction to a set of circumstances. Consider these two arguments, and evaluate the impact this might have on the employment relationship.

Unlawful industrial action

If unlawful industrial action is taken (which could be action following a void ballot, or could be action taken without a ballot – known as a 'wild-cat' strike) the employer can apply for an injunction to stop any further action being taken.

Given the immediacy of the situation (ie the desire to stop unlawful action that is already occurring) it is usual for an employer to start by trying to obtain an interim injunction. This gives an order for the unlawful action to cease until a particular date. It is hoped that, by the given date, the matter will have been considered at a full hearing and either the application will have been refused or a permanent injunction will have been granted.

In deciding whether to grant an interim injunction, the courts will consider first whether there is a serious issue to address. The courts will then need to consider the balance of convenience – in other words, is the granting of an interim injunction in the interests of both parties (and is there any relevant public interest)? The court also needs to consider the likelihood of the trade union being able to give a defence under the immunities that we examined earlier in this chapter.

If it can be shown that an employer has suffered loss as a result of unlawful industrial action they can bring an action for damages. Claims are usually brought against trade unions, although they can be brought against individual participants.

The level of damages that can be awarded by the court is subject to limits imposed by Section 22 of TULRCA. The limits vary according to the size of the union:

- £10,000 – if the union has fewer than 5000 members.
- £50,000 – for 5000–25,000 members.
- £125,000 – for 25,000–100,000 members.
- £250,000 for 100,000+ members.

Picketing

Section 220 of TULRCA 1992 allows for a person who is contemplating or acting to further a trade dispute to attend at or near their place of work or (if they are a trade union official) at or near the place of work of a member of the trade union they are representing for the purpose of peacefully communicating information or peacefully persuading a person to abstain from working.

Picketing, therefore, is not unlawful in itself although there are situations in which actions taken in relation to picketing may be deemed to be unlawful. It should be noted that mass picketing is likely to be unlawful, because it may no longer be picketing for the purposes of 'peaceful persuasion'. This is illustrated in the next case.

Thomas v *National Union of Miners (South Wales)* [1985] IRLR 136

This case took place during the Miners' Strike. When a number of miners started to return to work, although the dispute continued, large groups of pickets assembled at the entrances to the mines. Although there were only six official pickets groups, 60–70 miners would gather shouting abuse at those who crossed the picket lines. It was found that this was no longer 'peaceful persuasion' and was also restricting the miners from using the highway to get to work. An injunction was placed on the NUM restricting it to the placing of just six pickets at the mine gates.

There are other civil and criminal offences that could potentially be committed in the process of picketing:

Civil

- *Inducing a breach of contract.* This could occur if a driver from another organisation is persuaded not to cross a picket line. In this situation the driver is being induced to breach his contract of employment.
- *Trespass to the highway.* This could occur if the regular passage along the highway is disrupted.
- *Private nuisance.* This could be interference with a person's use of nearby land or premises. It could also be action that makes it unpleasant for a person to access premises, such as using foul language or beating on cars as they drive through.

Criminal

- Obstruction of the highway.
- Causing a breach of the peace.
- Obstruction of a police officer in the execution of their duty.
- Riot, affray, violent disorder.
- Public nuisance.
- Criminal damage to property.
- Harassment.

Further Exploration

Students wishing to consider the issue of industrial action in more detail would be well advised to look at any current employment disputes and consider what is occurring. Although there are not always high-profile disputes happening, a careful read of any newspaper over a number of days will usually result in some dispute being identified. Alternatively, read about recent disputes such as with the Royal Mail (November–December 2003), The Fire Brigade (2002) or various train companies (2002–2003).

Read the summaries of the actions taken and the reasons for them. Then apply the relevant legislation. In applying legislation, try to understand any limitations that were placed on either the employers or the trade unions in their activities.

Dismissal of employees

The Employment Relations Act 1999 provides that it is unfair to dismiss those involved in strike action for the first eight weeks of any strike. After that time the dismissal is fair if the CAC judges that all reasonable action has been taken by the employer to end the strike.

If an employer dismisses all employees involved in industrial action and then re-engages a selection of those employees within a three-month period the dismissal of those who are not re-engaged is likely to be unfair.

It is automatically unfair to dismiss an employee because he is a member (or proposes to become a member) of an independent trade union, or has taken part (or proposes to take part) in activities of an independent trade union or refuses to join, or proposes to resign from, a trade union.

CONSULTATION

Transnational Information and Consultation of Employees Regulations 1999

The European Works Council Directive was implemented in the UK by the Transnational Information and Consultation of Employees Regulations 1999, which came into force on 15 January 2000.

The regulations require that a European Works Council (EWC), or an alternative process for consulting and informing employees, is set up for 'community-style undertakings' if a valid request to do so is received. A valid request must include at least 100 employees from at least two member states. A community-style undertaking is defined as an undertaking with at least 1000 employees within the Member States, with at least 150 members in each of at least two of the States.

From 15 January 2000 any undertaking that has not already set up a voluntary EWC must start negotiations about setting up an EWC within six months of receiving a request to do so. If the undertaking refuses to commence negotiations it can be ordered by the EAT to set up a statutory EWC as defined in the regulations.

The purpose of the EWC is for the employees to receive information on, and to consult about, matters that interest the company as a whole. These include issues such as business structure, economic and financial situation, mergers, cutbacks, redundancies, production and sales.

There should be a minimum of three members of an EWC and a maximum of 30. The EWC is required to meet at least once every year. The organisation is required to pay the costs of the EWC, which can include costs relating to travel, accommodation, interpretation, and any resources required for members to carry out their duties.

Members of the EWC are entitled to paid time off for the carrying out of their duties. Any dismissal or detriment relating to membership of an EWC will be automatically unfair.

Information and Consultation Directive 2002

Clearly the EWC regulations apply only to multinational companies. The Information and Consultation Directive (No. 2002/14) addresses the need to establish a general framework for the rights to information and consultation of employees in undertakings within the European Community. As with Works Councils, there is the requirement to take action only if a valid request is made. In this case, to be valid the request must come from at least 10 per cent of the employees (or at least 15 employees if the workforce comprises fewer than 150 staff, or at least 2500 employees if it comprises more than 25,000 staff). In July 2003 the UK Government published a consultation document on this directive, and specific proposals for the implementation of the directive are now expected.

Further Exploration

Students wishing to read the consultation document can access it at www.dti.gov.uk/er/consultation/perf_work.htm. The DTI website will also contain more information about the implementation of the directive as this becomes clearer.

Initially the directive will apply to businesses with 150 or more employees. Such businesses will be required to have met the necessary requirements by March 2005. The directive will be extended to businesses with 100 or more employees by March 2007, and to all businesses with 50 or more employees by March 2008.

The rights given to employees within the directive are to receive information relating to such issues as activities within the organisation, economic position, the development of employment (particularly when this might involve a threat to employment) and any proposed substantial changes in work organisation or contractual relations. The information must be given in sufficient time to allow the employees to prepare for consultation.

Consultation must then be carried out with appropriate timing and content at the relevant level of management. The consultation must involve the employees' representatives having ample opportunity to express their opinions, and take place with a view to reach agreement.

Specific requirements of organisations will become more evident as the Government releases further guidelines.

RELATIONSHIP BALANCE

The purpose of the European Works Councils and the directive on national consultation is to ensure that employers and employees enter meaningful discussions about matters that affect both the employees and the organisation. Clearly, some organisations already have effective ways of approaching this issue of consultation. Greater consultation should lead to less conflict between the employer and employees, particularly if consultation is entered into with a clear intention to reach agreement. However, some employers might resent the formality of the negotiation and consultation structure that is being imposed on them. Do you think there is a situation in which the formality of the consultation process could actually damage employee relationships?

CHAPTER REVIEW

1 A trade union is a group of workers who are concerned with the relationship between the workers and employers.

2 A certificate of independence is issued to a trade union by the Certification Officer.

3 Recognition of a trade union means that the employer and trade union negotiate on issues covered by collective bargaining.

4 There are four routes to recognition – voluntary, semi-voluntary, automatic and by ballot.

5 If the employer and trade union cannot agree on the definition of a bargaining unit they can ask the Central Arbitration Committee (CAC) for assistance.

6 The Central Arbitration Committee is an independent body with statutory powers.

7 An application for derecognition of a trade union can be made only three years or more after the declaration of recognition.

8 A trade union representative is allowed a reasonable period of paid time off work to carry out his duties.

9 An employer is required to disclose to the trade union any information without which the trade union would be impeded in the process of collective bargaining, or information that should be disclosed in accordance with good employee relations.

10 If a trade union takes lawful industrial action it has immunity from certain torts, as long as the relevant actions are taken in contemplation or furtherance of a trade dispute.

11 For lawful action to take place, a process must be followed that involves notifying the employer of a ballot, holding a ballot and giving notice of any industrial action.

12 If unlawful action takes place, the employer may seek an injunction to halt the action.

13 Picketing is lawful as long as it is done with the aim of 'peaceful persuasion'.

14 Although picketing is lawful, certain actions that might take place during picketing could breach civil or criminal legislation.

15 An organisation that has at least 1000 employees within the Member States of the European Community, and at least 150 employees in each of at least two of the States, is required to form a European Works Council.

16 Directive number 2002/14 gives further requirements for consultation arrangements within all organisations within the European Community.

WEBSITES REFERENCED IN THIS CHAPTER

www.acas.org.uk   Advisory, Conciliation and Arbitration
                                                    Service
www.cac.gov.uk   Central Arbitration Committee
www.dti.gov.uk/er/consultation/perf_work.htm   Information and Consultation Directive
                                                    draft legislation

FURTHER READING

- *Camellia Tanker Ltd* v *International Transport Workers Federation and Another* [1976] ICR 274 – a claim that there had been an inducement to breach a contract of employment.

- *Crofter Home-Woven Harris Tweed Company* v *Veitch* [1942] AC 435 – a case looking at immunity relating to the tort of conspiracy.

- *Monk Staff Association* v *Certification Officer and ASTMS* [1980] IRLR 431 – a case looking at the issue of the independence of a trade union.

- *News Group Newspapers Ltd* v *SOGAT '82* [1986] IRLR 227 – a case where the torts of nuisance and intimidation were committed.

- *Post Office* v *Union of Communication Workers* [1990] IRLR 143 – when specific action has been specified on a ballot paper, only the action that has received the majority vote can be pursued.

EXAMPLES TO WORK THROUGH

1   You are the personnel manager for an organisation of 100 employees. You have received an application from a trade union to receive recognition. They claim that 65 per cent of the employees in the proposed bargaining unit are members of the trade union. Your Managing director wants to resist the application and has asked your advice on the process to be followed, and ways to avoid recognition. What advice would you give him?

2   The trade union that is recognised within your organisation has informed you that it is carrying out a ballot of its members about a proposal to take industrial action. The trade union has not been clear about which of your employees might be involved in any potential action. What action can you take, and what protection have both you and the trade union got?

3   Your employees are currently taking strike action. A neighbour has complained to you that she was late taking her children to school this morning because she could not get her car off her drive due to the number of pickets at your gates. What legislation might be relevant and what action could your neighbour take?

4   The trade union representatives within your organisation have approached you, the personnel manager, asking that a European Works Council be formed. Your managing director maintains that the current consultation arrangements are quite adequate. How should you proceed in considering the request?

Privacy and Confidential Information

CHAPTER 11

The objectives of this chapter are to:

■ Understand the provisions of the Human Rights Act that are relevant to employment law;

■ Explore the provisions of the Data Protection Act;

■ Outline the main issues relating to inventions, patents and copyright;

■ Understand the importance of restraints of trade;

■ Explain the relevance of Public Interest Disclosures;

■ Outline the requirements imposed by the Access to Medical Reports Act.

HUMAN RIGHTS ACT 1998

Of the 14 articles within the Human Rights Act (HRA) there are six that have potential relevance to employment law. It is those six articles that we shall examine in this section. The Act, which came into effect in England and Wales on 2 October 2000, incorporates the provisions of the European Convention on Human Rights (ECHR) into UK law. Since this date the UK courts have been required to take into account any decision or judgment from the ECHR when interpreting legislation.

Article 6 (1): The Right to a Fair Trial

This article states that everyone is entitled to a fair and public hearing in the determination of civil rights and obligations within a reasonable time by an independent and impartial tribunal established by law.

This article is of particular relevance to the Employment Tribunals system. As we noted in Chapter 2, one proposal to reduce the number of applications to the Employment Tribunals is to give the ET greater powers to 'strike out' cases that have very little chance of success. In doing so the applicant is not allowed to bring the case before the Tribunal, and there is the possibility that the applicant could argue that his rights under Article 6 have been ignored.

It is also important to note the requirement the article places to hear any case within a 'reasonable period of time'. This was challenged in the following case.

Somjee v *United Kingdom* [2002] IRLR 886

Somjee was a doctor who worked for a hospital in Merseyside. She brought cases against the hospital relating to race discrimination and unfair dismissal. The applications went through a series of hearings and appeals, and there were a number of delays in the proceedings. The cases were reasonably complex, and the reasons for the delays were varied. Somjee took a complaint to the ECHR relating to the length of time taken to hear the cases: there were three claims she had brought – the first took eight years and nine months to reach a conclusion, the second took seven years and eleven months and the third took eight years and eight months. The ECHR ruled that there had been unreasonable delays, although they did note that some of the reasons for the delays were the fault of Somjee.

These delays were unusually long, but it should be noted that Article 6 does bring in the requirement to deal with claims in a timely manner.

Further Exploration

The reasons for the many delays in the above case are complex. Students who wish to understand the requirements of Article 6 (1) in more detail would be advised to read a full synopsis of the case to gain further insight.

RELATIONSHIP BALANCE

Think back to the issues we discussed in Chapter 2 relating to the efficiency and best use of the Employment Tribunals. Do you think that Article 6 (1) affects the balance of the relationship between the employer and the employee as we discussed in that chapter?

Article 8: The Right to Respect for Private and Family Life

The first part of this article determines that everyone has the right to respect for his family life, home and correspondence. However, this first part of the article is subject to the provisos included in the second part, which allow for there to be 'interference' with this right when it is necessary for reasons of public safety, national security, economic well-being of the country, prevention of crime or disorder, protection of health of morals or the protection of the rights and freedom of others.

The next case related to events that took place before the Human Rights Act became part of UK legislation. However, in making their judgment the EAT gave a ruling on what would have been the decision had the HRA been legislation at the time.

O'Flynn v *Airlinks The Airport Coach Company Ltd* [2001] EAT 0269/01

O'Flynn was employed as a customer case assistant. Her job could involve assisting drivers in manoeuvring coaches and serving hot drinks on coaches, although these were not regular features of her job. Airlinks introduced a 'zero tolerance' of drugs policy, and also introduced random screening. When O'Flynn was asked to attend for a drugs test she informed the organisation that she had recently used both cannabis and cocaine. She tested positive for cannabis (but not for cocaine) and was called to a disciplinary hearing at which she was dismissed. She took a claim for unfair dismissal.

Her dismissal was found to be fair. With particular relevance to the HRA the EAT commented that the dismissal would still have been fair because the testing for drugs was acceptable due to the need to uphold public safety.

RELATIONSHIP BALANCE

What impact do you think that Article 8 could have on the relationship between the employer and the employee? Do you think that the provisos given in the second part of the article give a fair balance between the rights of the employee and the needs of the employer?

The issue of surveillance and monitoring of employees has been debated in some detail in recent years, partly because of the increased ability to carry out sophisticated surveillance. The use of CCTV (closed-circuit television) is becoming increasingly common. In addition, the use of e-mails and the Internet has become widespread and some employers do have concerns about the use that employees might be making of such tools.

There has been specific legislation to address these issues. The Regulation of Investigatory Powers Act 2000 made it a civil wrong to intercept communications on private and public systems. However, the Telecommunications (Lawful Business Practice) (Interception of Communications) Regulations 2000 allowed exceptions for 'legitimate business purposes'. There is considerable breadth to the legitimate business purposes allowed, which include monitoring quality, investigating unauthorised use and ensuring compliance with internal procedures. There is the concern that employers can apply the concept of legitimate business purposes to almost anything – but they still must have regard to the Data Protection Act 1998, which we shall examine later in this chapter.

TASK Find out if your organisation, or an organisation with which you are familiar, has a policy relating to privacy in the workplace. If there is a policy, do you think it adequately addresses all the issues? If there is no policy, what problems might the organisation face in addressing any issues relating to privacy?

Further Exploration

Given the current relevance of the topic, students might find it interesting to explore the issue of privacy relating to e-mails, Internet use, etc in more detail. An interesting publication is 'Employee Privacy in the Workplace' published by IDS (Incomes Data Services Ltd) in May 2001 (see www.idsbrief.co.uk).

Article 9: Freedom of Thought, Conscience and Religion

This article gives the freedom of thought, conscience and religion, and the freedom to manifest the religion or belief. This freedom is subject to limitations prescribed by law, and those limitations necessary for public safety, public order, health or morals, and the protection of rights and freedom of others.

There is likely to be some overlap between the provisions of this article and the legislation relating to discrimination on the grounds of religion or belief that was introduced in December 2003.

An interesting aspect of this article is the issue of 'manifesting' the religion or belief, particularly where this clashes with work obligations. This is illustrated in the next case.

Ahmad v *Inner London Education Authority* [1982] ICR 490

Ahmad was a schoolteacher and a devout Muslim. He worked under a contract of employment that required full time service, but also allowed time off with pay on special religious days, when his religion determined that no work should be done. He was refused permission for a 45-minute absence every Friday to attend the mosque. He resigned and claimed unfair dismissal. The case was referred to the ECHR that found that there was no breach of Article 9 because Ahmad had known the terms of the contract of employment when he commenced work.

The issues to be considered here are similar to those examined in Chapter 6 in relation to discrimination on the grounds of religion or belief. The ruling in this case (and in the case of *Stedman* v *UK* – see Further Reading) seems to suggest that the ECHR are not sympathetic to the employee when the request to worship clashes with reasonable work obligations.

Further Exploration

This case seems to suggest that the employer is not required to allow time off during regular work commitments for the purpose of regular worship. Do you think that this conclusion contradicts the Employment Equality (Religion and Belief) Regulations 2003 in any way? Take note of any cases that are brought under the 2003 legislation and contrast them with the Ahmad and Stedman cases.

Sunday working

Certain retail workers are protected for refusing to work on Sundays. 'Protected Shop Workers' cannot be required to work on Sundays, and cannot be dismissed or suffer any detriment for refusing to work on Sundays. Those who fall into this category are those who were employed as shop workers when the Sunday Trading Act 1994 came into force (25 August 1994). They lose this protection if they agree to work on a Sunday, or by giving written agreement to the employer to work on Sundays.

Workers who commenced after 25 August 1994, or who have lost this protection, are known as 'opted-out shop workers'. They can give their employer notice that they object to working on a Sunday. Three months after this notice is given they receive the same protection as protected shop workers.

These provisions do not apply to any employee who has specifically agreed to work on a Sunday.

Article 10: Freedom of Expression

This article allows everyone the freedom of expression including the right to hold opinions and to give and receive information relating to these opinions without interference. Again, there are restrictions given in the second part of the article relating to the interests of such things as national security, public safety, the prevention of disorder or crime and the protection of health, morals and the reputations of others.

The ECHR has determined that freedom of expression can relate to the way the employee dresses – because dress can be a form of expression. However, there will be circumstances in which an employer can show that a dress code at work is reasonable because of the nature of the work. This could include the need to tie back long hair for hygiene reasons. Less clear could be a dress code that the employer justifies on the grounds of the 'reputations of others', ie the employer's reputation is related to the appearance of the employees.

RELATIONSHIP BALANCE

Consider a range of organisations that have dress codes. Try to determine the reason that the dress code is in place. Do you think that the dress code meets the needs of both the employer and the employee? Can you think of any dress codes that might contravene Article 10 of the HRA?

Freedom of expression can also relate to the employee's interests outside of work. This is shown in the following case.

Pay v Lancashire Probation Service [2003] ICR 1138

Pay was employed as a probation officer specialising in the treatment of sex offenders. His employers became aware that he was involved in an organisation that promoted the sale of items relating to sado-masochism and also that he performed acts in hedonist and fetish clubs. The employers decided to dismiss Pay, because they considered that these outside activities were inconsistent with his role of a probation officer, particularly given his work with sex offenders. Pay applied to the Employment Tribunals, claiming unfair dismissal, and contravention of Articles 8 and 10 of the Human Rights Act.

It was ruled that the dismissal was fair. In specific relation to Article 10 it was agreed that the continuing employment of Pay, given his outside interests, was not justified given the need to protect the reputation of others – in this case the reputation of the Probation Service.

In considering the case it is important to note the relevance of the nature of Pay's job. If his employment had not involved work with sex offenders it might well be that any dismissal would have been found to be unfair.

Article 11: Freedom of Assembly and Association

This article gives everyone the right to peaceful assembly and association with others, and includes the right to form and join trade unions for the protection of one's interests. Again, there are provisos that include potential restrictions on the grounds of national security or public safety interests, protection of health or morals and the rights and freedoms of others, and the prevention of disorder or crime.

The restrictions that can be imposed on this article are clearly illustrated by the decision in the next case, which was later referred to the ECHR for its judgment.

Government Communications Staff Federation v Certification Officer and the Council of Civil Service Unions [1992] ICR 163

In 1984 the rights of employees of the Government Communications headquarters (GCHQ) to join a trade union were withdrawn. The employees were allowed to join a staff association, which was set up at GCHQ, known as the Government Communications Staff Federation. In 1989 the Federation applied for a certificate of independence (as explained in the last chapter) but was refused because it was not truly independent – the GCHQ director could 'interfere' with its operation, and indeed its existence was subject to the approval of the GCHQ director.

The UK Government argued that the refusal to allow GCHQ employees to join an independent trade union was justified because of the employees were involved with matters of national security. Therefore, their rights to freedom of association under Article 11 were restricted by the interests of national security. This case was referred to the ECHR, which ruled in favour of the UK Government.

> ## Further Exploration
>
> The impact of Article 11 on trade union recognition and activities is potentially wide ranging. Exploring this matter further, the student should consider the impact on:
>
> - the right to picket.
> - the unlawfulness of the closed shop
> - the right to strike
> - the refusal to recognise a trade union.
>
> (See the previous chapter for some relevant case law to start the exploration.)

Article 14: Prohibition of Discrimination

Article 14 specifically relates to discrimination relating to one of the articles within the HRA. It does not, therefore, give protection against discrimination in any circumstance. The areas of discrimination covered in the article are sex, race, colour, language, religion, political or other opinion, national or social origin, association with a national minority, property, birth or other status.

To illustrate the essential relationship between the discrimination and an article within the Human Rights Act, consider this example.

If an organisation introduced random drug testing for all employees aged over 50 years, this would be discrimination in contravention of Article 14. This is because the random drug testing relates to Article 8 – the right to privacy – and discrimination on the grounds of age is specifically listed within Article 14.

However, if the organisation introduced the requirement that all employees aged over 50 years who applied for promotion had to give a presentation to the senior management this would not be in contravention of Article 14 because the issue of giving a presentation does not fall under any Article of the Human Rights Act.

> ## Further Exploration
>
> Students wishing to explore the issues of the Human Rights Act and the work of the European Court of Human Rights in more detail would be advised to start by looking at the ECHR website (www.echr.coe.int). This website will give summaries of recent judgments, and advise on further reading.

DATA PROTECTION ACT 1998

As already mentioned, the Data Protection Act (DPA) has some relevance to Article 8 of the HRA – the right to privacy. The DPA is specifically concerned with the safe handling and use of personal data that are held about individuals.

In UK legislation, issues relating to the safe handling of the data were initially addressed in the Data Protection Act 1984. Subsequent to this the UK government was required to implement the Directive on the Protection of Personal Data 1995. This has resulted in the Data Protection Act 1998.

The Directive applies to a wider remit than employment, although we shall concentrate on employment in this chapter. The Directive widened the definition of data that was previously held in the DPA 1984. This addressed automated data. The definition of data in the Directive, and hence in the DPA 1998, is much broader and means:

1   Any information that is processed by equipment operating automatically in response to instructions given for that purpose.

2   Any information that is recorded with the intention that it should be processed by means of such equipment.

3   Any information that is recorded as part of a relevant filing system, or that is intended to form part of a relevant filing system.

4   Any information that forms part of an accessible record, but is not covered in the earlier definitions (points 1–3).

It is clear from this definition, therefore, that the Act covers information that is held manually as well as electronically.

 Find out if your organisation, or an organisation with which you are familiar, has a data protection policy. If there is such a policy, read it and consider whether it meets the requirements of the Data Protection Act 1998.

For any processing of data to be lawful *one* of the following criteria must be met:

1   The subject of the data has unambiguously given his consent.

2   The processing of the data is necessary for the performance of a contract or in order to enter into a contract requested by the subject of the data.

3   The processing is required by law.

4   The processing is necessary to protect a vital interest of the data subject.

5   The processing is necessary in the performance of tasks carried out in the public interest or by official authorities.

6   The data can be processed where the employer has a legitimate interest to do so, and this is not overridden by the interest of protecting rights of the subject, such as the right to privacy.

Within the DPA 1998 is a list of eight data protection principles. The Act requires each data controller (in the case of employment this will be the employer) to abide by these principles in all keeping and processing of personal data. The eight principles are:

1   All personal data must be processed lawfully and fairly. To achieve this the processing of the data must be necessary for the reasons already listed, or the data subject (the employee) must give permission for the data to be processed. The employee should be made aware of the processing of the data that is to take place. Without this knowledge the employee cannot give informed consent, and hence the processing is unlikely to be fair.

2   The personal data must be obtained only for specific and lawful purposes. The Act does allow an employer to list such purposes in a note to employees.

3   The personal data must be adequate, relevant and not excessive in relation to the purpose for which they are required.

4   The personal data should be accurate, and be kept up to date. The employer must keep an accurate record of the information provided by the employee. There should be opportunity for the employee to advise the employer of any changes, but the employer is not necessarily at fault if the information is inaccurate due to the employee not notifying the employer of changes. It is important that the employer takes 'reasonable steps' to ensure the ongoing accuracy of the data.

5   Personal data should not be kept for longer than is necessary. This is particularly relevant to employees who have left employment. Some information must be kept in case an employee makes a claim against an employer, and in case there is a need to supply references. The employer must consider what information to keep – it might not be necessary to keep all information for an extended period of time.

6   The personal data must be processed in accordance with the rights of the employee (which are listed below).

7   The employer must take reasonable steps against unauthorised or unlawful processing of data and loss of or damage to data. This will include considering who needs to have access to the data and including some sort of protection against unauthorised access such as password protection.

8   Personal data should not be transferred outside the European Economic Area unless the country in question can ensure adequate levels of protection for the data.

As well as abiding by these eight principles, the employer is required to inform the Data Protection Registrar of the type of records he holds containing personal data. The employer is also required to inform the Data Protection Registrar of the use that is made of these records.

The main rights of the data subjects are:

■   to have access to personal data. The employee is allowed to ask the employer to inspect all records held about him, and the employer may charge a small fee (not usually greater than £10) for allowing this. Some information is exempt from inspection, such as any references that have been given in confidence by the employer.

■   to correct any data that are inaccurate.

It should be noted that there are additional restrictions relating to the holding and processing of 'sensitive personal data'. This is data relating to such things as racial or ethnic origin, political opinions, religious belief, trade union membership, health, sexuality and committing a criminal offence. Before any such data can be processed specific consent must be obtained from the employee.

RELATIONSHIP BALANCE

In order to administer the employment relationship the employer does need to have a certain amount of information about the employee. Do you think that the provisions of the Data Protection Act 1998 give sufficient protection to the employee? Can you think of any situations in which the Act might give insufficient protection, allowing the employer to use information in a way that the employee might never have intended?

In determining the restrictions placed by the Data Protection Act, the reasons for processing the data must be considered. This is shown in the following case.

> ### Blackpool and the Fylde College v National Association of Teachers in Further and Higher Education [1994] IRLR 227
>
> In this case the trade union (NATFHE) had informed the college of the intention of its members to take industrial action. However, the college argued that it did not know the full list of the teachers that were members of NATFHE and hence the trade union had not met its obligations under TULRCA 1992 – see previous chapter. The College successfully applied for an injunction against the industrial action. NATFHE challenged the injunction, claiming that to disclose the names of its members would contravene the Data Protection Act. NATFHE were unsuccessful in their challenge because although they were trying to adhere to the Data Protection Act, in doing so their actions had breached the legislation relating to industrial action and ballots. It was noted that they could ask members to give their permission for their names to be given to the college, as this detail was required by law when giving notice of proposed industrial action.

Another example of the correct use of information is illustrated in the next case.

> ### Dalgleish v Lothian and Borders Police Board [1991] IRLR 422
>
> In this case the local authority asked the employer to provide details of employees' names and addresses to help them trace those who were in arrears with their community charge payments. The employees applied for an injunction stopping the employer from complying with this request. It was ruled that the information held by the employer was for the sole purpose of employment related issues and was not information that was generally available to the public. Hence, the employer did not have the right to disclose the information to the local authority.

Further Exploration

Any student wishing to examine the legislation relating to data protection in more detail, or wanting to understand further the role of the data protection registrar, is recommended to refer to the Information Commissioner's Office website (www.dataprotection.gov.uk).

ACCESS TO MEDICAL RECORDS ACT 1998

This Act covers any medical report that is supplied before employment commences or during employment by a medical practitioner who is or has been responsible for the clinical care of the individual.

Therefore, the Act covers any information sought from an employee's GP because that medical practitioner is responsible for the clinical care of the individual. However, if the employer asks an independent doctor for a report on an employee (for example, if the employee has had long periods of absence due to illness) the report is not covered by this Act, unless the doctor is going to be involved in treating the employee in some way.

If an employer wants to apply for a medical report that is covered by the Act then the employer must seek the consent of the employee and specifically inform the employee that:

- he has the right to refuse consent for the application for the medical report
- he can request access to the medical report before the employer sees the report
- he can request that the report is amended or is allowed to record, in writing, a difference of opinion over any details within the report
- he can refuse consent for the report to be disclosed to the employer.

An employee can be denied access to a medical report if the medical practitioner considers that the disclosure would be likely to:

- cause serious physical or mental harm to the employee
- reveal information about another individual
- reveal the intentions of the practitioner in relation to the individual
- reveal the identity of another person (non-medical) who has supplied information to the medical practitioner.

If the medical practitioner decides to withhold part or all of a report he must inform the employee. The employee then has the right to refuse consent to the report being disclosed if he wishes.

PATENTS, INVENTIONS AND COPYRIGHT

Section 39 of the Patents Act 1977 provides that an invention made by an employee shall belong to the employer if *one* of the following conditions is met:

1 The invention was made in the course of the employee's normal duties and an invention might reasonably be expected to result.

2 The employee had a special obligation to further the interests of the employer's undertaking because of his duties and the particular responsibilities arising from those duties.

3 Although the invention was not made in the normal course of duties it was made in the course of duties specifically assigned to the employee so that an invention would be expected to result.

In every other situation the patent will lie with the employee.

The issue of 'normal duties' was examined in the following case, which we looked at briefly in Chapter 1.

> ### *Reiss Engineering* v *Harris* [1985] IRLR 23
>
> Harris was manager of a department within a company that sold and assembled valves. It provided an after-sales and advice service to its customers, but it had never designed a valve or a modification to a valve.
>
> Harris was given six months' notice of his impending redundancy. During this time he invented a new valve that overcame some of the problems that existed with valves currently sold by Reiss Engineering. There then was a dispute over who owned the patent to the valve. Reiss Engineering argued that Harris had developed the valve in the course of his 'normal duties' and, in addition, that he had a special obligation to further the interests of his employer. Hence, the patent should belong to them. Harris challenged this.
>
> The High Court ruled that the patent should belong to Harris. As Reiss Engineering was not involved in any way with the design or modification of valves, it was not correct to claim that Harris had developed the valve in the course of his normal duties.
>
> In addressing the issue of his responsibility the Court held that this requirement had to relate to some extent to the employee's status and responsibilities within the organisation. Harris was not employed in a senior role, and it was also noted that he was actually under notice of redundancy when he made his invention. On this basis, Harris had no special obligation placed upon him.

Clearly it can be difficult to determine exactly what might result from an employee's normal duties. However, it is unlikely to be found that an invention belongs to an employer for this reason if the employer does not design and develop products similar to the invention.

If it is found that a patent does belong to an employer the employee can still apply to the Controller of Patents for compensation on the grounds that the invention is of 'outstanding benefit' to the employer. The Controller can then consider whether the employee is entitled to a share of the benefits giving regard to the nature of the employee's duties, the effort and skill involved in making the invention, the effort and skill of any third party and the significance of any contribution made by the employer towards the invention.

If an employee produces any literary, musical, dramatic or artistic work in the course of employment the copyright will be owned by the employer unless there is any agreement to the contrary (Section 11 of the Copyright Designs and Patents Act 1988).

RESTRICTIVE COVENANTS

There are situations in which an employer might wish to restrict the activities of an employee. This is normally after the employee has left the employer's employment, but it might refer to the desire to restrict an employee from engaging in certain other work. If the employer wishes to restrain the employer in some way then a restrictive covenant is put in place within the contract of employment.

However, a restrictive covenant must be reasonable, otherwise it will be deemed to be void. To be reasonable, the covenant must be in the interests of both parties and the public. There must be a clearly enforceable interest to protect. This could include the knowledge of trade secrets, particular influence over customers, or cases when the employee might entice other employees away from the employer after his employment has terminated. If a restrictive covenant simply seeks to restrict competition it will not be deemed to be reasonable.

An example of a restraint that was not reasonable is shown in the next case.

Greer v *Sketchley* [1978] IRLR 445

Greer was a director of Sketchley's dry cleaning business. At the time of this case Sketchley operated only in the Midlands and the South of England. After Sketchley was taken under new management Greer proposed to leave and join a competitor. Sketchley tried to stop him because there was a restrictive covenant in his contract of employment. This covenant restricted Greer from working in any organisation where his knowledge of trade secrets/special processes was of relevance. The restriction was in place for 12 months and geographically the restriction applied to the whole of the UK.

Greer successfully applied for a declaration that the restriction was invalid. The Court of Appeal ruled that the geographical restriction was unreasonable (primarily because Sketchley did not operate throughout the UK) and hence the restraint was void.

It is important to note that the whole restrictive covenant was ruled invalid because of the unreasonableness of one aspect of the restraint.

RELATIONSHIP BALANCE

In assessing the reasonableness of a restrictive covenant the courts have regard to the interest of both parties. It is usually straightforward to see the requirements of the employer, which usually relate to the fear of negative impact on the organisation in some way. In what way could the interests of the employee be negatively affected by a restrictive covenant being breached?

Further Exploration

There are a number of additional cases that deal with the issue of restrictive covenants. It would be useful to consider the rulings in the following cases. In each, note carefully the reasons for the judgments that are made. Also note how strictly the courts tend to apply the test of 'reasonableness'.

- *Alliance Paper Group plc* v *Prestwich* [1995] IRLR 25.
- *J A Mont (UK) Ltd* v *Mills* [1992] IRLR 172.

- *Marley Tile Company Ltd* v *Johnson* [1981] CA M.2818.
- *Office Angels Ltd* v *Rainer-Thomas and O'Connor* [1991] IRLR 214.
- *Rock Refrigeration Ltd* v *(1) Jones and (2) Seward Refrigeration Ltd* [1996] IRLR 675.

 Find out if your organisation, or an organisation with which you are familiar, uses restrictive covenants. If possible, read one. Do you think that the provisions within the covenant would be judged to be reasonable by a court? If not, what problems do you foresee?

CONFIDENTIAL INFORMATION

An employee has an obligation not to disclose or misuse confidential information. The obligations were explained specifically as a result of the following case.

Faccenda Chicken Ltd v *Fowler* [1986] IRLR 69

Faccenda Chicken Ltd prepared and sold chickens to a range of customers. Fowler was the sales manager. He left Faccenda and set up an organisation in competition – selling chickens to customers in the same area. His eight recruits included five salesmen from Faccenda. In setting up his business he used information he had gained from Faccenda, including names and addresses of customers, their usual requirements and the prices they were charged. Faccenda brought an action for damages against Fowler.

Faccenda Chicken was unsuccessful in its application. In making its judgment the Court of Appeal gave some clear guidelines about the use and misuse of confidential information:

1. When assessing what is confidential information it is first important to consider the express terms of the contract of employment. In this case there were no express terms clearly stating what was to be considered to be confidential information.

2. When the employment ends the requirement to keep information confidential applied only to information that can be clearly defined as a trade secret.

3. In determining what is a trade secret, regard must be given to the nature of the employment, the nature of the information, and whether the employee was clearly told that the information was confidential. In this case the sales information was freely available to a wide range of employees and they had never been told that it was classed as confidential information.

This case demonstrates, therefore, that the employer must address the issue of confidentiality by an express term within the contract of employment. This can relate back to the introduction of a restrictive covenant, as discussed in the previous section. Again, it is important to be specific and reasonable – and this can be difficult for employers as it is difficult to consider the varied range of information to which the employee might be exposed during employment.

RELATIONSHIP BALANCE

The case of *Faccenda Chicken Ltd* v *Fowler* [1986] IRLR 69 seems to clearly suggest that it is the employer's responsibility to determine what information is confidential and inform the employee accordingly. Do you think that this approach adequately addresses the needs of both the employer and the employee? Given the wide range of information used in organisations, does this approach give adequate protection to the employer?

PUBLIC INTEREST DISCLOSURES

The Public Disclosure Act 1998 (PDA) makes additions to the protection already offered to employees in Sections 43 and 47 of the Employment Rights Act 1996. The Act specifically addresses situations where the employee knows of (or suspects) some wrongdoing within the organisation.

In order to gain the protection offered by the Act, disclosures must be made in good faith. The employee must reasonably believe that the information and any allegations being made are true. The employee must not make the disclosure for any personal gain and must have already disclosed very similar information to their employer. If the employee believes that the employer might disrupt evidence if made aware of the disclosure, or is concerned of any potential detriment, the employee does not have to make such a disclosure to the employer.

The employee must act reasonably in making the disclosure. In determining this reasonableness, regard will be given to issues such as the identity of the person to whom the disclosure has been made (if the employee has gone straight to the media it is quite likely that the disclosure will not be protected), the seriousness of the matter, the likelihood of the issue recurring (and the number of times it has already occurred) and whether the disclosure results in a breach of a duty of confidence.

If the disclosure deals with a failure of an exceptionally serious nature the employee is not obliged to work through any existing internal procedures. In this case the employee can go straight to an appropriate body.

The type of disclosures that will be protected include those where the employee has a reasonable belief that a criminal offence has been committed, where there has been a failure to comply with a legal obligation, where health and safety is endangered, or where a miscarriage of justice has occurred.

The need for an employee to have a reasonable belief of the truth of his allegations was illustrated in the next case.

Darnton v *University of Surrey* [2003] IRLR 133

Darnton was employed as a lecturer at the University of Surrey. He accused the head of department of serious academic malpractice. Darnton claimed that his contract of employment was terminated unlawfully and also claimed that the head of department had subjected him to harassment, intimidation and had been dishonest.

He argued that his dismissal was unfair because he had made a protected disclosure. The Tribunal did not agree that Darnton could have reasonably believed that his allegations amounted to a criminal offence, and hence he had not made a protected disclosure. The EAT disagreed. They found that the Tribunal had erred by looking at the facts to determine whether they believed that the allegations amounted to a criminal offence. What was relevant was whether Darnton could have reasonably come to the conclusion that there was a criminal offence. On this basis the case was referred back for a newly constituted Tribunal to consider.

Although the final ruling on this case is not yet available it is important because it shows that the reasonable belief of an employee is paramount.

An employee should not be subjected to any detriment as the result of making a protected disclosure. Any dismissal as a result of making a disclosure will be automatically unfair.

RELATIONSHIP BALANCE

An employee making a disclosure that is protected by the Public Disclosure Act 1998 is protected against any detriment. Do you think this is reasonable, given the need for an employer and an employee to work together to further the interests of the business? If you do not think it is reasonable what alterations would you make to current legislation?

CHAPTER REVIEW

1 Article 6(1) of the Human Rights Act 1998 (HRA) determines the right to a fair trial.

2 Article 8 of the HRA determines the right to respect for private and family life.

3 Article 9 of the HRA determines the right to freedom of thought, conscience and religion.

4 Article 10 of the HRA determines the right to freedom of expression.

5 Article 11 of the HRA determines the right to freedom of assembly and association.

6 Article 14 of the HRA prohibits discrimination.

7 The Data Protection Act 1998 defines what information can be kept about an individual, and how it should be processed and stored.

8 The Access to Medical Reports Act 1998 covers medical reports made by a medical practitioner who is responsible for the clinical care of the employee.

9 The Patents Act 1977 specifies when an invention will belong to an employer.

10 A restrictive covenant can protect an employer against certain activities of an employee once that employee has left employment – but all aspects of the restriction must be reasonable.

11 An employer must determine what information is confidential as an express term within the contract of employment.

12 An employee must suffer no detriment from making a public interest disclosure, as long as the disclosure is protected and is made in good faith.

WEBSITES REFERENCED IN THIS CHAPTER

www.dataprotection.gov.uk	Information Commissioner's Office
www.echr.coe.int	European Court of Human Rights
www.idsbrief.co.uk	IDS employment resources

FURTHER READING

- *ACAS* v *UKAPE* [1980] IRLR 124 – Article 11 of the HRA does not give a trade union the right to recognition.

- *Ahmed* v *United Kingdom* [1999] IRLR 188 – senior local government employees are restricted in participation in political activities.

- *Aspinall* v *MSI Mech Forge Ltd* [2002] EAT 891/01 – an employee claimed he had suffered detriment due to making a protected disclosure.

- *Halford* v *UK* [1997] IRLR 471 – the Assistant Chief Constable of the Merseyside force claimed that there was an invasion of her privacy contrary to Article 8 of the HRA.

- *London Borough of Harrow* v *Knight* [2002] IRLR 140 – an employee claimed he had suffered detriment because of making a protected disclosure.

- *Stedman* v *UK* [1977] 23 EHRR CD 168 – an employee claimed she was dismissed for refusing to work on Sundays, and this dismissal was contrary to Article 9 of the HRA.

EXAMPLES TO WORK THROUGH

1 You are the personnel manager in an organisation that develops computer games. All employees have regular access to a computer, which includes access to e-mail and the Internet. The operations manager has contacted you expressing suspicions that some employees are spending long periods of time using the Internet, and possibly e-mails, for non-work related matters. He wants to investigate this. The organisation has no policy on the use of computers at work. How should you proceed, giving thought to the requirements of the Human Rights Act 1998?

2 The organisation for which you work has entered into discussions with another organisation about a possible merger. As part of these discussions the other organisation has asked for a number of details about your employees. What steps would you take to ensure that the giving of such data did not contravene the Data Protection Act 1998?

3 John works for you as a research physicist. It is likely that he will invent new ways of controlling emissions into the environment, which is the main business of your organisation. Who is likely to own any inventions that John might make? How can your organisation be sure to protect its interests?

4 You work for a hotel chain. You have recently been working in the kitchens and you are concerned that certain procedures are in breach of hygiene regulations. Six months ago there was an outbreak of food poisoning following a function at the hotel, but there was a major clean up of the kitchens before any inspection was made. You have mentioned your concerns to the head chef, who shouted at you to 'keep your nose out'. You are still concerned. What should you do? What is the likely impact of your actions on your employment?

Health and Safety Legislation

CHAPTER 12

The objectives of this chapter are to:

■ **Overview current health and safety legislation;**

■ **Explore the duties of the employer in relation to health and safety;**

■ **Explore the duties of the employee in relation to health and safety;**

■ **Understand the issues relating to stress in the workplace;**

■ **Overview the potential penalties for breaching health and safety legislation;**

■ **Outline the legislation to support good health and safety practices.**

HEALTH AND SAFETY LEGISLATION

In this chapter we shall be examining a range of issues relating to health and safety. The legislation underpinning all that we look at is summarised as follows:

■ Health and Safety at Work Act 1974 (HASAWA). This is the main statute relating to health and safety. It sets out the main duties of the employer and the employee. It also provides for a variety of means of enforcement of the legislation, which are wide ranging and can include criminal action.

■ Workplace (Health, Safety and Welfare) Regulations 1992. The regulations impose a duty on employers to maintain places of work, equipment and systems in an efficient state of good order and repair.

■ Personal Protective Equipment at Work Regulations 1992. An employer must identify the protective equipment that is needed by the employee, provide that equipment and ensure that it is kept in a good state of repair. The employee must be trained in the correct and appropriate use of the equipment.

■ Health and Safety (Display Screen Equipment) Regulations 1992. These regulations focus on the specific risks associated with the use of display screens. They specify the need for regular breaks when using display screens, the appropriate layout of work stations, and the need to provide regular eye examinations if necessary.

■ Reporting of Injuries, Diseases and Dangerous Occurrences Regulations 1995 (RIDDOR). These regulations set out the need to report events arising from events at work, ranging from injury requiring hospital treatment to the death of the person involved in the incident. There is also the requirement to report the occurrence of certain diseases at work.

■ Manual Handling Operations Regulations 1998. The regulations require an employer to examine all work involving lifting and manual handling, looking at ways to eliminate the amount of lifting and handling involved, and ensuring that all employees are trained in the correct ways to lift and move heavy objects.

- Provision and Use of Work Equipment Regulations 1998. These regulations specify the need to supply appropriate equipment for use at work, with special emphasis on particular dangers such as fires and explosions. There is a duty to give employees information and training with regard to the equipment.

- Management of Health and Safety at Work Regulations 1999. The main object of these regulations is to use risk assessments to improve health and safety at work. Employers are required to look at each activity within the organisation, consider the potential risks and look at ways to reduce or to eliminate those risks.

- Control of Substances Hazardous to Health Regulations (Amendment) 2002 (COSHH). These regulations set out the requirements for the storage, usage and risk assessments of materials that can be hazardous if used incorrectly.

From this list you will note that whereas HASAWA addresses a full range of general issues associated with health and safety, the other legislation focuses on specific areas of health and safety activity.

It should be noted that the Working Time Regulations 1998 could also have been included in this list. As we noted when we examined these regulations in Chapter 5, their basis is in health and safety concerns.

TASK	Talk to the person responsible for health and safety in your organisation, or an organisation with which you are familiar. Find out what processes the organisation has in place to ensure that it meets the requirements of health and safety legislation.

DUTIES OF THE EMPLOYER

Section 2 (1) of HASAWA clearly states that the employer has a duty to ensure, as far as is reasonably practicable, the health, safety and welfare at work of all employees. This requirement includes the following aspects of work:

Safe and adequate plant and equipment

Bac v *Austin* [1978] IRLR 332

Austin's job required the wearing of eye goggles. She had to wear these over her own spectacles, which resulted in the goggles becoming misted up and light reflecting. She complained but her employers did nothing. She was left with the option of dropping her complaint, not wearing the goggles and risking an eye injury, or leaving her job. She chose to leave her job and took a claim of constructive dismissal. Her claim was successful because her employers had breached the implied contractual requirement to provide safe equipment for her use at work.

Safe premises and/or place of work

Latimer v AEC Ltd [1953] AC 643

Latimer slipped on an area of floor where oil had become mixed with water. The employer was aware that this had happened, and had put sawdust across the floor to make the place of work safe. However, they had not had enough sawdust to cover the whole floor. Latimer argued that they had breached the requirement to provide a safe place of work. However, it was ruled that the employer had acted as far as was practicable, as the only alternative would have been closing the factory. In this case the emphasis is on the requirement to act as far as is 'reasonably practicable'.

Competent and safe fellow employees

Hudson v Ridge Manufacturing Co Ltd [1957] QB 348

An employee had carried out practical jokes for many years, which included tripping up fellow employees. He had been warned against such behaviour by his foreman, but no further action had been taken. He tripped up Hudson, who was disabled, and he sustained an injury. It was found that the employers had breached the requirement to provide a safe environment for employees because they were aware of the employee's behaviour and had not stopped it.

A safe system of work

Jagdeo v Smiths Industries Ltd [1981] ICR 47

Jagdeo was transferred to work in the soldering area, following a reduction of work in her usual department. She soon became ill and had a period of sickness absence. On her return to work she was soon taken ill again. When she returned to work she refused to work in the soldering area, and the employer was advised that it was possible to be allergic to soldering fumes. After some time of discussion and trial of protective equipment, Jagdeo was dismissed. The EAT found that her dismissal was unfair because the employer had breached the requirement to provide a safe system of work.

RELATIONSHIP BALANCE

Do you think that the requirements on the employer are too onerous, or too lenient? In which professions might it be difficult for the employer to meet the requirements? If an employee enters one of these professions knowing of the increased risks, is it fair for him to expect a high standard of protection against health and safety? How can the needs of the employer to get the job done, and the needs of the employee for a healthy and safe place of work, be balanced?

In addition to these primary requirements, there have been two specific requirements that have attracted a significant amount of attention in recent years:

- employee's health damaged by smoking in the workplace
- employee has suffered from repetitive strain injury.

We shall examine these in turn.

Smoking

It is an implied term of the contract of employment that the employer will provide a workplace that is, as far is reasonably practicable, suitable for the employee to perform their contractual duties. If the employee is subjected to poor quality of air because of the smoking habits of colleagues, the employer could be in breach of this implied term.

Waltons and Morse v *Dorrington* [1997] IRLR 488

Dorrington worked as a secretary in a firm of solicitors. She worked in an open-plan area with other secretaries, some of whom smoked. She also worked near the offices of solicitors who smoked, and their smoke drifted to her place of work. After her complaint the solicitors decided to ban smoking in open-plan areas, but solicitors were still allowed to smoke in their offices and a smoking area was set up for other smokers. Unfortunately, Dorrington had to work near one of these smoking areas. She asked to be moved, but her request was refused – and when she moved her own desk she was instructed to move back. Eventually she resigned and claimed constructive dismissal.

The Employment Tribunal, supported by the EAT upheld Dorrington's claim. They decided that there was a requirement to provide a suitable place of work in comparison with other similar places (ie other offices based in London). They decided it was not enough to consider how the needs of non-smokers could be balanced with smokers, because the choice of an employee not to smoke had no adverse impact on smokers, whereas the choice to smoke did have an adverse impact on non-smokers. They found, therefore, that the employer had breached the contract of employment and hence there had been a constructive dismissal.

It is interesting to note the way the courts defined a suitable workplace in this case. They compared the situation Dorrington was working in with what could generally be expected of offices in London. Clearly, different workplaces have different levels of noise, smells and other potentially irritating factors. This case suggests we have to consider what might be reasonable, given the type of workplace in which the employee is operating.

TASK Does your organisation, or an organisation with which you are familiar, have a policy relating to smoking at work? If so, read the policy. Do you think that it protects the employer? Does it address the needs of both the smoker and the non-smoker?

Further Exploration

Following a number of cases relating to smoking at work, many employers have banned smoking in the workplace. However, if an employee is a heavy smoker it might not be possible for that employee to refrain from smoking for a full working day. To accommodate this, many employers have considered the use of dedicated smoking areas, allowing smoking breaks and providing help for employees in quitting smoking. There are a number of issues that are raised by such approaches – for example: Is it fair that smokers are allowed more breaks from work than non-smokers? Is it fair to require smokers to work longer at the end of day to make up time lost due to smoking breaks? If an employee does not want to give up smoking can the employer still insist that the employee attends 'quit smoking' courses? What legislation affects the way the employer must address these issues (and any others that you might identify)? What safeguards should the employer put in place?

Repetitive strain injury

Repetitive strain injury (RSI) is also known as WRULD (work-related upper limb disorder). If the employee is involved in highly repetitive work that results in damage to the upper limbs it is possible that the employer has breached the requirement to provide a safe system of work. The issue of proof has been key in the cases that have been brought in this area.

Pickford v *ICI* [1998] WLR 1189

A Secretary brought a claim for WRULD on the basis that her employer had failed to ensure that she took regular breaks from prolonged spells of typing. However, she was unable to prove that she was actually suffering from WRULD – and that the problem was not 'in her mind'. Hence, her claim failed.

In contrast, a successful claim for damages resulting from WRULD was made in the following case.

Alexander and other v *Midland Bank plc* [2000] ICR 464

The employees were encoders working in the bank. They were required to input data at great speeds, which was emphasised by the league tables run by the bank. The employees complained of damage to their necks, arms and hands. In this case the employees were able to prove that the most likely probability was that the work regime had caused the damage, and hence the claim was successful.

TASK Earlier in this chapter we considered the use of risk assessments. How could they be used to reduce the potential number of claims of WRULD from employees?

DUTIES OF THE EMPLOYEE

Section 7 of HASAWA states that employees have a duty to:

- take reasonable care for the health and safety of themselves and others who may be adversely affected by their acts or omissions at work
- co-operate with their employer as is necessary to enable health and safety requirements to be met.

More specific duties on employees are laid down in other health and safety legislation that was cited at the start of this section. Examples include:

- the requirement to use any personal protective equipment that is provided, to ensure it is stored correctly, and to report any loss or obvious defect of the equipment (from the Personal Protective Equipment at Work Regulations 1992)
- to follow appropriate systems of work laid down by the employer to ensure safety during manual handling operations (from the Manual Handling Operations Regulations 1992)
- to inform the employer of any serious and imminent dangers to health and safety, and to inform the employer of any shortcomings in the employer's protection arrangement for health and safety (from the Management of Health and Safety at Work Regulations 1999).

An employer is expected to bring to the attention of employees the requirements that are placed upon them. The Health and Safety Information for Employees (Modifications and Repeals) Regulations 1995 require employers to inform employees of their requirements through the distribution of leaflets, or the displaying of posters giving the appropriate information.

Although any prosecutions relating to health and safety are more typically brought against the employer, employees can be prosecuted for not complying with certain safety laws. In a Magistrate's Court there can be a fine awarded of up to £50,000, whereas claims in the Crown Court can bring the penalty of an unlimited fine.

RELATIONSHIP BALANCE

The demands on the employee, with relation to health and safety, are less onerous than the demands on the employer. Is this fair? In answering this question consider whether most accidents at work happen because of breaches of the duties on the employer or breaches of the duties on the employee. To get more information about accidents that do occur look at the Health and Safety Executive website (www.hse.gov.uk).

EMPLOYER'S LIABILITY RELATING TO CLAIMS OF WORK-RELATED STRESS

Work-related stress claims is an area of health and safety that has attracted a number of high-profile claims in recent years. Claims for stress have been based on the tort (wrong) of negligence – that the employer's duty of care to the employee has been breached. Most of the claims have related to the duty to provide a safe system of work.

One of the first, and often quoted, claims relating to stress, which we looked at briefly in Chapter 1, was the following.

Walker v *Northumberland County Council* [1994] IRLR 35

Walker was a social worker. There was a heavy workload in the area that he worked, largely because of the increased reporting of child abuse cases. On a number of occasions Walker discussed the workload with his employer, expressing his concern at the pressure he was under. No solution was found. In November 1986 Walker suffered a nervous breakdown, and he was absent due to this breakdown until March 1987. During his period of absence he discussed the workload with his employers again, and certain support mechanisms (including the temporary assignment of extra staff to help with the work) were agreed. When Walker returned to work most of this support mechanism did not appear, and any that did was withdrawn within a month. Walker suffered a second breakdown, and in February 1988 was dismissed on the grounds of permanent ill-health.

He claimed that the employers had been negligent in not providing him with a safe system of work. The High Court ruled that the employers were not liable for Walker's first breakdown because it was not reasonably foreseeable that this would occur. However, they were liable for the second breakdown because he had already suffered the first breakdown, and the agreed support mechanisms had been withdrawn. An out-of-court settlement of £175,000 was eventually agreed.

The fact that the damages were awarded for the second breakdown only is very significant. For an employer to be liable for damages resulting from the stress of an employee, the illness resulting from the stress must have been reasonably foreseeable.

This point was emphasised further in the following judgement given by the Court of Appeal when considering appeals on four cases that were grouped together.

Sutherland Chairman of the Governors of St Thomas Becket RC High School) v *Hatton and three other cases* [2002] IRLR 263

In this appeal, damages had been awarded in four unrelated cases, and in each one the employer was appealing against the decision.

1   Hatton had been awarded £90,766. She was a teacher who had suffered stress and depression and had eventually retired early on the grounds of ill-health. Her workload had not been exceptionally heavy, and she had not told the school she was struggling. The history of events included her being attacked in the street in January 1994, and suffering the anxiety of her son being hospitalised in April 1994 for a considerable period. Neither of these events related to her work. In August 1994 she first saw a stress counsellor, but did not tell the school. In October 1995 she went absent due to sickness, and never returned to work. She eventually took ill-health early retirement in August 1996. The appeal of the

employer succeeded, and the award of damages was withdrawn. There could be no liability because the illness relating to stress was not foreseeable, because the school had not been made aware that she was struggling.

2   Barber was also a teacher. He worked at a difficult school, but did not have a particularly heavy workload in comparison to other teachers. He became depressed in August 1995, and did not tell his employers at that time. In October 1995 he talked to the deputy headteacher and told him he was struggling, and he helped Barber to prioritise and delegate some work. He continued to experience symptoms of stress but did not tell anyone (not even his doctor) until his collapse in November 1996. In March 1997 he took early retirement on the grounds of ill-health. He took a claim for damages relating to stress-induced injury and was awarded £101,042. The employers won the appeal. Barber had not told anyone he was suffering medical symptoms as a result of stress, and hence the employer could not foresee the problem and hence could not be liable.

3   Jones worked as an administration assistant. Hers was a unique job in the organisation that involved working very long hours. The employer commented that it was a gamble to expect one person to do the job, which was really two or three people's work. She complained of the workload and was offered extra help – but that never materialised. She then wrote a five-page document explaining the problems in detail and invoked the formal grievance procedure. She was threatened with the loss of her job if she continued to complain. In January 1995 she became ill with anxiety and depression and never returned to work. Towards the end of 1996 the centre where she worked closed and hence she was made redundant. She was awarded £157,541 upon her claim for damages relating to stress-induced illness on the grounds of the employer's negligence. The employers lost this appeal. The outcome was clearly foreseeable – Jones had complained in detail about the problems, and the employer had accepted that the workload was too great.

4   Bishop was a factory worker. His organisation was bought by another and there was a reorganisation. He had to move to a new job, and found it hard to adjust. He complained and asked for his old job back, but it no longer existed. The pressures in the new job were not seen to be excessive, but Bishop could not cope with the changes. He saw his GP due to symptoms of depression, but did not tell his employer. His employer knew he was unhappy, but was not aware of any medical impact this was having on him. In February 1997 he had a breakdown and attempted suicide. In 1998 his employment was terminated. He brought a claim for damages relating to a stress induced illness, and was awarded £7000 plus loss of earnings. The employer won the appeal. At no time had the employer been made aware that the difficulties at work were having any impact on Bishop's health, and hence the outcome was not foreseeable.

These rulings are important because they result in some clear guidelines for dealing with claims of negligence relating to stress. The key points to note are:

■   The ordinary principles of employer's liability apply to any psychiatric injury, in the same way as they apply to any physical injury.

■   An essential question is whether the harm was reasonably foreseeable – in particular, was an injury to health attributable to stress at work (as opposed to stress from personal difficulties).

- Foreseeability has to depend on what the employer knows (or ought to know – the employer cannot decide to ignore obvious signs, and then claim ignorance). If the employer is not aware of any problems he is entitled to assume that there are none.

- In considering whether an event was reasonably foreseeable consideration must be given to the type of work being carried out, and the demands placed upon an employee in comparison to other employees in similar work.

RELATIONSHIP BALANCE

Do you think that the clear focus on the issue of foreseeability is fair for both the employer and the employee? If the employee is truly suffering from stress, is it reasonable to expect him to have to raise the issue with the employer (a process that could be stressful in itself)?

TASK Find out what safeguards your organisation, or an organisation with which you are familiar, has put in place to guard against claims of work-related stress. Do you think that sufficient has been done?

Further Exploration

Read other cases about stress-induced illness, and damages sought for the employer's negligence. Apply the guidelines given by the Court of Appeal in the above four appeals. Try to understand what the courts see as 'reasonably foreseeable' when dealing with these cases. Cases that might be of interest can be found in the Further Reading section at the end of this chapter.

PENALTIES FOR BREACHES OF HEALTH AND SAFETY

Tort of negligence

As we have seen from the cases that we have examined so far, the focus in determining the outcome of a claim has been on the breach of the employer's duty of care. As explained at the start of the second section, the employer's duty of care extends to a range of different aspects of health and safety (eg a safe system of work, a safe place of work).

These claims are based on the tort (wrong) of negligence. In order to show that the tort of negligence has occurred, and hence succeed in a claim for damages, the employee must be able to show that:

1 The employer owed the employee a duty of care.
2 The employer breached that duty through negligence.
3 The employee suffered damage as a result of that negligence.

Having established that the employer has been negligent in some way, the courts will consider any contribution that the employee has made to the situation, before determining what damages should be awarded. This is known as contributory negligence.

The Law Reform (Contributory Negligence) Act 1945 provides that, where an employee has contributed to his injuries by his own negligence, their damages may be reduced by the percentage by which they are to blame. An example of such is not wearing the protective equipment that has been provided by the employer.

In addition, the courts will give consideration to any consent the employee has given to the act concerned. This is known as *volenti non fit injuria* – the employee was aware of the risk associated with a particular act and voluntarily consented to continue. In reality, there are difficulties with this defence, because it can be argued that an employee never gives completely 'voluntary' consent to anything. However, if this defence is successfully argued any compensation will be reduced to nil.

A claim for damages for negligence is brought in the County Court if the amount claimed is less than £50,000 and the County or the High Court if the amount claimed is greater than £50,000.

Contractual claims

As we have also seen, in the cases we have looked at in this chapter, there is the possibility of bringing a claim of constructive dismissal if the employee has resigned as a result of the employer's breach of the duty of care. As we explored in Chapter 8, the employer's breach must go to the root of the contract and the employee's resignation must be as a result of that breach.

Criminal action

If the employer is successfully prosecuted under HASAWA the penalty is either a fine or imprisonment. The maximum penalty will depend on the actual breach of the legislation that has been proven.

In deciding on the level of fine to be imposed the courts will consider the penalty that the offence merits. However, the fine will not usually be so large as to create a risk of the organisation collapsing – unless the breach is so serious that the organisation should not be trading. The courts will also consider such things as whether any warnings had been given (and if so, whether any action was taken), any profit the employer made from the failure to take adequate health and safety measures, prompt admission of guilt, action that has since been taken to remedy the problem and the previous safety record.

ENFORCING GOOD STANDARDS OF HEALTH AND SAFETY

Much of the health and safety legislation is focused on putting systems in place to ensure that employers are providing healthy and safe places of work. Within that legislation there are specific requirements placed on the employer.

Written statements

Section 2 (3) of HASAWA requires every employer who employs more than five people to prepare (and revise as often as required) a written statement of the general policy with respect to the health and safety at work of the employees, and the process in force for carrying out that policy. The statement, and any revisions of it, must be brought to the attention of all employees.

No guidance is given in the HASWA as to what the statement should include, or how it should be brought to the attention of employees. However, advice is available from the HSE (see later in this section). Generally, the statement should include the responsibilities of all employees in relation to health and safety, and general safety precautions.

Safety representatives

Section 2 (4) of HASAWA refers to the appointment by recognised trade unions (see Chapter 10) of safety representatives. The safety representatives must be employees, and may be elected or appointed. The employer has a duty to consult with these safety representatives about all measures to ensure the health and safety of employees at work.

The main duties of the Safety Representatives are to investigate potential hazards and dangerous occurrences, investigate complaints by their colleagues about health and safety-related issues, make general representations regarding health and safety to their employer, carry out inspections and attend safety committees.

A trade union safety representative is allowed paid time off to carry out his duties during normal working hours. The safety representative is also allowed paid time off for relevant training.

Safety Committees

If at least two trade union safety representatives submit a written request, employers must establish a safety committee. This must be formed after consulting with those who made the request, and any other representatives of recognised trade unions, and within three months of the request being made. The function of the committee is to review measures being taken to ensure the health and safety at work of employees.

 TASK Find out if your organisation has a safety committee. If it has, ask if you can attend a meeting to see what issues are discussed and the decisions that are made.

RELATIONSHIP BALANCE

In an earlier Relationship Balance question we considered whether the balance of the demands placed on the employer and the employee is fair. If a safety committee is working effectively do you think that helps to bring balance to the demands?

Health and Safety Executive (HSE) and Health and Safety Commission (HSC)

The Health and Safety Executive (HSE) (www.hse.gov.uk) and the Health and Safety Commission (HSC) were set up by HASAWA to help enforce the requirements of the Act.

The role of the HSC is to carry out research into health- and safety-related issues, to provide information and training, to advise employers and employees with regard to health and safety issues and to develop and submit proposed regulations.

The HSE's role is to enforce HASAWA. The HSE appoints inspectors who have the right to enter an employer's premises at any reasonable time and to carry out any necessary investigations. If there has been an incident that requires investigation they have the authority to demand that premises are left undisturbed for as long as it takes them to carry out any investigation and to take any necessary evidence. They also have the right to see any documents or books that contain information relating to the issue under investigation.

If an inspector is concerned that a practice is contravening a statutory requirement, such that the contravention is likely to continue, then the Inspector can serve an Improvement Notice. The Notice must specify the area of concern, the reasons that the Inspector has the concerns and must give a time period within which action must be taken to address the issue. The period must not be less than 21 days (if the employer wishes to appeal against the Notice he must also do so within 21 days).

If the inspector believes that the contravention of the statutory requirement is such that there is a risk of serious personal injury he may serve a 'Prohibition Notice'. Again, the Notice must specify the issue and the reasons for the concerns. This Notice usually takes immediate effect – and the activity cannot continue until the problems have been remedied.

An employer who has received an Improvement Notice or a Prohibition Notice can appeal to the Employment Tribunal – who can cancel the Notice, affirm the Notice or modify it. If an appeal is made against an Improvement Order it is suspended until the appeal is heard. If an appeal is made against a Prohibition Order it is suspended only if the Employment Tribunal specifically directs that this be so. Failure to comply with either order is an offence under HASAWA, and could lead to a fine or imprisonment.

Further Exploration

Read the annual reports of the HSC and the HSE (both on the HSE website – www.hse.gov.uk). Study some of the incidents that they cite. What legislation has been breached, or could be breached in these incidents?

CHAPTER REVIEW

1   The main duties of the employer and employee, with relation to health and safety at work, are set out in the Health and Safety at Work Act 1974 (HASAWA).

2   In addition to HASAWA there are a number of pieces of legislation concentrating on specific aspects of health and safety at work.

3   The employer has a duty of care to the employee that includes the duty to provide a safe place of work, a safe system of work, safe equipment and safe fellow employees.

4   The employee has a duty to take reasonable care of his own health and safety, and to co-operate with the employer in all matters relating to health and safety.

5   In assessing the employer's liability in cases of alleged work-induced stress a key is whether the psychiatric illness caused by the stress was foreseeable.

6   Potential claims relating to the breach of health and safety legislation include damages under the tort of negligence, claims for breach of contract (eg constructive dismissal) and prosecution.

7   Processes to enforce good standards of health and safety include written statements, safety representatives, safety committees and the support of the HSE and HSC.

WEBSITE REFERENCED IN THIS CHAPTER

www.hse.gov.uk   Health and Safety Executive

FURTHER READING

- *Barlow* v *Borough of Broxbourne* [2003] EWHC 50 (QB) – a case looking at whether the stress related illness of an employee was reasonably foreseeable.
- *Costain Building and Civil Engineering Ltd* v *Smith and another* [1999] ICR 215 – a Safety Representative must be an employee of the company.
- *Duthie* v *Bath and North Somerset Council* [2003] EAT 0561/02 – a case examining the right of a Safety Representative to attend a training course.
- *Johnstone* v *Bloomsbury Health Authority* [1990] QB 333 – a Junior Doctor claimed that the hours he was required to work are damaging to his health.
- *Marshall Specialist Vehicles Ltd* v *Osborne* [2002] EAT 0101/02 – an employee suffering from stress resigned and claimed constructive dismissal.
- *Morland* v *London Borough of Tower Hamlets* [2003] High Court 1.5.03 – another case examining the issue of stress-related illness being foreseeable.
- *Thanet District Council* v *Websper* [2002] EAT 1090/01 – an employer who did not find an alternative job for an employee suffering from stress had not provided a safe system of work.

EXAMPLES TO WORK THROUGH

1 Due to sickness absence amongst other employees Fred is asked to move to work to a different section. He is expected to work in the section only for a maximum of three days. Following a risk assessment it has been agreed that all employees working in this section should wear steel-capped boots. Unfortunately, Fred has very large feet and there are no boots available that will fit him. As he will be working in the section for only three days the employer is unwilling to purchase a pair of boots for him, so Fred starts work in his ordinary shoes. On the second day Fred drops a heavy item on his foot, breaking three toes. He takes a claim for negligence against his employer. Advise the employer on the likelihood of Fred's claim succeeding.

2 Mary successfully applied for a new job within your organisation. At the interview it was agreed that she would be provided with training if she were successful in her application. She has now been working in the new job for three months and still has not received any training. Her job involves a lot of interaction with dissatisfied customers, which she fully understood at the interview stage. Yesterday she phoned saying she did not feel well, and today she has submitted a medical note covering four weeks' absence on the grounds of 'anxiety and stress'. What action should the employer take, and why?

3 A line manager has complained to you (personnel manager) that Joe, a safety representative, is constantly interfering in production processes. Joe has informed the manager that he is entitled to investigate any issue of concern relating to health and safety. The line manager wants you to stop Joe 'interfering'. What response would you give?

Useful Websites

www.acas.org.uk	Advisory, Conciliation and Arbitration Service
www.cac.gov.uk	Central Arbitration Committee
www.cbi.org.uk	Confederation of British Industry
www.cipd.co.uk	Chartered Institute of Personnel and Development
www.cre.gov.uk	Commission for Racial Equality
www.curia.eu.int	European Court of Justice
www.dfes.gov.uk	Department for Education and Skills
www.drc-gb.org	Disability Rights Commission
www.dti.gov.uk	Department of Trade and Industry
www.dti.gov.uk/er/individual/taskforce.htm	Employment Tribunal System Taskforce
www.dwp.gov.uk	Department for Work and Pensions
www.echr.coe.int	European Court of Human Rights
www.employmentappeals.gov.uk	Employment Appeal Tribunal
www.eoc.org.uk	Equal Opportunities Commission
www.ets.gov.uk	Employment Tribunals Service
www.europa.eu.int	European Union
www.europa.eu.int/comm	European Commission
www.europarl.org.uk	European Parliament
www.hse.gov.uk	Health and Safety Executive
www.incomesdata.co.uk	Incomes Data Services Ltd
www.irsonline.co.uk	Industrial Relations Service
www.lawreports.co.uk	Incorporated Council of Law Reporting
www.scottishlaw.org.uk	Scottish Law
www.Scottish.parliament.uk	Scottish Parliament
www.tuc.org.uk	Trades Union Congress
www.womenandequalityunit.gov.uk	Women and Equality Unit

Index

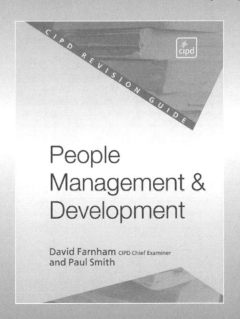